playful graphics

Graphic Design that Surprises
Des graphismes saisissants
Diseño gráfico que sorprende

Wang Shaoqiang (ed.)

promopress

playful graphics

Graphic Design that Surprises
Des graphismes saisissants
Diseño gráfico que sorprende

Editor: Wang Shaoqiang
English preface revised by: Tom Corkett
Translators of the preface:
Marie-Pierre Teuler French translation /
Jesús de Cos Pinto Spanish translation

PROMOPRESS is a brand of:
Promotora de Prensa Internacional S.A.
C/ Ausiàs March, 124
08013 Barcelona, Spain
Phone: 0034 93 245 14 64
Fax: 0034 93 265 48 83
info@promopress.es
www.promopresseditions.com
Facebook: Promopress Editions
Twitter: Promopress Editions @PromopressEd

Sponsored by Design 360°
– Concept and Design Magazine

Edited and produced by
Sandu Publishing Co., Ltd.
Book design, concepts & art direction by
Sandu Publishing Co., Ltd.
info@sandupublishing.com

Cover design:
spread: David Lorente

ISBN 978-84-15967-74-3

Printed in China

CONTENTS

INTERACTION AND PLAY

By Claire Hamilton_Filter Studio_Australia

What an incredible world we live in. We are connected, through the Web, with unlimited digital information. And we can reconnect with friends through social media, tell stories, share our lives with strangers, or interact in a digital landscape to collaborate and innovate, despite being separated by distance.

It's amazing and really quite a wonderful mess of limitless creativity.

However, now that the world is constantly accessible 24/7, are we becoming fatigued with an overload of correspondence, images, videos, and online content? Are branded messages becoming less effective in an increasingly brand-aware digital world? And are we drowning in a sea of millions of ideas that make us cynical and unimpressed?

Ours is an age of flourishing digital information. It is also an age when a tactile and playful approach can bring us back to simple communication and human nature. We have the opportunity to genuinely connect with people in an honest and fun way that can empower ideas. As designers, we have the responsibility to think differently and to offer clear messaging and engagement. If we can do this in a way that is tactile and interactive, then we are able to help our clients, the community, and brands to communicate in a far more effective, creative, and memorable way.

A couple of years ago, one of Filter's clients, Bryan Crawford (Longbow Productions), asked if I could design a business card for him. He needed an identity that would both excite recipients and create a memorable experience—a card that would stand out and result in more calls for his work. Bryan is a brilliant photographer who works with creative agencies, so the target was a highly creative, brand-aware audience that needs to access an equally creative commercial photographer for collaborative projects.

What we created was a simple laser-etched and cut mahogany card that splits into three parts. Two of the sections create identical slim-line cards. Each features Bryan's contact details (on one side) and logo (on the other side) when the main card is broken apart, with one card for the recipient to keep and one for referrals. The third and most fun piece of the deconstructed card is a thin section that transforms into a mini longbow with the help of a rubber band. With the addition of any appropriate projectile, Bryan's clients began playing and shooting each other in a childlike frenzy with their mini bow and arrow devices.

The impact of this simple and playful card became evident as people started sharing stories about it and the experiences that it had created within their offices. Photographs of the card were uploaded to creative blogs and spread around the creative online community.

Requests for Longbow business cards came via email and online, and Bryan was asked to send his cards via mail to potential clients because they wanted one of their own.

This kind of impact for such a simple project can give businesses the opportunity to really connect with consumers to create a real and tangible conversation. When we combine a visual and sensory offering with a simple message, we create a memorable experience that we can all share. At Filter, we offer creative problem-solving and playful concepts that connect and empower our clients and their brands.

The best creatives develop relationships and communication through inspiring ideas that connect with people.

Playful Graphics is a celebration of great ideas that offer interactivity and play to convey their messages. In this book, you'll find designers from all over the world who've taken this approach for their projects and created playful and impactful designs.

As you look through their work, I encourage you to feel inspired and open yourself up to see possibility in your own projects. By searching for inspiration in everything you feel, touch, and see, it becomes easier to consider how you can create a memorable experience for consumers in a tactile and effective medium for your message.

Be genuine, collaborate, invent, and create.

PRÉFACE

INTERACTION ET JEU

Par Claire Hamilton_Filter Studio_Australie

Nous vivons une époque formidable. Grâce au web, nous avons accès à un nombre illimité de données. Nous pouvons renouer contact avec des amis à travers les médias sociaux, raconter des histoires, partager notre quotidien avec des étrangers, interagir dans le paysage numérique pour collaborer et innover malgré la distance qui nous sépare.

C'est une magnifique et incroyable pétaudière de créativité sans fin.

Cependant, dans ce monde connecté accessible 24/7, ne croulons-nous pas sous les courriers, images, vidéos et autres contenus web ? Sommes-nous aujourd'hui moins sensibles aux slogans traditionnels et plus accros aux marques qui brillent sur la toile ? Sommes-nous devenus des êtres cyniques et blasés pressés par les millions d'idées qui pullulent sur le net ?

Nous vivons à l'ère de l'information numérique. Toutefois, les solutions tactiles et ludiques que nous avons développées démontrent que nous sommes encore capables de communiquer simplement et de rester fidèle à notre nature humaine. Aujourd'hui nous pouvons échanger avec nos semblables sur un mode direct et amusant qui favorise la créativité. Notre rôle, en tant que designers, est de penser autrement et de proposer des messages et des orientations clairs. Et lorsque nous misons sur une solution tactile et interactive, nous donnons à nos clients, à la communauté toute entière et aux marques les moyens de communiquer d'une manière plus efficace, plus originale et plus impactante.

Il y a deux ans, un des clients de Filter, Bryan Crawford (Longbow Productions), m'a demandée de concevoir sa carte de visite. Il voulait un design qui interpelle et marque les esprits – une carte qui sorte du lot et lui attire des commandes. Bryan est un photographe de talent qui travaille avec des agences de création. C'est un public dédié au monde des marques qui recherche des photographes commerciaux créatifs pour leurs projets collaboratifs.

Nous avons créé une carte en acajou gravée et découpée au laser constituée de trois parties distinctes détachables. Deux des volets étaient de minces cartes identiques portant au recto les coordonnées de Bryan et au verso son logo. Le contact en conservait une partie et pouvait donner l'autre à un tiers pour recommander les services de Bryan. Le troisième élément de la carte était le plus amusant. C'était une étroite bande de bois qui se transformait en mini arc à l'aide d'un simple élastique. Les clients s'amusaient comme des gamins à s'envoyer des projectiles avec leurs arcs improvisés.

L'impact de cette carte à la fois simple et ludique était évident. Les gens ont commencé à en parler autour d'eux et à raconter les batailles qu'ils avaient organisées au bureau. On a vu apparaître des photos de la carte dans différents blogs, puis elles se sont diffusées parmi toute la communauté créative en ligne.

Les demandes de cartes de visite Longbow commencèrent à affluer par email et internet. Bryan envoyait sa carte de visite par courrier à ses clients potentiels qui voulaient tous en avoir un exemplaire.

L'impact d'un projet aussi simple permet aux entreprises de forger un lien réel avec les consommateurs et d'établir un dialogue tangible. Lorsque l'on associe un message à un objet visuel qui stimule les sens, l'on crée une expérience mémorable pouvant être partagée par tous. Chez Filter, nous proposons des concepts apportant des solutions créatives sur un mode ludique qui renforce l'image et l'impact de nos clients et de leurs marques.

Les meilleurs créatifs sont ceux qui favorisent les échanges et la communication à partir d'idées stimulantes qui interpellent les gens.

Playful Graphics est un recueil d'idées géniales qui font passer le message sur un mode interactif et ludique. L'ouvrage présente des réalisations de créatifs du monde entier qui ont adopté cette approche pour concevoir des designs à fort impact.

Inspirez-vous de ces exemples pour élargir votre horizon et n'hésitez pas à adopter cette démarche pour vos propres projets. Imprégnez-vous de ce que vous touchez, sentez et voyez pour créer une expérience unique chez le consommateur. Votre message sera d'autant plus marquant qu'il sera accompagné de différentes sollicitations des sens.

Soyez authentiques, collaboratifs, inventifs et créatifs.

INTERACCIÓN Y JUEGO

De Claire Hamilton_Filter Studio_Australia

Vivimos en un mundo increíble. Estamos conectados con una cantidad ilimitada de información a través de internet, y podemos comunicarnos con los amigos en las redes sociales, contar historias, compartir nuestras vidas con extranjeros o interactuar en entornos digitales para colaborar e innovar aunque nos separen grandes distancias.

Es realmente asombroso, un fantástico caos de creatividad ilimitada.

Sin embargo, ahora que tenemos acceso constante al mundo, 24 horas al día y siete días a la semana, empezamos a cansarnos de la sobrecarga de correspondencia, imágenes, vídeos y contenidos en línea. En un mundo digital cada vez más consciente de las marcas ¿se están volviendo menos eficaces los mensajes relacionados con ellas?

En esta era de florecimiento de la información digital en la que vivimos, un enfoque táctil y divertido puede devolvernos la comunicación simple y la naturaleza humana. Tenemos la oportunidad de entrar en contacto con la gente de una manera sincera y divertida que dé fuerza a las ideas. Como diseñadores, nuestra misión es pensar diferente y ofrecer mensajes claros y atractivos; si podemos hacerlo de una manera táctil e interactiva seremos capaces de ayudar a nuestros clientes, a la comunidad y a las marcas a comunicarse de una manera mucho más eficaz, creativa y memorable.

Hace un par de años, uno de los clientes de Filter, Bryan Crawford (Longbow Productions), me pidió que diseñara su tarjeta de negocios. Necesitaba una identidad que fuera estimulante para quienes la recibieran y, al mismo tiempo, creara una experiencia memorable: una tarjeta que destacara y que produjera más encargos profesionales. Bryan es un fotógrafo brillante que trabaja con agencias creativas, y su mensaje debía llegar a personas altamente creativas y conscientes de las marcas que buscaran a un fotógrafo comercial igualmente creativo para colaborar en sus proyectos.

Nosotros realizamos una tarjeta color caoba, grabada y cortada por láser, que se dividía en tres partes. Cuando estas partes se separaban, se obtenían tres piezas: por un lado, dos tarjetas delgadas idénticas con los datos de contacto de Bryan (por una cara) y su logo (por la otra cara) destinadas una al cliente y la otra para posibles referencias; la tercera y más divertida pieza de la tarjeta desmontada era una sección que se transformaba en un pequeño arco con la ayuda de una goma elástica. Añadiendo cualquier proyectil adecuado, los clientes de Bryan empezaban a jugar y a lanzarse disparos entre ellos con sus arcos y flechas con entusiasmo infantil.

El impacto de esta sencilla y divertida tarjeta se hizo evidente cuando la gente empezó a compartir historias sobre ella y sobre las experiencias que había creado en sus oficinas. En los blogs creativos aparecieron fotos de la tarjeta que se difundieron entre la comunidad creativa en línea.

Empezaron a llegar peticiones por correo electrónico y en línea para recibir la tarjeta de Longbow, y posibles clientes le pedían a Bryan que les enviara sus tarjetas por correo porque querían tener una propia.

Con un proyecto muy simple, este tipo de impactos ofrece a los negocios la oportunidad de conectar de verdad con los consumidores y entablar una conversación real y tangible. Cuando combinamos una propuesta visual y sensorial con un mensaje simple, creamos una experiencia memorable que todos podemos compartir. En Filter ofrecemos conceptos creativos y divertidos para solucionar problemas, ideas que conectan y refuerzan a nuestros clientes y sus marcas.

Los mejores creativos desarrollan relaciones y comunicación mediante ideas inspiradoras que conectan con las personas.

Playful Graphics es un homenaje a las grandes ideas que transmiten su mensaje a través de la interactividad y el juego. En este libro encontrarás diseñadores de todo el mundo que han adoptado este enfoque en sus proyectos y han creado diseños impactantes y divertidos.

Te invito a inspirarte y abrirte a nuevas posibilidades en tus propios proyectos mientras recorres estos trabajos. Buscando inspiración en todo lo que percibas, toques y veas, te resultará más fácil pensar maneras de crear experiencias memorables para el consumidor en un medio táctil y eficaz para tu mensaje.

Sé auténtico, colabora, inventa y crea.

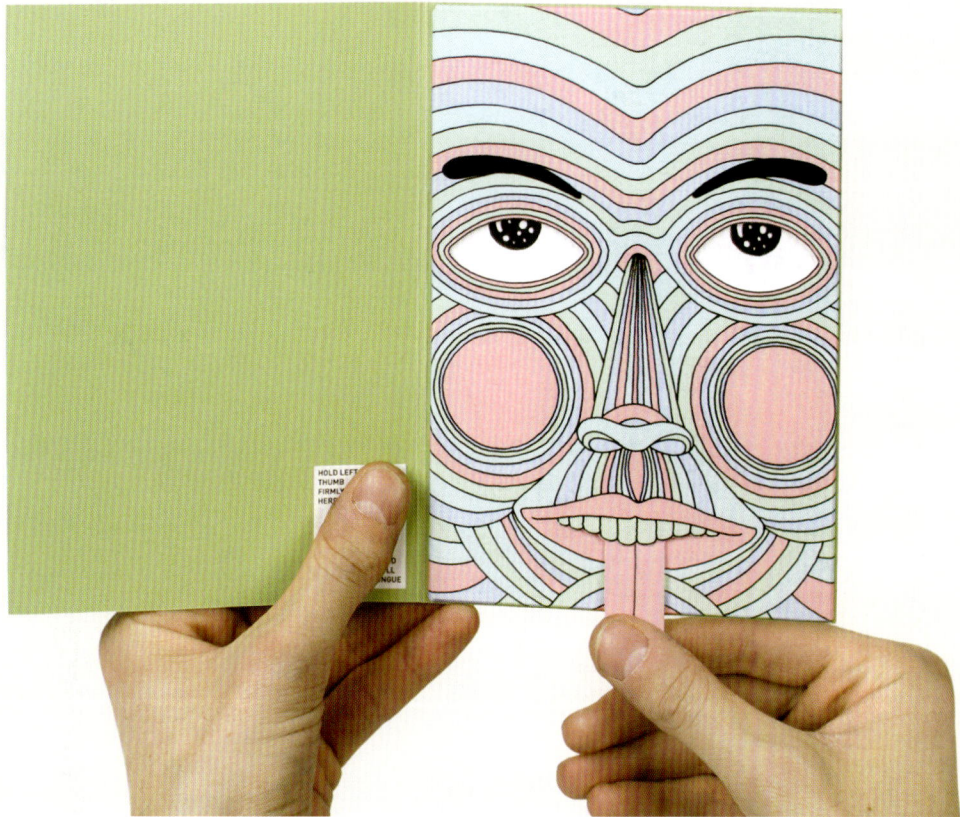

Personal Holiday Card

This a nnual personal holiday card consists of a pink envelope with a die cut face, which opens to reveal a green card. The card then opens to reveal colourful face with the tongue sticking out that functions as a pull tab. When the tongue is pulled, the character's eyes roll back in his head as the words "HAPPY HOLIDAYS," illustrated by hand, slide into view.

Designer / Joseph Veazey
Illustrator / Joseph Veazey

Adult Swim Comic-Con Brochure

The Adult Swim Comic-Con Brochure was designed to be seen through the attached polarized 3d glasses, which make more saturated colours seem closer and less saturated colours recede.

The brochure was given out to visitors at the booth, and was meant to function as a way to dispense the 3d glasses to the fans. Printed with fluorescent spot colours, the panel and signing information inside was designed to look really cool when viewed through the glasses.

Creative Director / Brandon Lively
Art Director / Jacob Escobedo
Designer / Joseph Veazey
Illustrator / Joseph Veazey

The Secret of Gods

"The Secret of Gods" is a project that portrays, with some humour and irony, the great Gods of the Olympus, and satirizes their deeds and unreachable powers. The twelve most powerful Olympians (Zeus, Hera, Poseidon, Aphrodite, Apollo, Hermes, Demeter, Artemis, Athena, Ares, Dionysus and Hephaestus) are individually presented through illustrations that cover the boxes' exterior. Each box is taken as the "head" of one of the gods, with the purpose of granting it personality. What can be found inside the boxes is in "the secret of Gods" — it's a surprise that each god was given a colour and an object which, for some reason, connects with and identifies it, accompanied by a small textual description of the character.

Designer / Helena Morais Soares

Toshiyuki Hirano and Danny / Oymaten

Toshiyuki Hirano and Danny / Oymaten is a flyer designed for the exhibition of two illustrators,
Toshiyuki Hirano and Danny. The theme of this exhibition is a mountain, so the two illustrators drew
two mountains on the flyer which can be folded diagonally to make the flyer stand as a mountain.

Design Agency / UMA/design farm
Art Director/ Yuma Harada
Designer / Midori Hirota
Photographer / Yoshiro Masuda

Bouquet Business Card

This is a business card designed to "put a smile on one's face." When folded, it turns into a flower bouquet.

Design Agency / Latona Marketing Inc.
Designer / Kazuaki Kawahara
Photographer / Sugar Bee Flowers

Latona Marketing
Kazuaki Kawahara
122-2 Ooka, Numazu-shi, Shizuoka, 410-0022, Japan
http://www.latona-m.co.jp

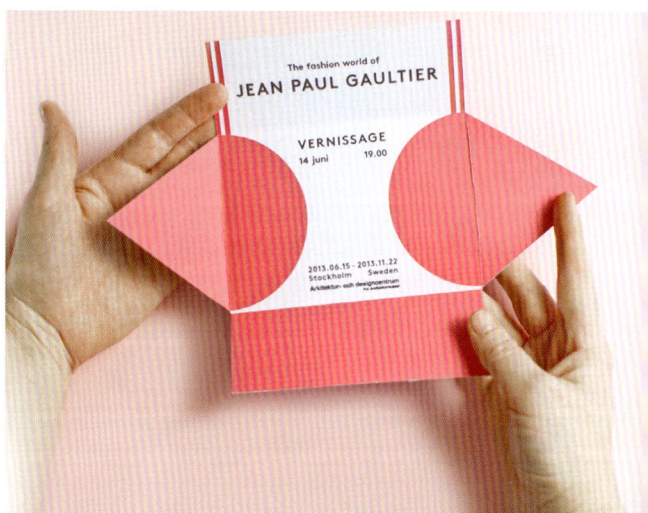

The Fashion World of Jean Paul Gaultier

This project was made as an application assignment for Beckmans College of Design. It was an assignment to make a poster and an invitation for the exhibition The Fashion World of Jean Paul Gaultier in Stockholm 2013.

Designer / Anna Dormer Volgsten

Dear Diary | Cheeky Notebook

Dear Diary is a small pamphlet stitched, bi-fold artist book. This cheeky notebook is a play on an idiom that one better share with friends than polite company: he has his head up his butt. This old saying is applied colloquially to denote someone's (or one's own) state of denial. The use of this idiom as a context for a journal enriches the physical joke beyond the category of juvenile humour.

Designer / Jacy Nordmeyer

Food Fight

Food Fight is a notepad with food skin texture designed to bring amusement to office hour. Tear a sheet from the pad, scrunch it into a ball of spaghetti, cake or fries, and launch them across the room to create the ultimate food fight.

Design Agency/ Trapped in Suburbia
Designer / Cuby Gerards,
Karin Langeveld & Richard Fussey

Lisa Sanders Public Relations Brand Identity

The client asked for simple yet sophisticated messaging pieces communicating why hiring PR counsel is a wise move. The message needed to distinguish the client and her approach from the sea of rivals while also providing insight into the type of solutions Lisa Sanders Public Relations provides. And it had to be smart and pithy, communicating quickly, decisively — and most importantly — in an engaging manner.

Design Agency / Red Peak
Art Director / Stewart Devlin
Designer / Ryan Adair, Yong Joon Cho & Stewart Devlin
Writers / Ryan Adair, Stewart Devlin & Nate Dwyer

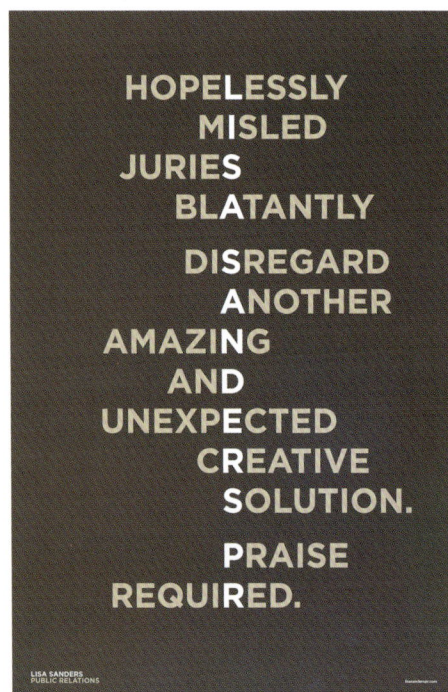

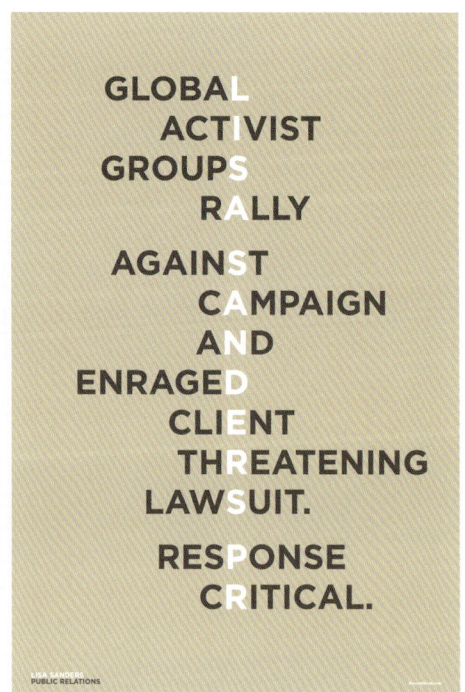

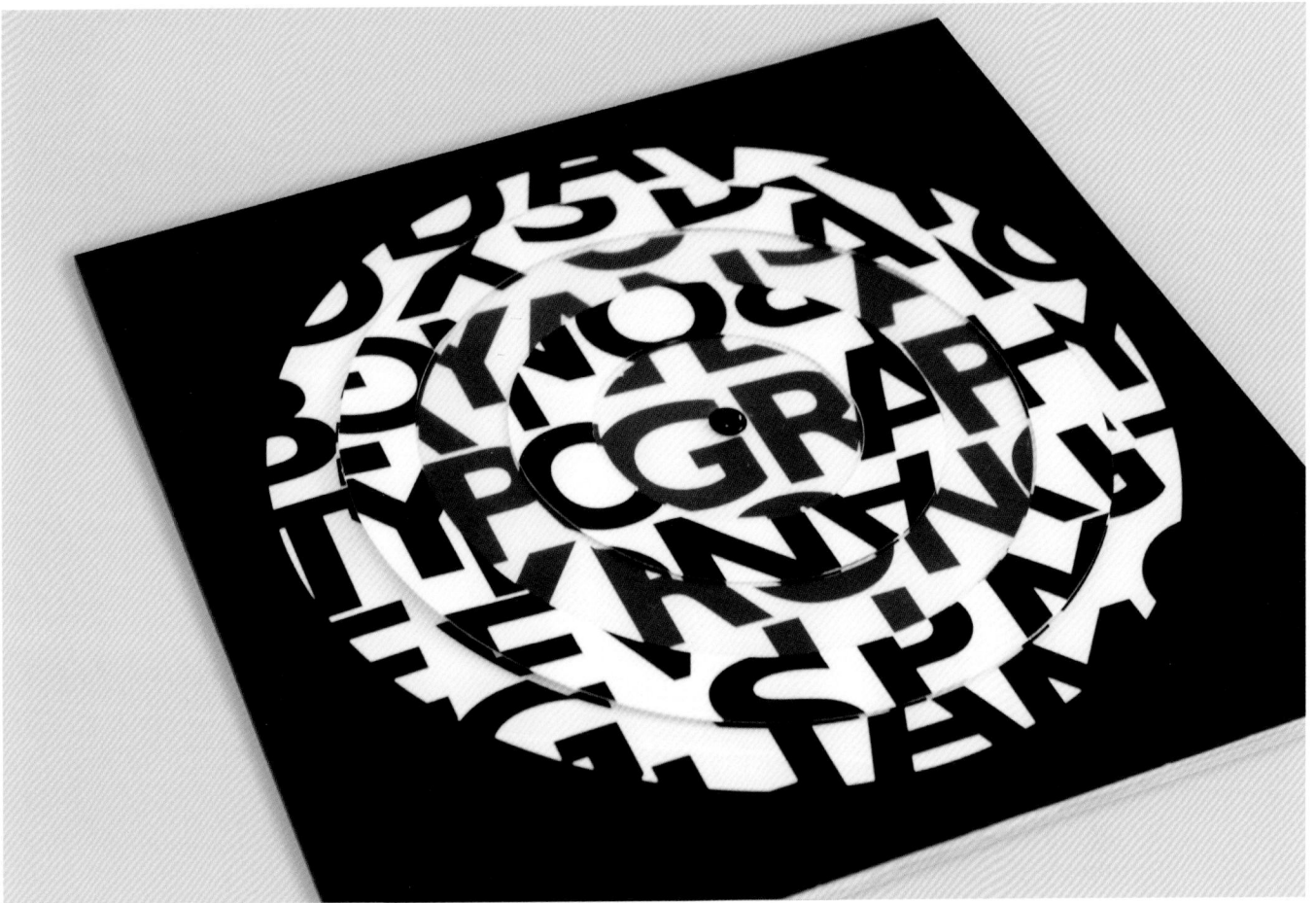

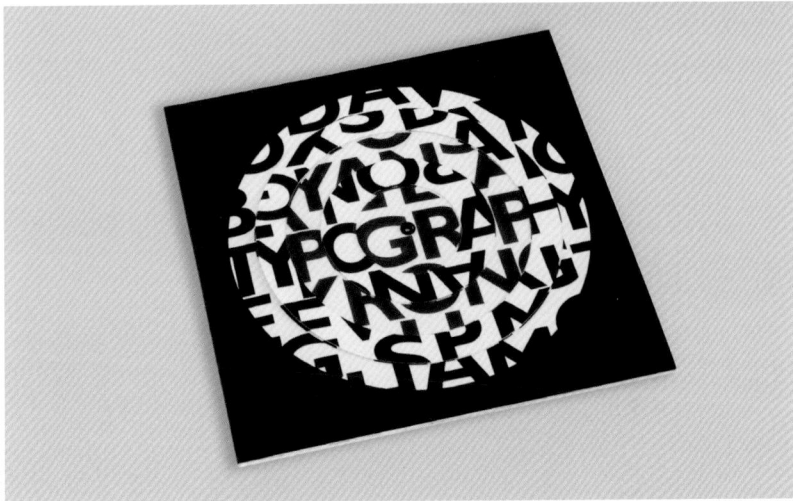

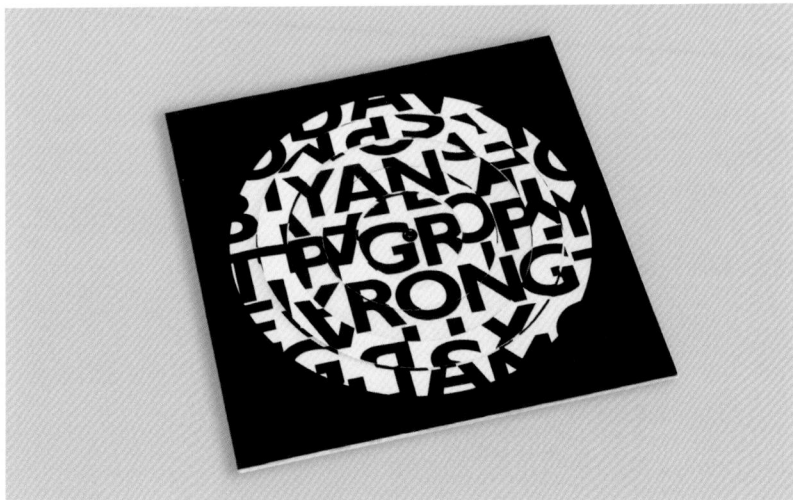

Type Puzzle

"Type Puzzle" is a book about exploring the compositions of letters, words, textures, and objects. The cover was created as a spinning puzzle that changes the letter order. When readers spin it they will find that the composition can change two separate compositional elements to reveal the full title of the booklet. By spinning at one direction, viewers will see the artist's name, and by continuing to spin, the word "Typography" will appear. By this means, Rong Yan aimed to create a fun way to engage the content before opening it.

Designer / Rong Yan

Handmade Structure

Nosigner managed art direction and venue arrangements for "Handmade Structure," an exhibition that gestured towards new attractions of paper.

For the direct marketing materials and the sample book, Nosigner chose a folding process. The finished product resembles a wooden shingle construction. Assembling the materials communicated the concept of the exhibition itself. The shingle-like construction was used for the venue to express the many possibilities when structural design and paper come together.

Design Agency / Nosigner
Art Directior / Eisuke Tachikawa
Designer / Eisuke Tachikawa & Toshiyuki Nakaie
Client / Takeo

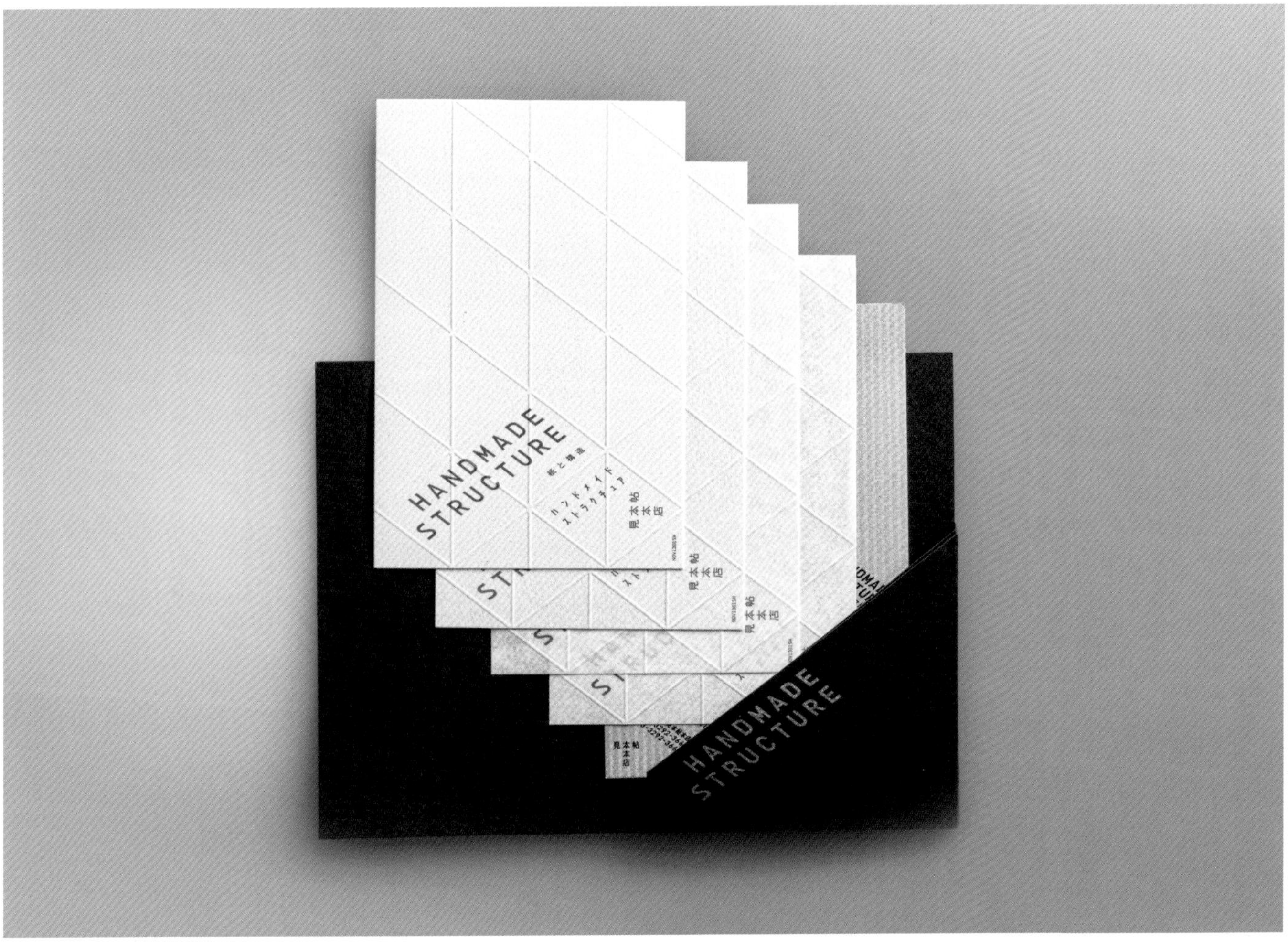
HANDMADE
STRUCTURE
見本帖
本店
HANDMADE
STRUCTURE

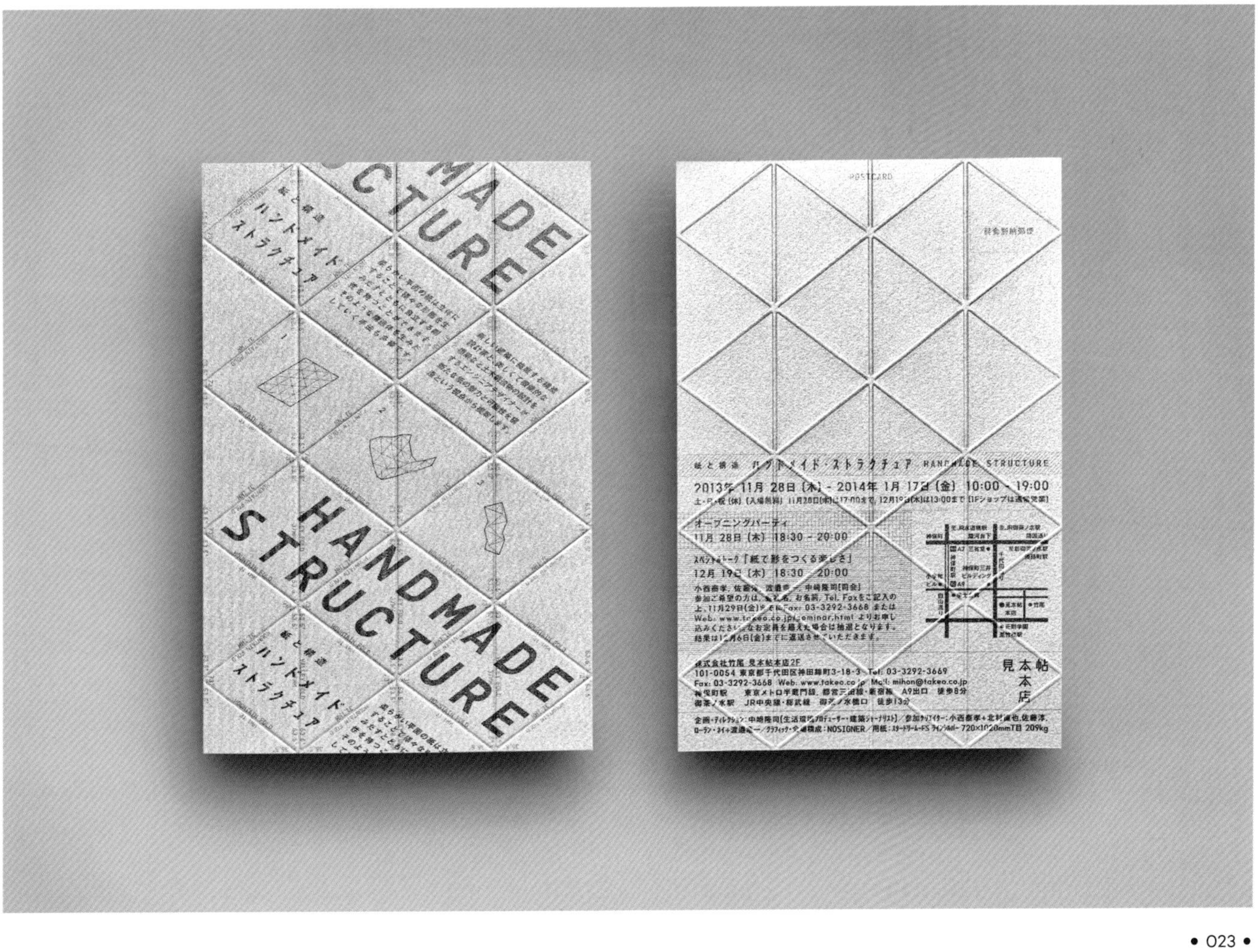
HANDMADE
STRUCTURE
ハンドメイド
ストラクチュア
HANDMADE STRUCTURE
2013年 11月 28日（木）- 2014年 1月 17日（金） 10:00 - 19:00
オープニングパーティ
11月 28日（木） 18:30 - 20:00
12月 19日（木） 18:30 - 20:00
株式会社竹尾 見本帖本店2F
Fax: 03-3292-3668 Web: www.takeo.co.jp
御茶ノ水駅 JR中央線・総武線 御茶ノ水橋口 徒歩13分
見本帖
本店

Bookmark

Paperlux began their work based on the concept that in today's age of high-technology, a bookmark can easily mark any place in a book: a paragraph, a line, or even a single word. Their aim for this project was to merge all of these options together with a generously playful element. The selection of the material did turn out to be a huge challenge: the punching had to be very precise in order to achieve the desired flexibility and haptics, because the thickness of fine paper is not as uniformly even as technical paperboard used for packaging. They also implemented two additional punched lines, in order to achieve even greater flexibility and to dramatize the playful effect. Three colour variations were printed in offset technique on Conqueror paper, and they produced one colour combination for themselves.

Design Agency / Paperlux GmbH
Director / Max Kuehne
Art Director / Carolin Rauen
Photographer / Michael Pfeiffer
Client / Arjowiggins

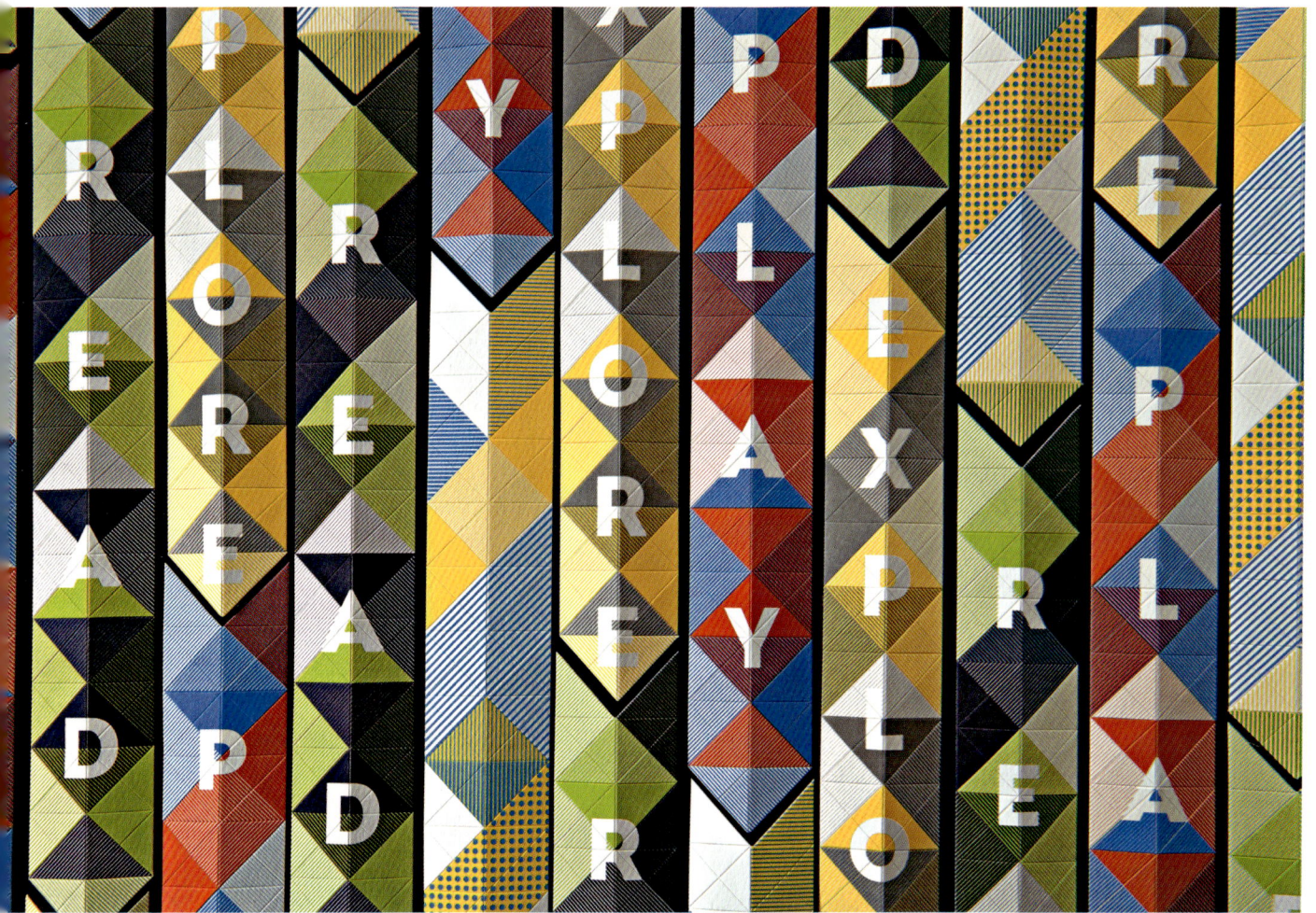

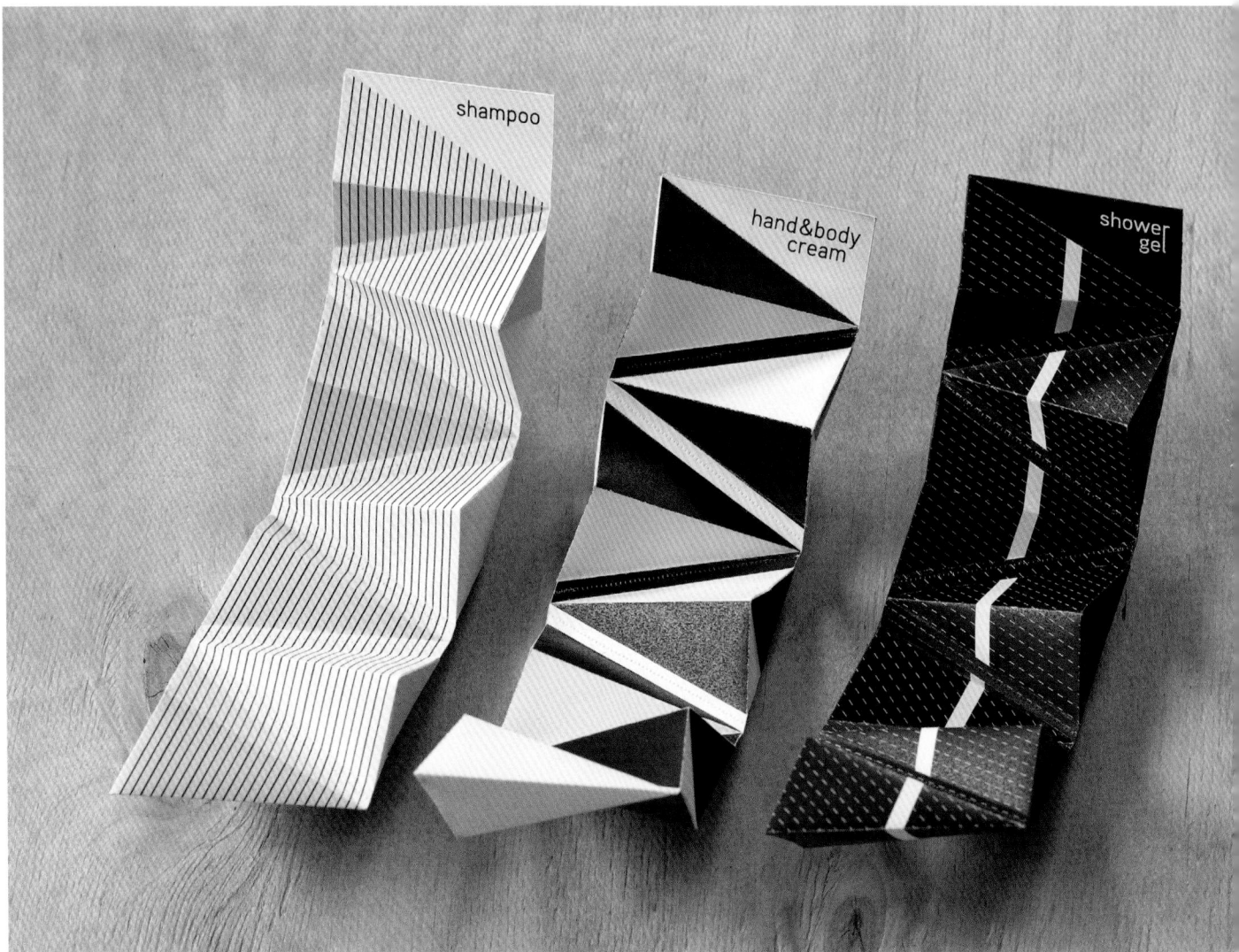

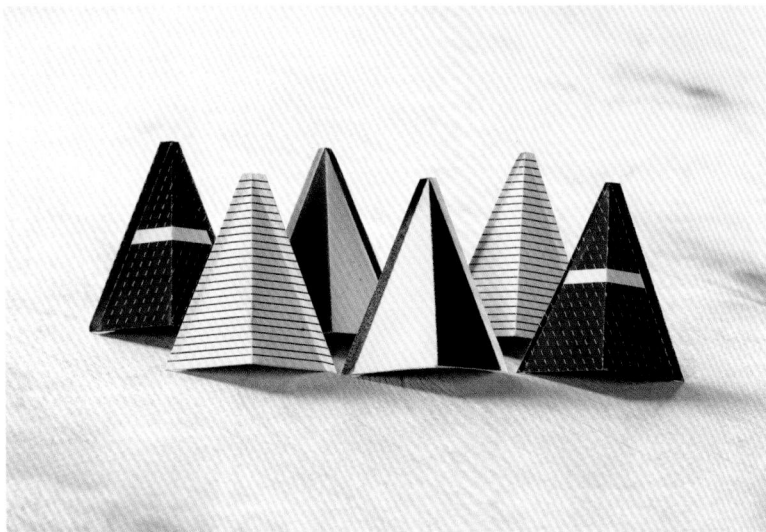

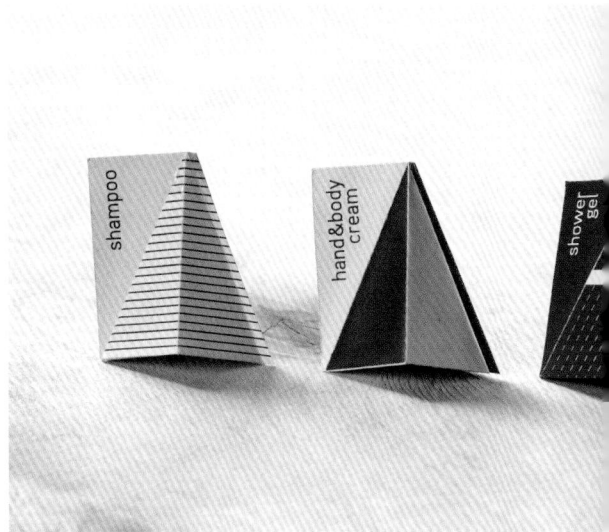

U SHAPE

U SHAPE is a packaging solution for 3 beauty products designed for travelling. The idea was to design a packaging, which can easily be changed the shape to better fit in suitcase and can be reduced with every day of the trip. A set of single use sachets for 7 days. The patterns were inspired by most common travel views: road, rain, wave, roughness, and peak.

Designer / Ewelina Orlowska

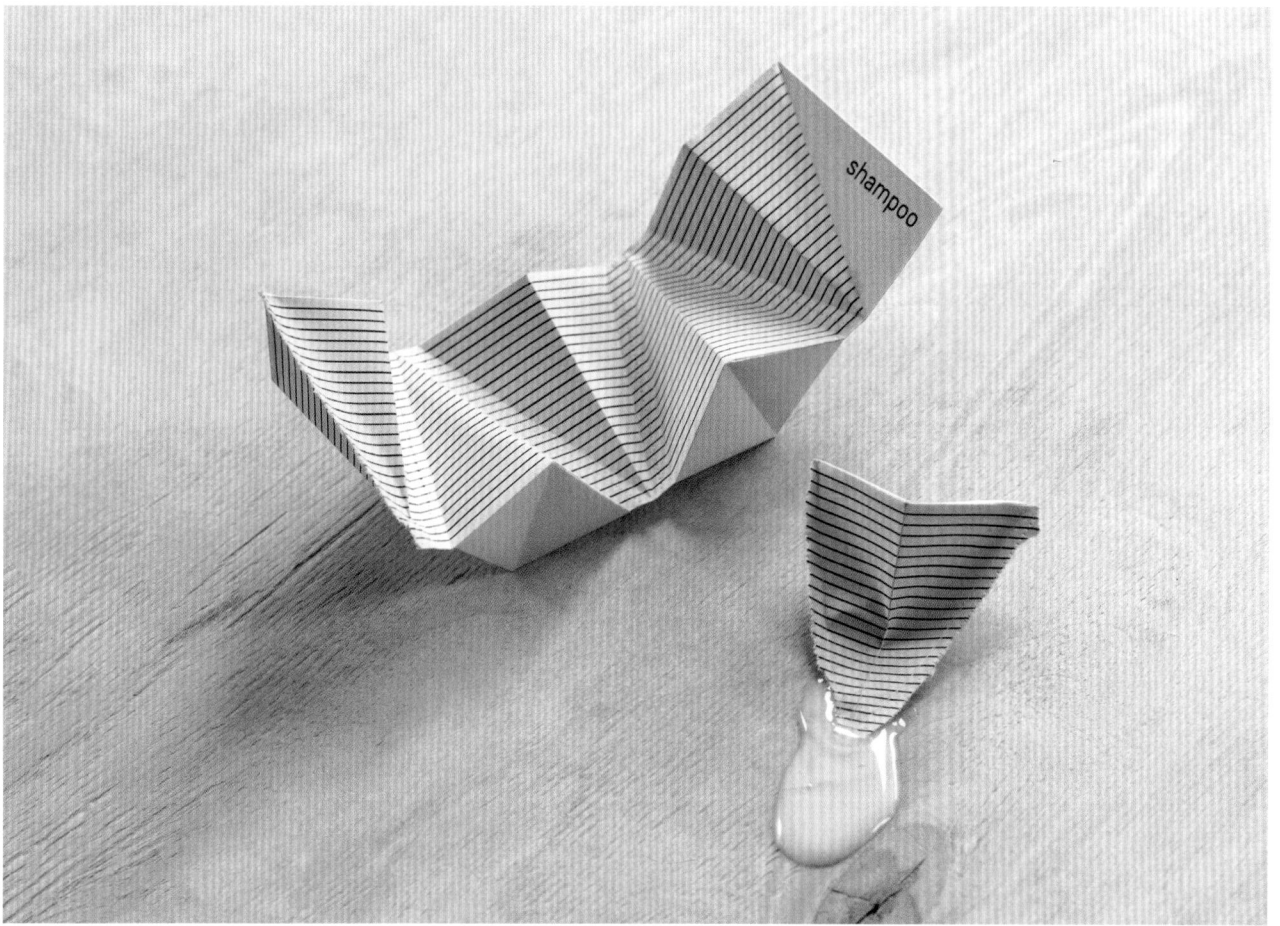

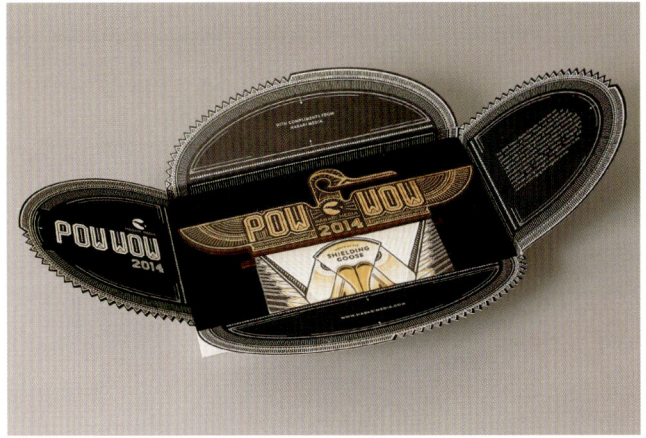

Habari Media - Pow Wow Calendar 2014

Each year, Habari Media creates and distributes an annual calendar showcasing 12 prominent media and marketing players in the industry, one for every month of the year. The brief was to create a direct mail calendar that promotes Habari Madia as an innovative and engaging media house. The result is an economically produced fold-out paper craft calendar entitled "Pow Wow" (meaning "gathering" in Narrangansett). Inspired by Native American totem poles, each media person is assigned a month and spirit animal, signifying the individuals' traits. Facial features of the spirit animals can be popped back and forth and are embedded with image recognition technology linking each spirit animal to the featured Linkedin profile. The promotion of various media players effectively links Habari Media, an innovative Media house, to some of the industry's greats.

Design Agency / Publicis Machine
Director / Gareth Mcperson, Jake Bester & Dani Loureiro
Art Director / Jacque Smit & Kaeli Justus
Designer / Nicole Dalton
Photographer / Travys Owen
Illustrator / Nicole Dlaton & Kaeli Justus
Writer / Gisele Human

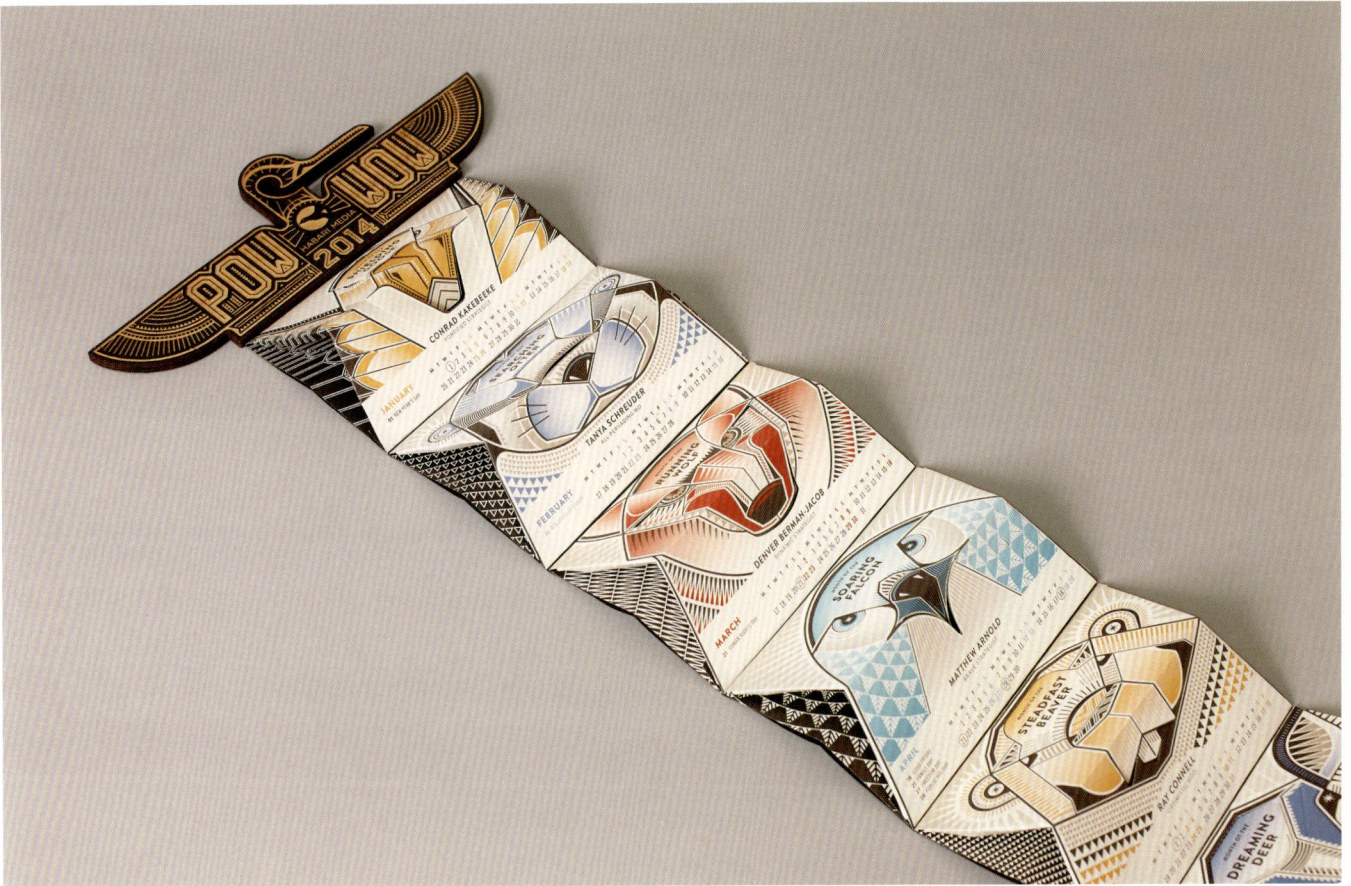

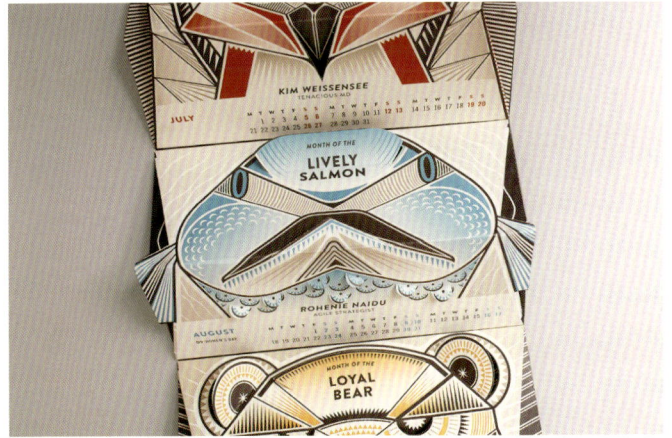

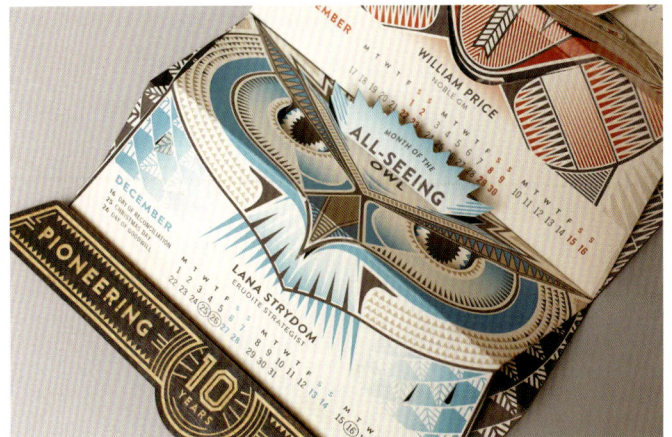

100% YELLOW · 100% PAPER
lemon, grapefruit, banana, pineapple, citrus, mango, orange, papaya and more.

Paper Field IRO IRO

Safari Inc. took over the directions for an exhibition of Heiwa Paper Co., Ltd to promote the "Fancy Paper" with its rich radiance of colour and use. Safari meanwhile displayed a series of fruits made with the yellow paper.

Design Agency / SAFARI Inc.
Designer / Jun Ogita

These are
not fresh.
However,
it does not
rot forever.

ONLY YELLOW FRUIT

lemon, grapefruit, banana, pineapple, citrus, mango, orange, papaya and more.
These are the yellow fruits made from paper. It is not deliciously. Please do not eat. Please appreciate, touch and enjoy these.

Teassert

Teassert is a food packaging that aims to create an enjoyable cultural and environmental friendly tea drinking experience. The package incorporates the idea of Dim Sum into packing tea leaves and snacks that are commonly enjoyed by Chinese while drinking tea.

The whole package is made without using any adhesive. It also has multiple reusable items, including a Dim Sum recipe, bookmarks, coasters, a set of bamboo steam basket for cooking, and a pair of tea leaves picking tool.

Designer / Lily Kao

Run Away to the Mountain: Pop Up Book

The pop up book is made from paper and it folds away flat into a small box, which is also its stand. As the lid is flipped open, one discovers a tiny cabin nestled in a three-dimensional mountain forest. The project concept is to create an object that goes beyond aesthetics to evoke an experience into which one can escape briefly and be delighted. Belying the initial simplicity and solitude of forest imagery are creatures hidden on the reverse side of the trees and artifacts buried under the mapped topography of the mountain. These contrasting elements invite the user to generate narrative.

Designer / Jacy Nordmeyer

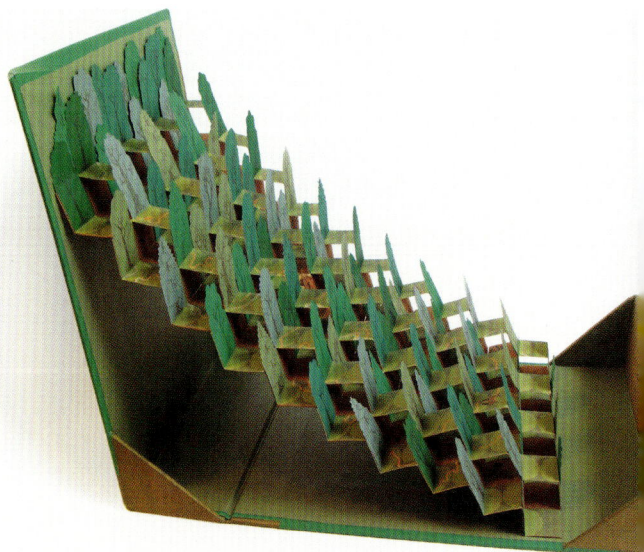

Interactive Invitation Masters of Photography

The invitation is developed in celebration of the Masters of Photography launched in Multimedia Art Museum, Moscow.

The invitation was inspired by the way how camera produces pictures that the message will be shown when the LED light passing through the plastic plate. In this way, it is indeed a playful invitation to show respect to the most influential living photographer, Elliott Erwitt, to capture the spirit of its heartland in his "Great Scottish Adventure."

Designer / Dina Lozovskaya

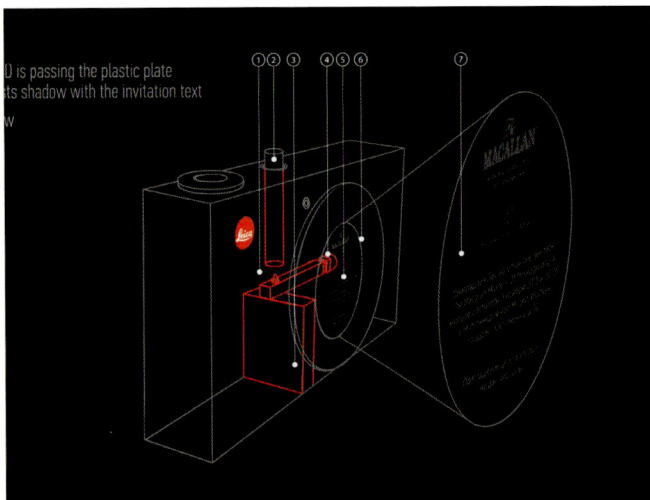

Fedrigoni Sirio Ultra Black

The aim of this project was to design a new marketing tool that would promote the new Sirio Ultra Black Fedrigoni paper range. The solution was to craft a pinhole camera mail out kit to designers and agencies with a single exposure made out of the paper. Once exposed, the magnetic lens can be adjusted back to place blocking any light that would further expose the emulsion paper inside the pinhole camera. The camera can then be sent out for development and followed up with a showcase of all the photos taken.

Designer / Katerina Kerouli

Wedding Invitation Card

Marriage represents the start of a family. So the card design takes "Home" as the concept. The new couple could make a house with the card and receive best wishes to them. After a house is made, it can also be used as a pen container.

Design Agency / Tu Design Office
Designer / Tu Ming-Shiang

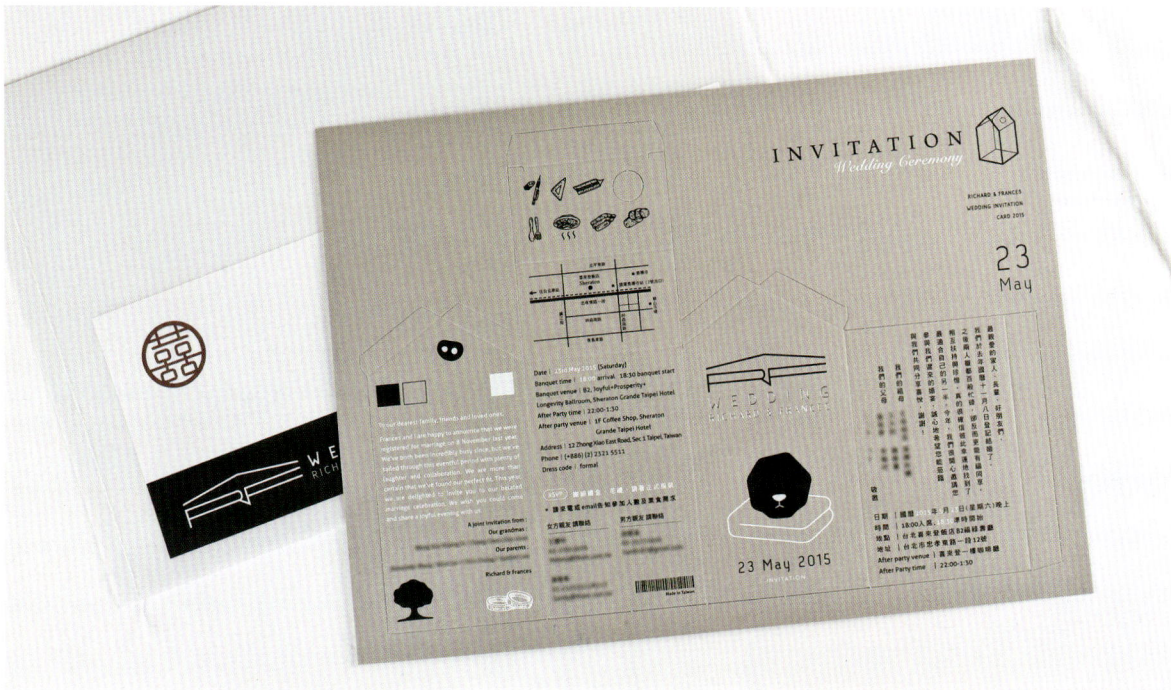

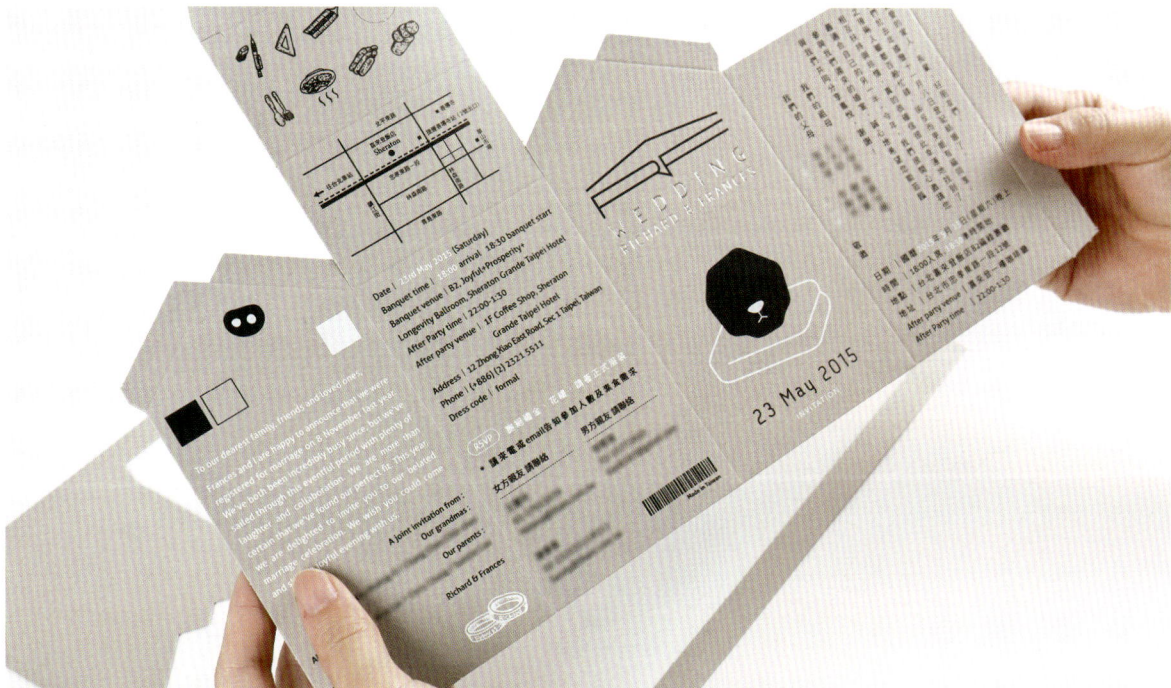

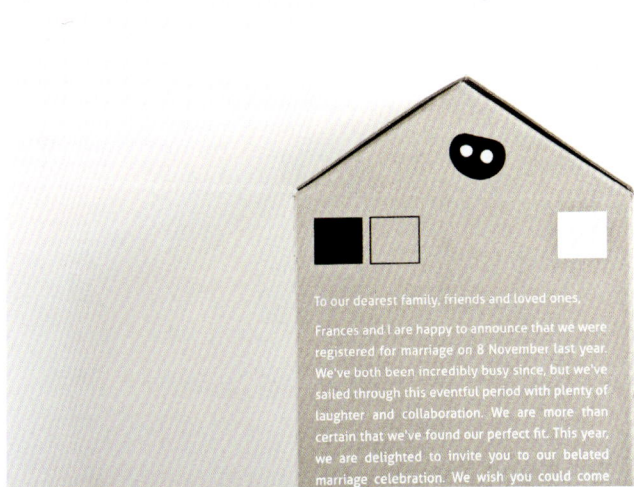

To our dearest family, friends and loved ones,

Frances and I are happy to announce that we were registered for marriage on 8 November last year. We've both been incredibly busy since, but we've sailed through this eventful period with plenty of laughter and collaboration. We are more than certain that we've found our perfect fit. This year, we are delighted to invite you to our belated marriage celebration. We wish you could come

Concresur

The project is a product catalogue designed in a simple and didactic way to show the benefits of concrete modules as well as the product versatility. The catalogue contains a die-cut piece that the reader can pull out and assemble in order to understand the modular system.

Design Agency / Hachetresele
Director / Horacio Lardies
Art Director / Patricio Kolar
Designer / Patricio Kolar
Photographer / Mike Mercau

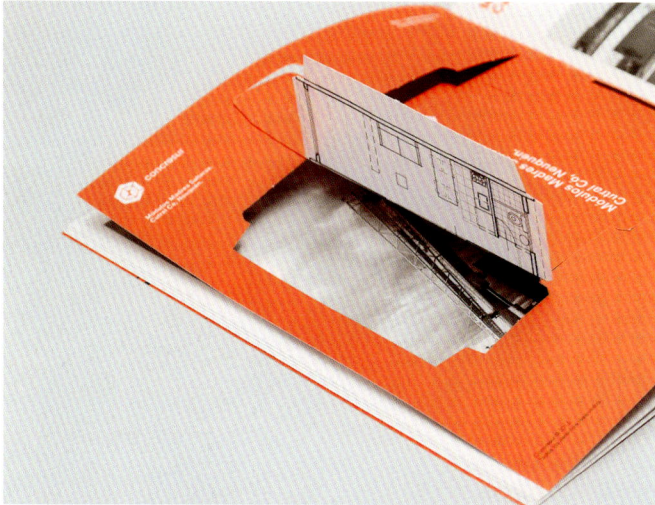

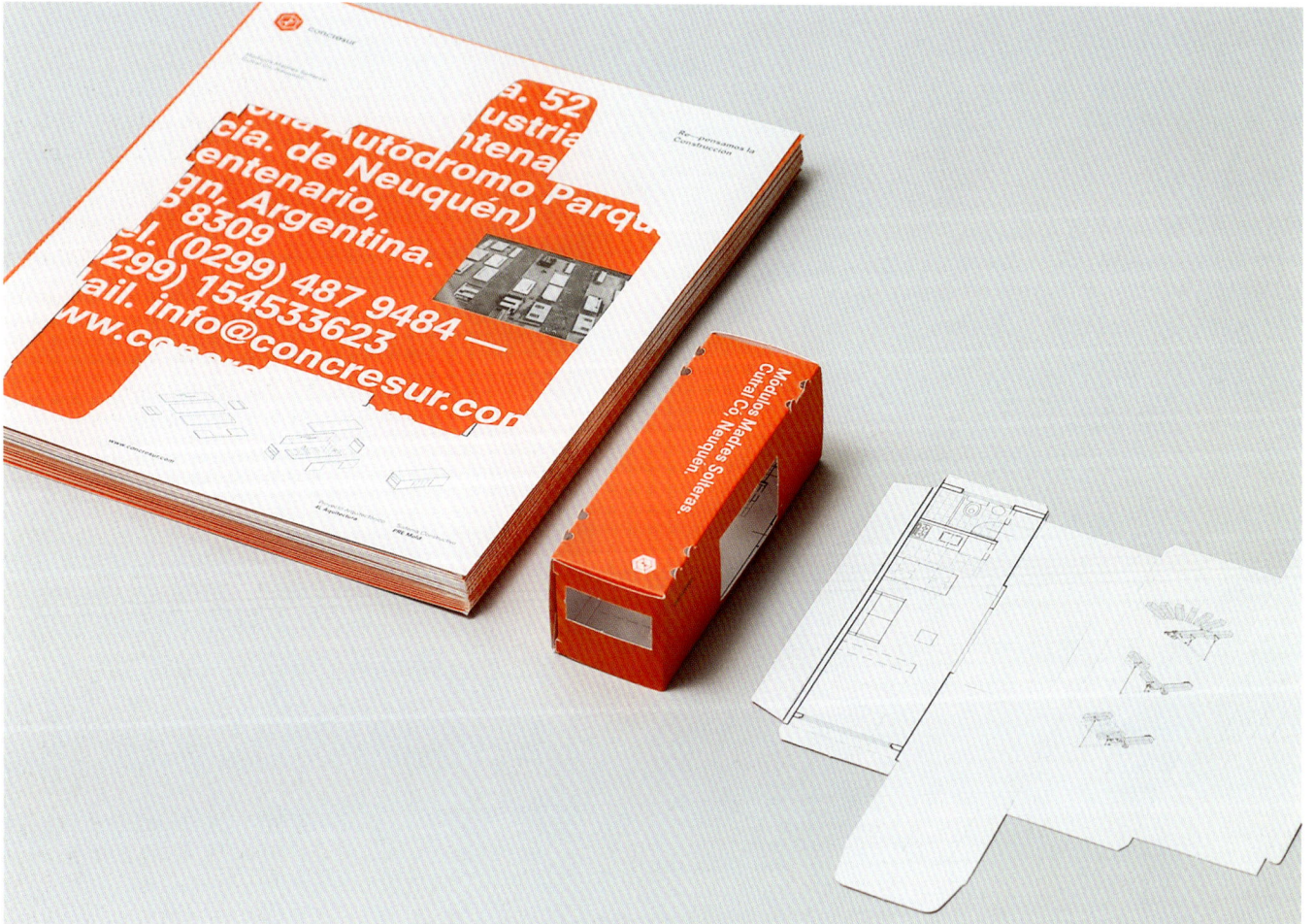

AHAB

AHAB is a collaboration between eskju and Pixeljuice 23. Their goal was to make a beautiful and independently produced T-Shirt package.

The concept was inspired by the story and the characters around Captain Ahab and Moby Dick, which are associated with childhood, book reading and fantasy dreams.

Design Agency / eskju | Bretz & Jung
Designer / Daniel Bretz (eskju)
Illustrator / Antonio Basilico (Pixeljuice 23)
Print / Oliver Jung (eskju)
Client / eskju

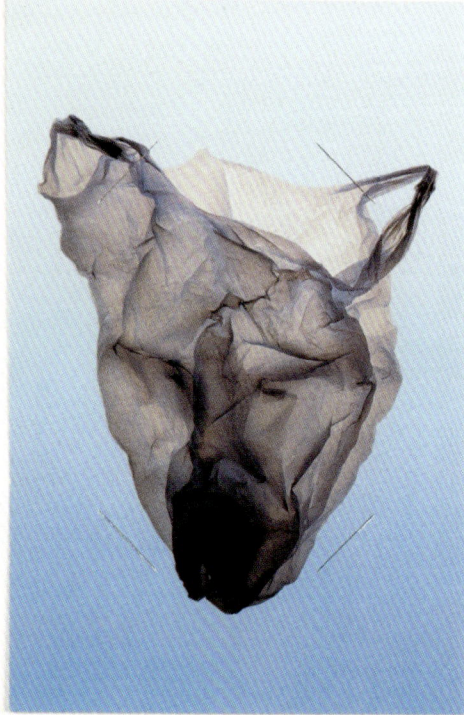

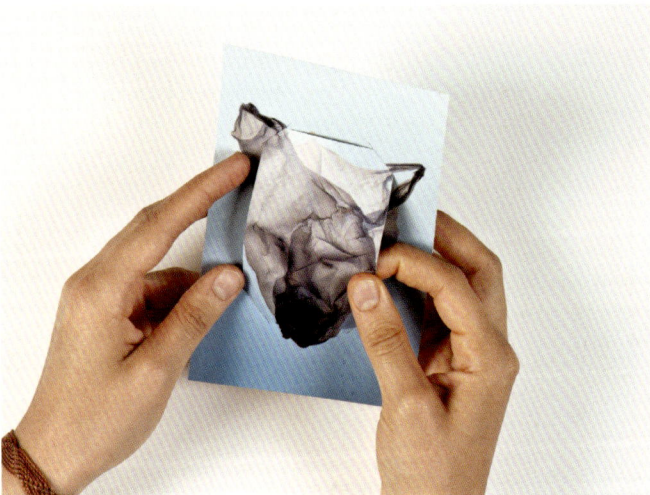

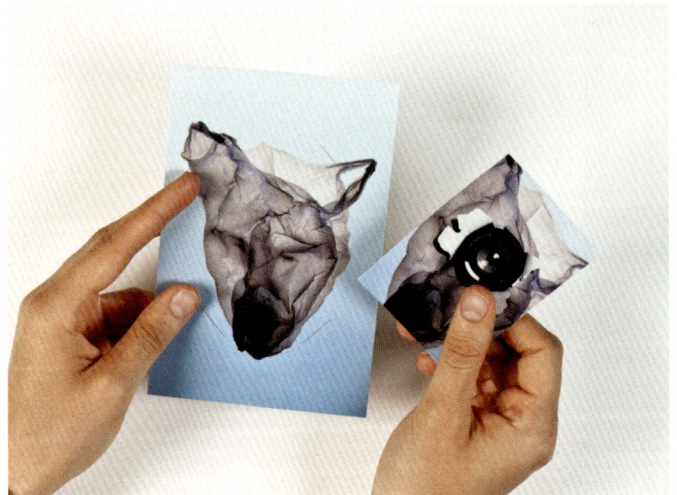

Invitation Card for an Exhibition

The aim of this project is to communicate a hypothetical exhibition about the work of Michal Batory. Roberta Donatini designed an invitation card based on the poster Tamerlan Le Grand by Batory for the Theatre National de Chaillot in Paris. She added an interactive element to create a new picture with a photographic lens cropping out the paper. In this way users can interact with the invitation to combine two different images, exploring another level of interpretation of Batory's work: photography within the poster.

Designer / Roberta Donatini

Giuseppe Giussani Identity

Giuseppe Giussani is an Italian craftsman specialized in bespoke wood flooring.

Everything starts from wood, so the idea is to combine his name and his raw material to create a personal brand identity. The result is an organic brand that represents the strong connection between the craftsman and his work.

Design Agency / 45gradi
Director / Marina Cattaneo & Silvia Grazioli
Designer / Valentina Ferioli

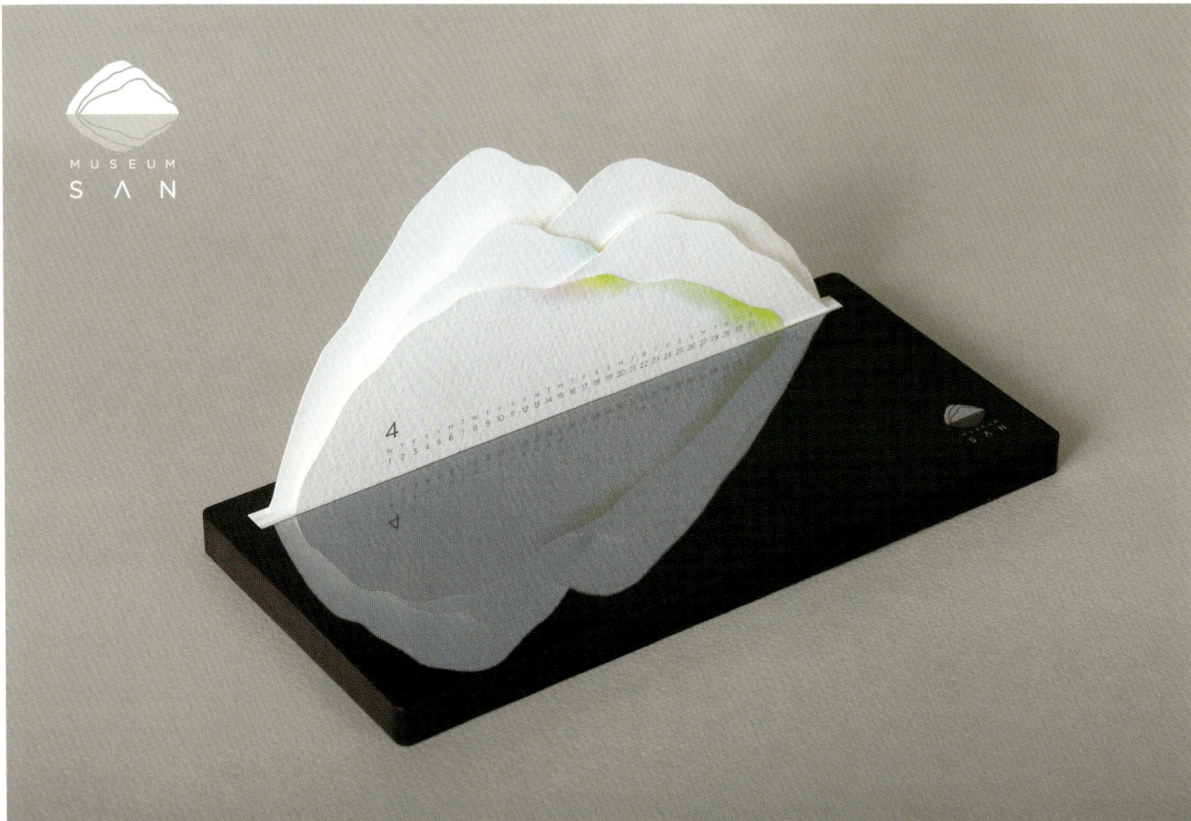

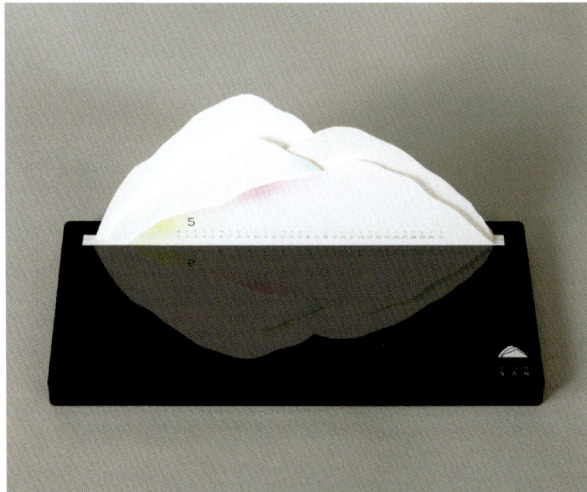

Museum SAN Calendar

Ando is an art museum located at the top of a mountain in the Republic of Korea. This calendar was created as the museum's opening invitation in order to promote the identity of SAN (mountain in Korean). It intends to communicate its special character as a place where art and culture are harmonized with natural surroundings and the four seasons. Therefore, the SAN logo on each monthly page was coloured differently referring to the mountain environment changing with the seasons.

Design Agency / Interbrand Seoul
Creative Director / Uzin Hwang
Designer / Hajin Jung & Miyoung Kim

BASIC   FLEXIBLE   DIGITAL

MUSEUM
SAN

MUSEUM   MUSEUM   MUSEUM
SAN   SAN   SAN

8
W T F S S M T W T F S S M T W T F S S M T W T F S S M T W T F
1 2 3 4 5 6 7 8 9 10 11 12 13 14 15 16 17 18 19 20 21 22 23 24 25 26 27 28 29 30 31

8

MUSEUM
SAN

MUSEUM
SAN

MUSEUM
SAN

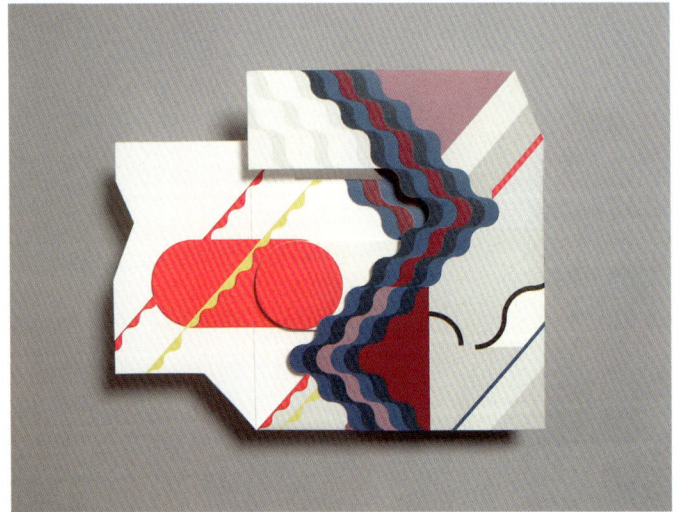

A HAPPY NEW YEAR Art Factory

A Happy New Year Art Factory is a postcard designed for art factory as a greeting for the year of Horse. When the recipient opens the first two layers, it shows a sun rising from the sea, while it becomes a horse when it is completely opened.

Designer / Naonori Yago

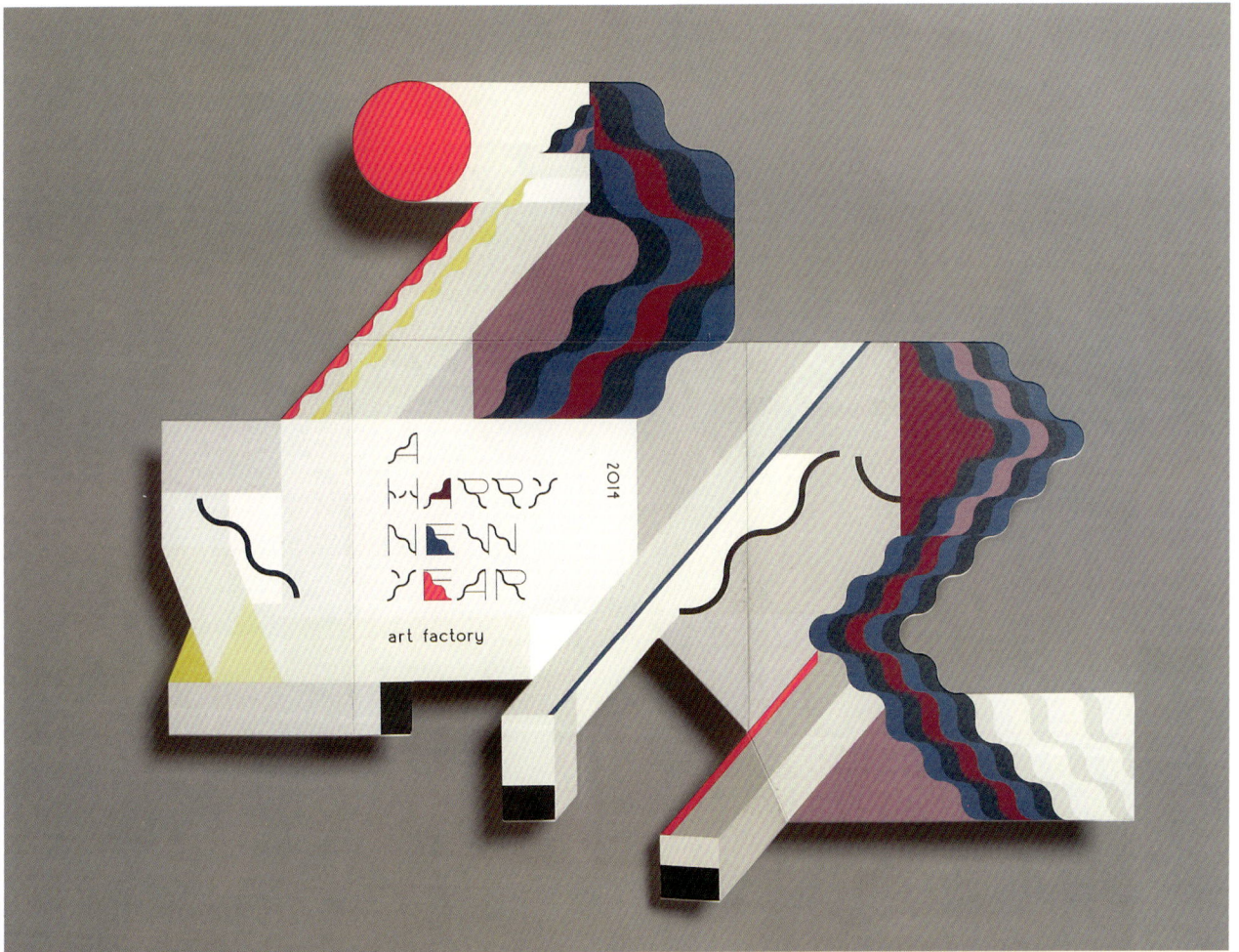

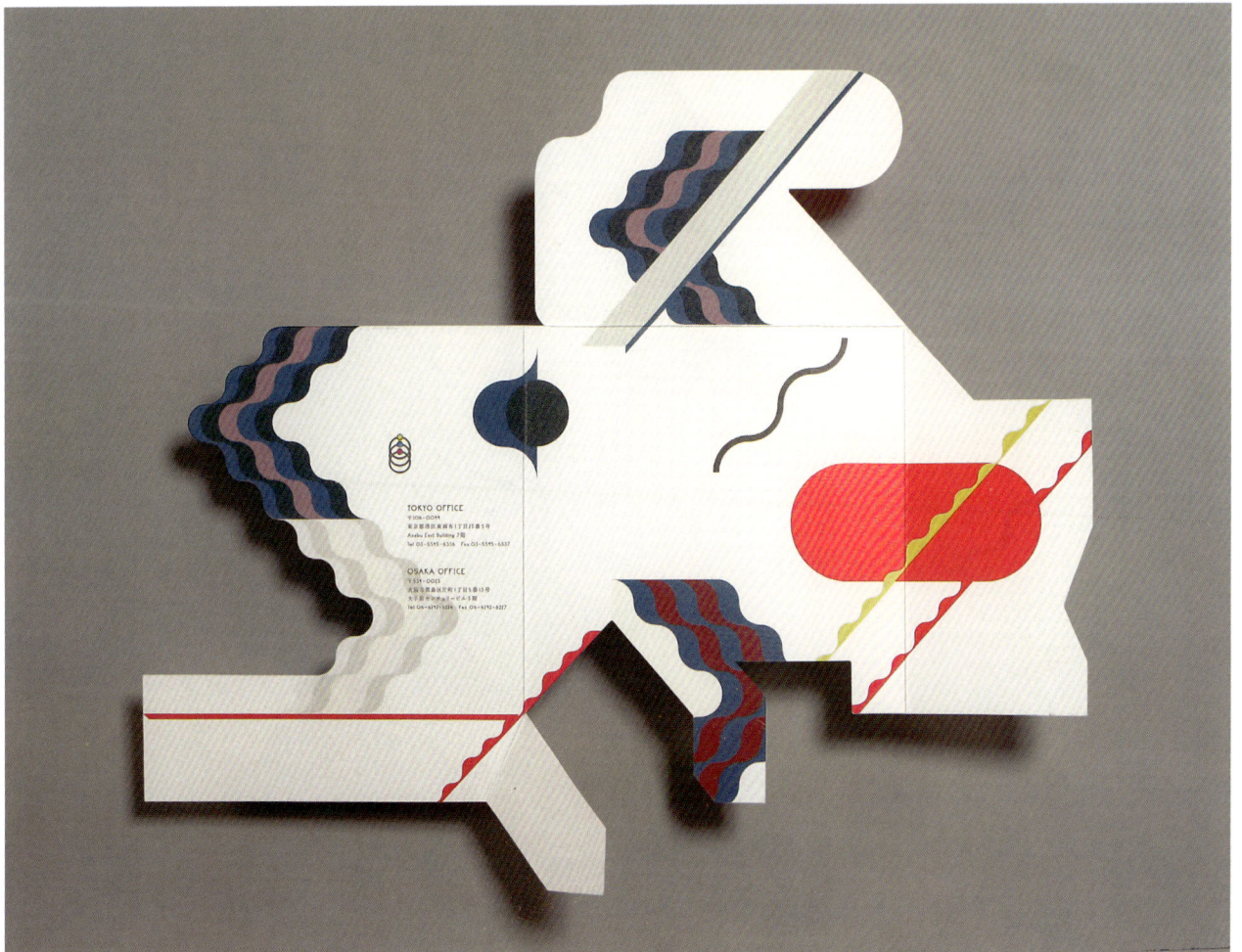

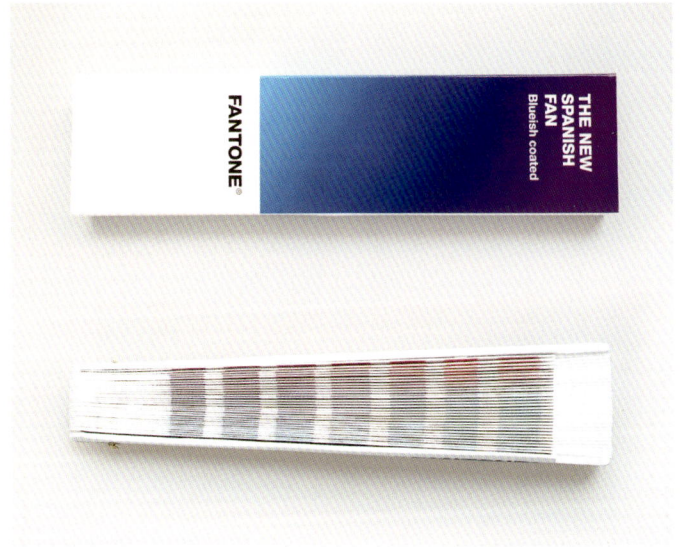

Fantone

Fantone was born from the combination of two concepts, the fan and Pantone®. The fan, a popular instrument and icon of Spanish culture, which is essential during hot summers, joins the colour guide, an indispensable tool for designers and creative types. The colour guide's applications have gone beyond its original use and became a design that has landed on such a variety of products from mugs to bicycles to hotels. The Fantone is not a colour guide and isn't intended to be one. Instead, it is an ironic approach to transform the famous colour guide to the form of a fan with an aim to make the fan to be a trend in the new generations and become a fashion essential.

Design Agency / IS Creative Studio
Designer / Richars Meza

Cora Hillebrand Visual Identity

Art photographer Cora Hillebrand extends her talents working with everything from video installations to portraits and still life, with the occasional commercial commission. Often carrying heavy equipment, Cora wanted something light to leave behind to her clients. Lundgren+Lindqvist designed a sturdy envelope, in the shape of a Polaroid picture, with an open front. On the envelope, they printed Cora's contact details. Pictures by Cora were printed on cardboard and perforated for easy detachment. This allows Cora to compose various mini portfolios customized for different client.

Design Agency / Lundgren+Lindqvist
Photographer / Cora Hillebrand
Printing / Göteborgstryckeriet

Micro Culture

Maryam Khosrovani created a microscopic art book, which consists of 300 pages. Only with a microscope you could see the writings and art works by famous international artists. The idea behind this work was that even if our culture was hidden and you would only see through a microscope, it would still be visible. Our culture can never be lost or vanished into thin air.

Designer / Maryam Khosrovani

Entre 20 Aguas

"Entre 20 Aguas" is a tribute album to flamenco artist Paco de Lucía. Mucho were asked to create the cover and interior concept for this piece with two things in mind: First, this was not a Paco de Lucía's album, but an album dedicated to his memorizing him. Second, it was important to remain faithful to sentimental and poetic nature of the tribute.

Their solution was to use water to form the silhouette of Paco de Lucía, one of the most recognizable figures in Spanish music, thus creating a specific, recognizable shape but from a medium as indomitable as water. The idea was to do it in a real and analogical way to stay faithful to the purity and the natural, patient spirit of his music and how he worked. It is both an ode of mourning for the death of this great artist and a celebration of his art.

Design Agency / Mucho
Photographer / Roc Canals
Typeface / Zarzuela (Carles Rodrigo)

**Entre
20 Aguas**
A la música
de Paco
de Lucía

Entre
20 Aguas
A la música
de Paco
de Lucía

EL PAIS

UNIVERSAL

casa
limón

PRISARADIO

"Paco de Lucía
ha ennoblecido
el flamenco, ha
ampliado su registro,
ha abierto ventanas
por donde otros
deben respirar."

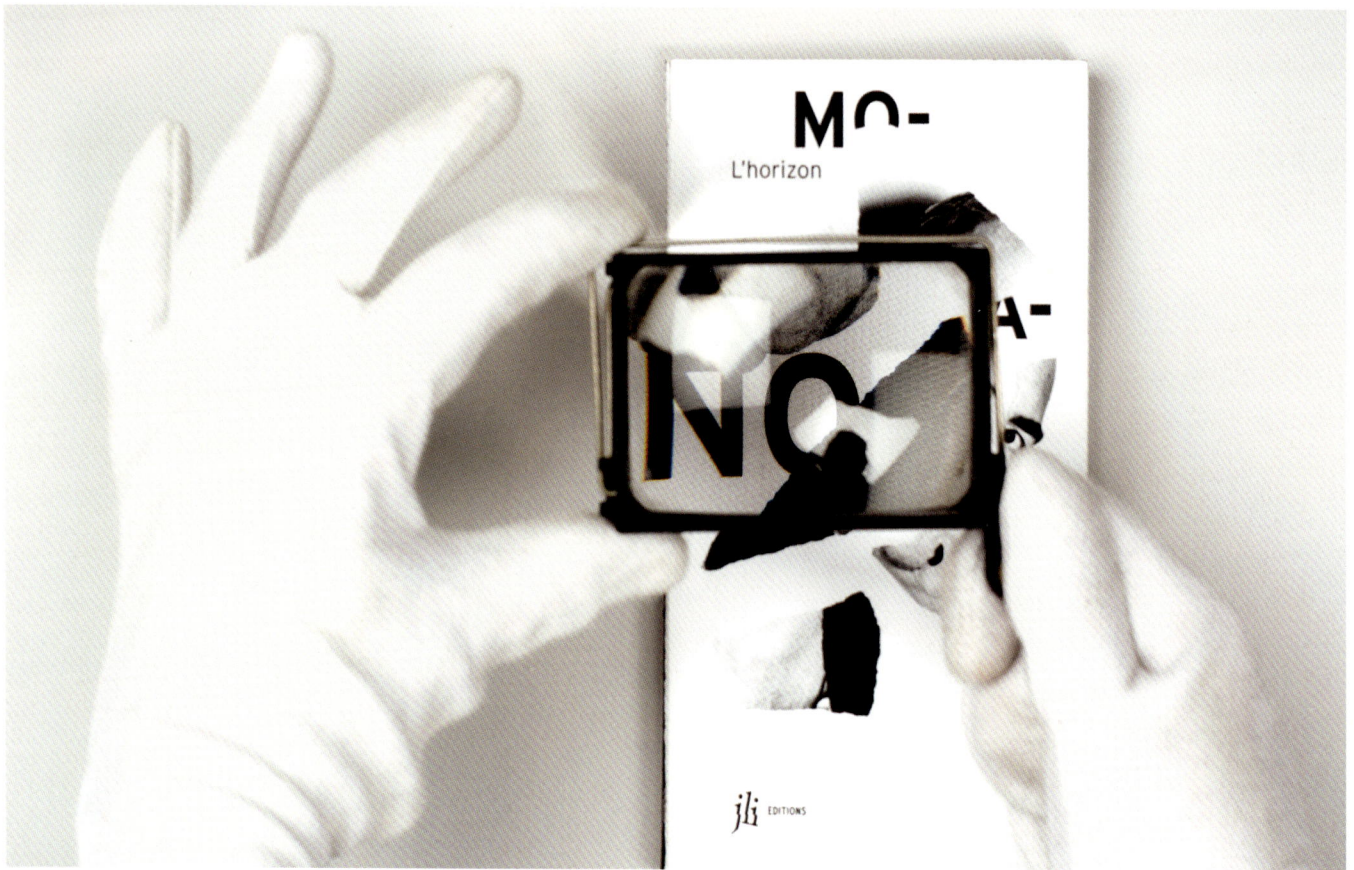

Horizon by P. Modiano Cover Book

The search for identity is a major theme in Patrick Modiano's work (French writer, author of about thirty novels). The book cover design of "Horizon" by Modiano attempts to recreate that atmosphere. A portrait of the author himself and his name are deconstructed on the cover which graphically reflects how Modiano, the narrator in most of his books, is very often an observer trying to identify every details that could guide him to rebuild his identity and understand what is around him. It strengthens the idea of research of self-identity and search for different clues by photographing the object with a magnifying glass and the photographic art direction.

Designer / Julie Soudanne
Photographer / Adrien Thibault

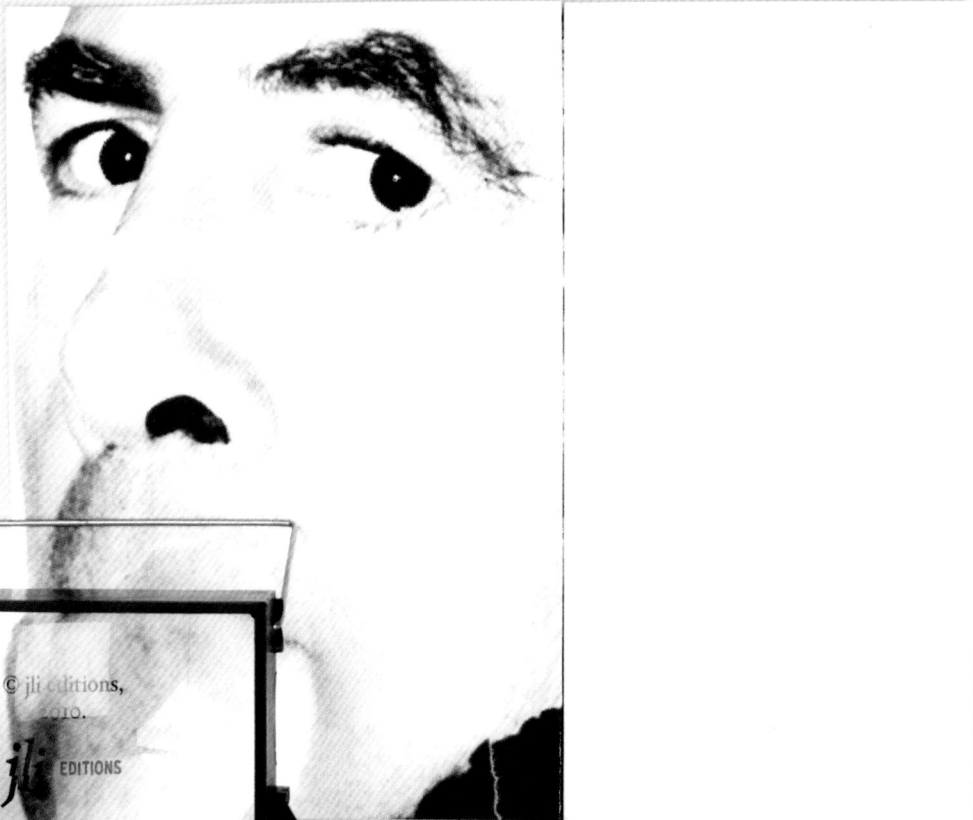

jli EDITIONS

POP – Personal Branding

POP is a self-branding based on popping bubble wrap. The concept stems from the obsessive tendency to press the pop that people can have when in contact with bubble wrap. Beneath each bubble is a unique self-portrait that seems to react as if being squeezed. This popping action highlights the way of thinking, which tends to grab attention and stand out among others.

Designer / Derek Dubler

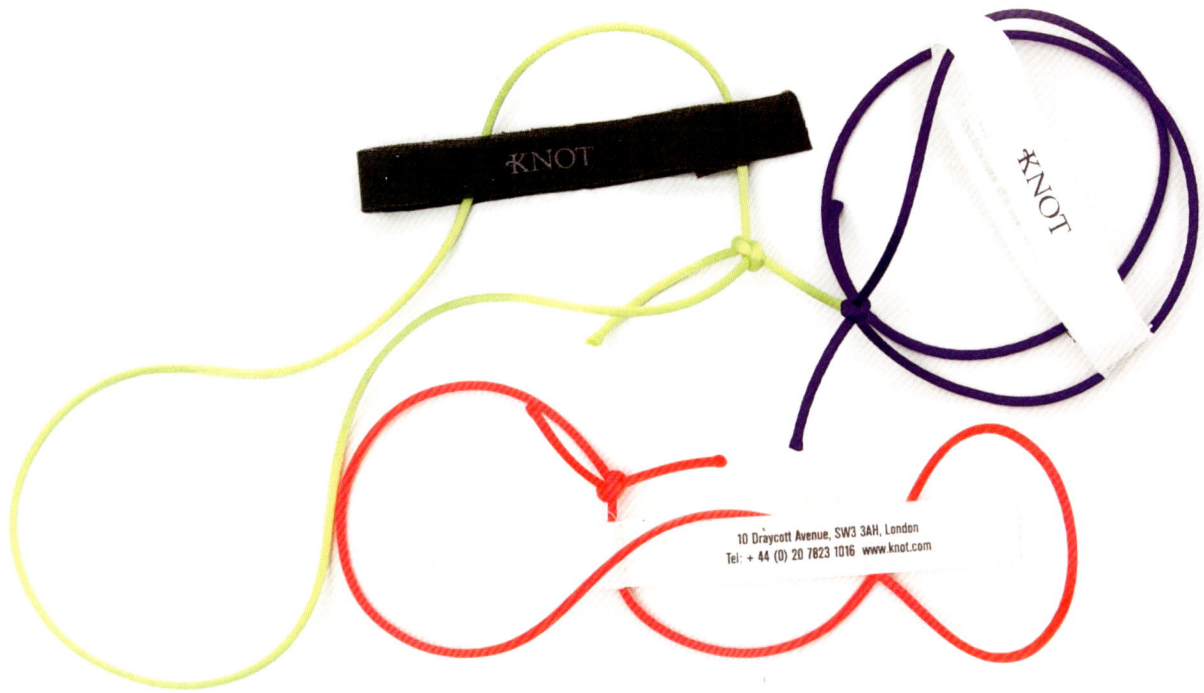

10 Draycott Avenue, SW3 3AH, London
Tel: + 44 (0) 20 7823 1016 www.knot.com

Knot

Knot is about creating longer and more meaningful relationships with clothes through quality and design to find value beyond the ephemeral and momentary pleasure, and to shape your identity in strategic decisions while contributing to a less materialistic lifestyle. When a costumer buys garment, a knot will be made as a ritual, forming a timelss memory.

Designer / Lucia Freire Coloma
Photographer / Anne Schwarz & Lucia Freire Coloma

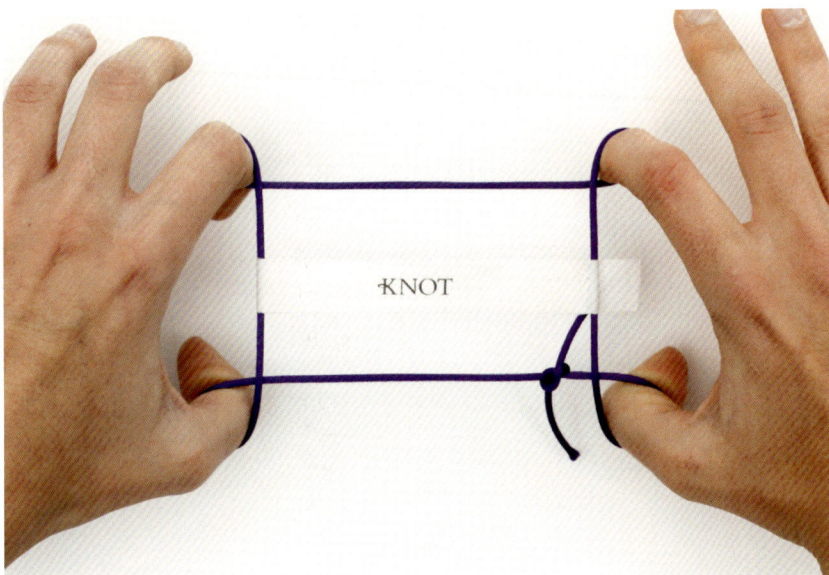

Your Cash Makes a Difference

Forest & Bird is a team to protect all of New Zealand's native species and wild places, but they receive no government funding. To continue this project and help increase their scale, Ogilvy & Mather New Zealand wanted people to see for themselves how just $5 could make a huge difference — it can literally put an endangered bird back in its natural environment. To maximize the revenue from this campaign, $10 and $50 executions were also created.

Design Agency / Ogilvy & Mather New Zealand
Director / Angus Hennah & Chris Childerhouse
Art Director / Martin Hermans
Designer / Stephen Fuller
Photographer / Forest & Bird

...yone is happy with the way the home's turned out
...an architect, to be able to live in a home you've des...
...analyse what works and what doesn't," says Jonatha...
...he girls think it's cool to live in a house their dad ha...
...ssive input into," says Justine. With two living areas...
...like having their own messy space. "The whole house...
...ks. I use it frequently as an exhibition space or show...
...t is a great home for entertaining.
..."People often say that contemporary architecture is c...
...erile. This house shows it can be far from that. I feel ver...
...f Jonathan's design when people visit and love our hous...
see Justine's work at justinehawksworth.weebly.com. ▥

Please visit forestandbird.org.nz/joinus today.

Forest & Bird®
GIVING NATURE A VOICE

Movies' Pop-up Book

This project is a pop-up book, which showcases the most famous lines from well-known movies. Those 7 quotes are illustrated, each one on a double page, with a simple graphic design based on 3 colours and the movies' universe. By folding out, rotating, and opening, readers can find the quotes which are combined with typographic works and strong symbols taken from the movies.

Designer / Amélie Valverde

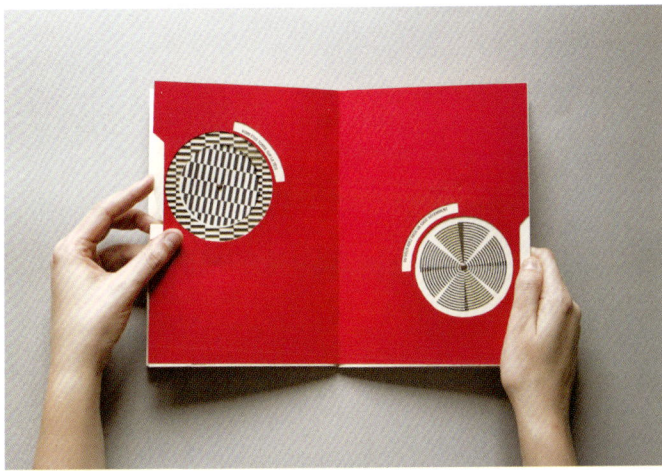 

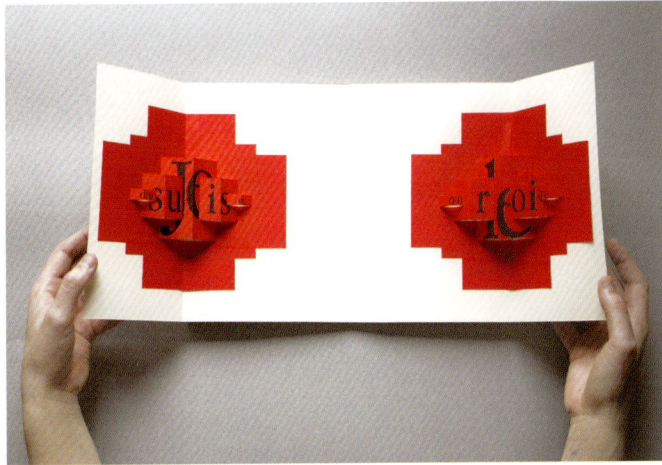 

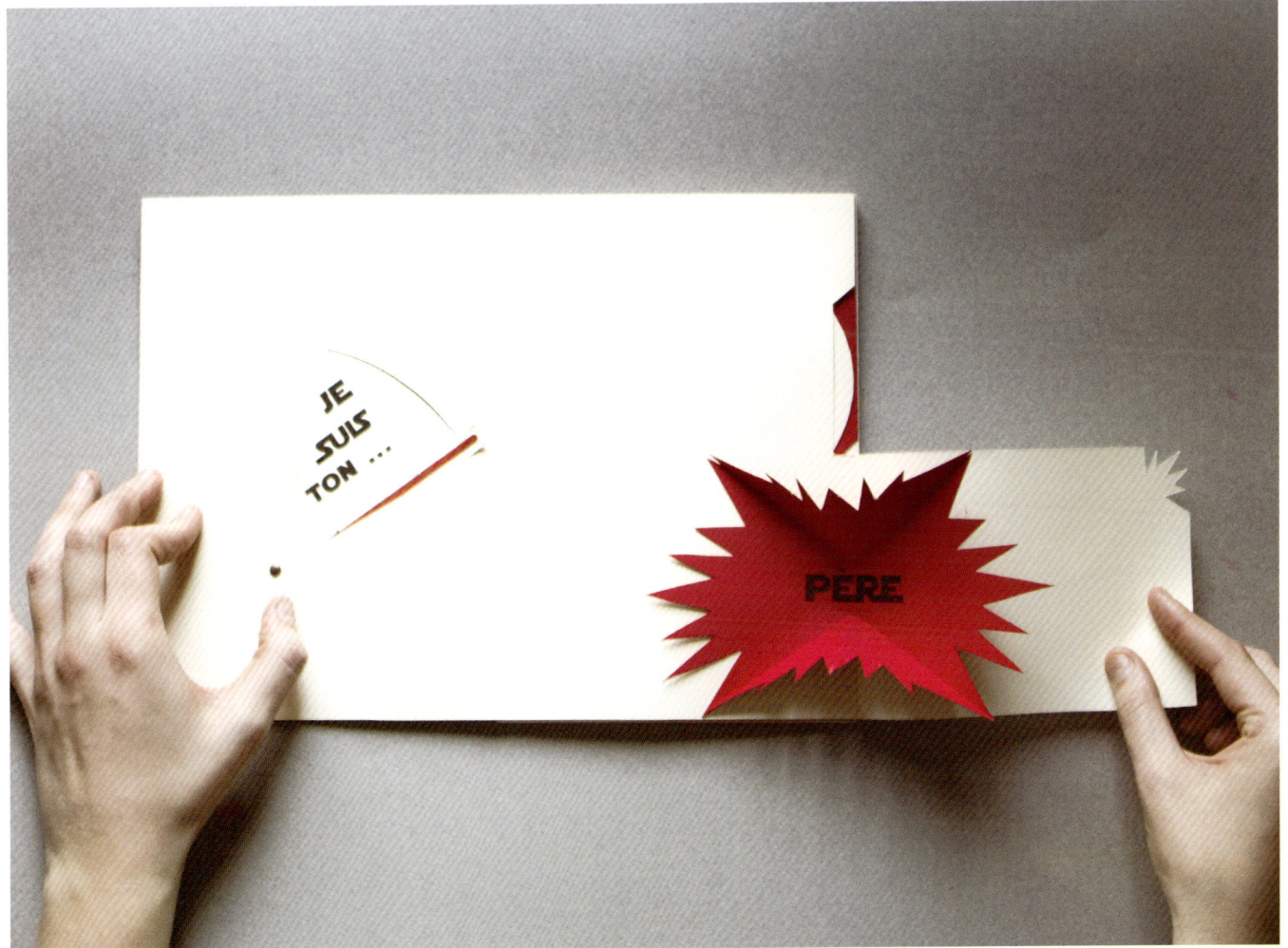

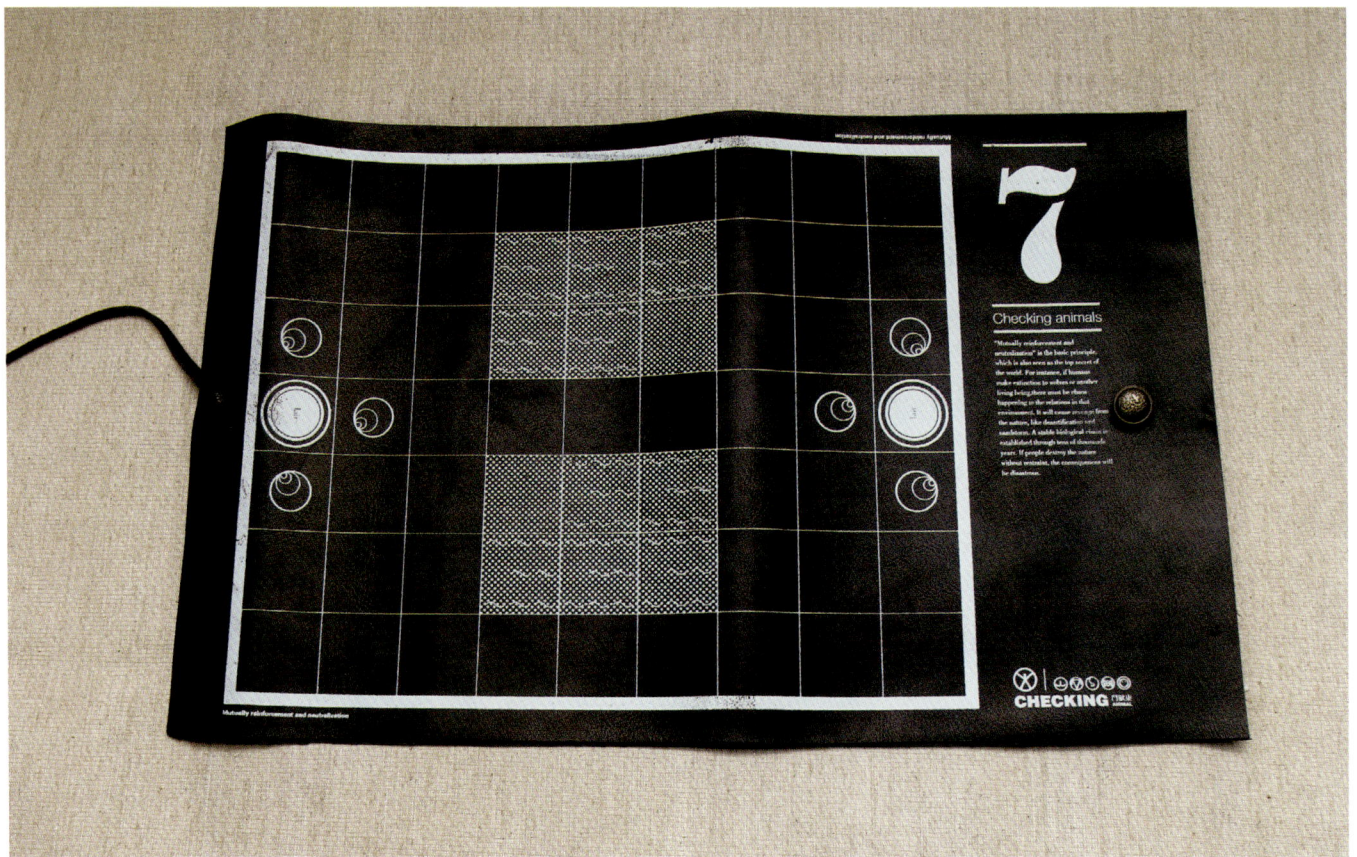

Chacking Seven Animals

This project was created by Gong Xinyu during his sophomore year in university. Inspired by the Jungle Chess, which is a Chinese traditional board game, the book cover was designed as the board, symbolizing a linear feeding relation in which human is mortal and merely a part in it.

Designer / Gong Xinyu

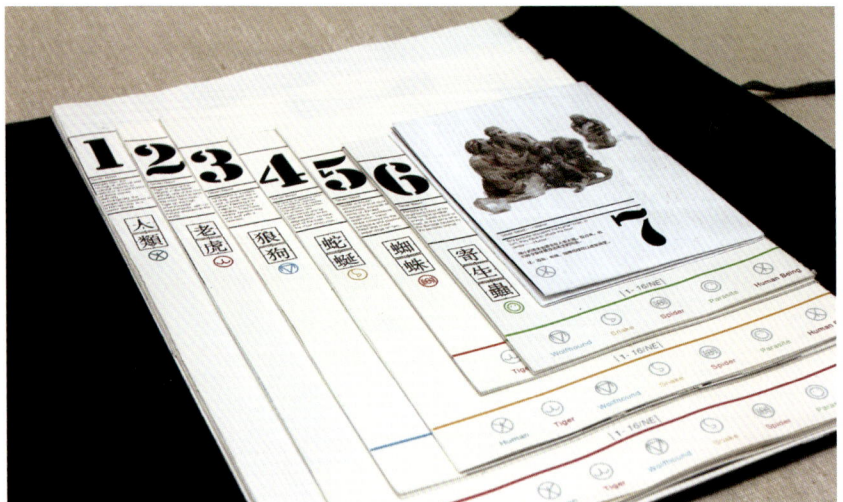

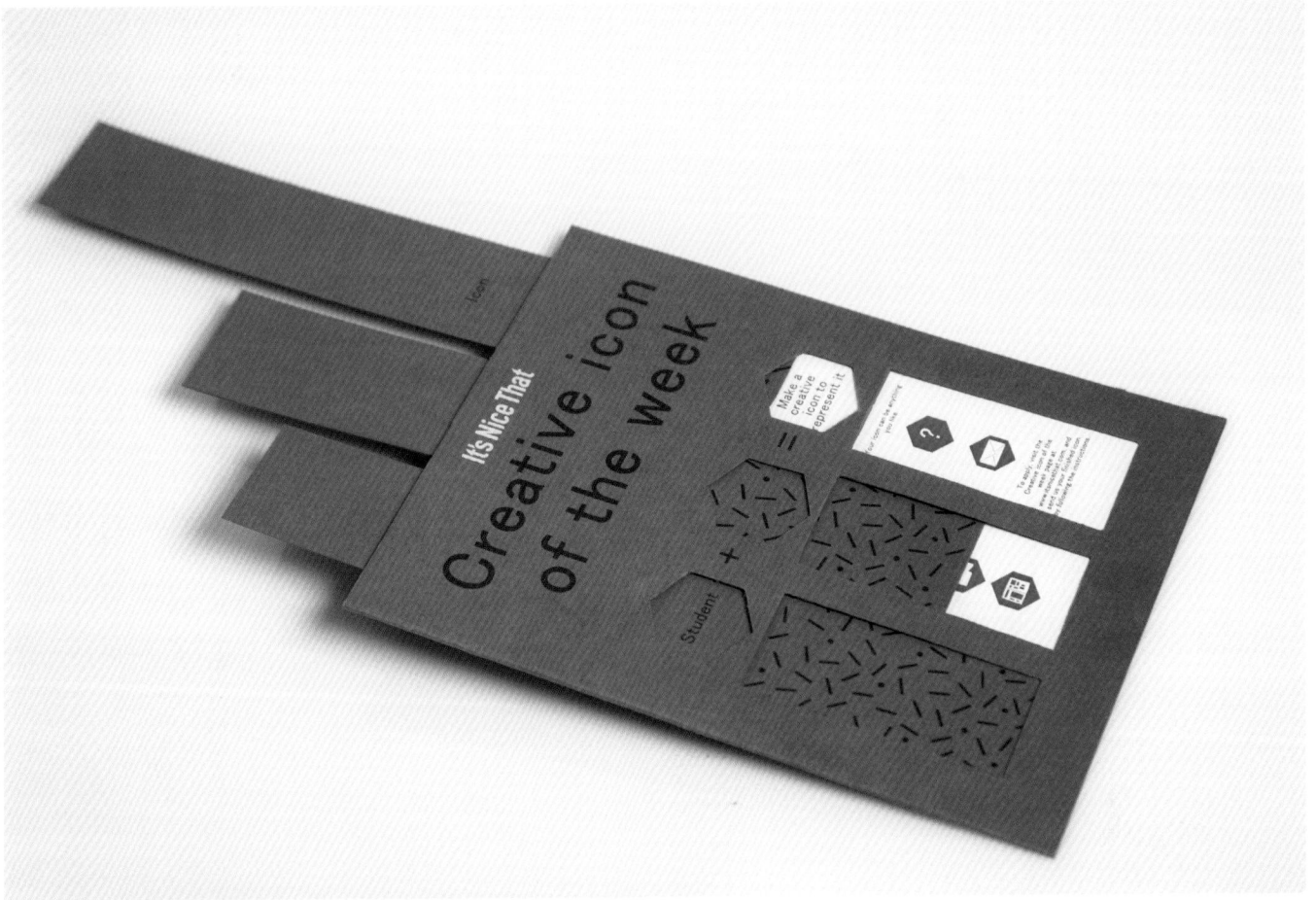

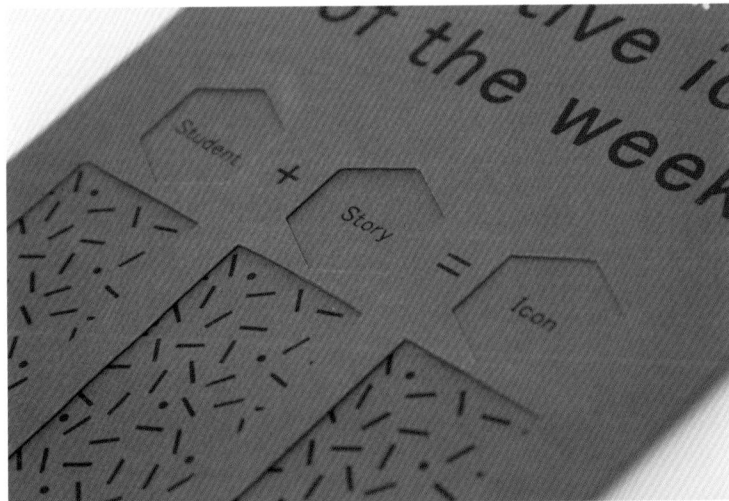

DandAD Student Awards 2013 - It's Nice That

The object is a flyer as well as a guidance to engage the existing and new student audience to submit and showcase their works on the It's Nice That website.

Designer / Chantelle Barnard-Rance

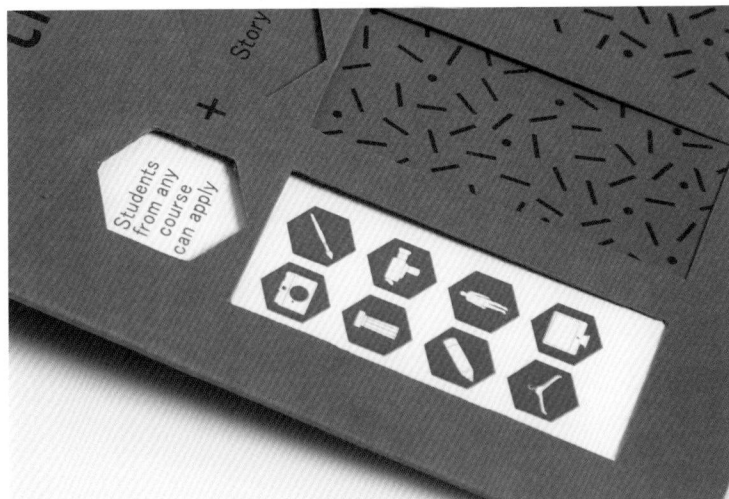

HEIWA PAPER | deep-mat

deep-mat is a project collaborated with a Japanese paper company and produced with high quality paper. artless selected 11 chic colours inspired by wine's colour, and designed these samples as bookmarks so that customers could feel their texture by using them for real.

Design Agency / artless Inc.
Designer / Shun Kawakami
Client / Heiwa Paper Co.,Ltd.
Photographer / Yuu Kawakami

upsetters architects: Corporate Identity

This project was designed for Japanese architect company with an aim to convey their business at first sight. The corporate card is designed with a cut-out shape of a building that the card is tactile and the clients could see different images from the front and the back. Also, the information on the card is able to be torn off and stuck to anything so as to allow business conversation at anywhere and in any time.

Design Agency / artless Inc.
Designer / Shun Kawakami
Photographer / Yuu Kawakami
Client / upsetters architects

Greeting Card

Commune aims to make their Greeting Card a surprising and exciting piece that people would be curious about the content before they open it. A series of photos is accordion folded as a flip-book movies in the postcard so as to bulge the words on the cover and bring amusement when the recipient flips through it.

Design Agency / Commune
Photographer / Tsubasa Fujikura

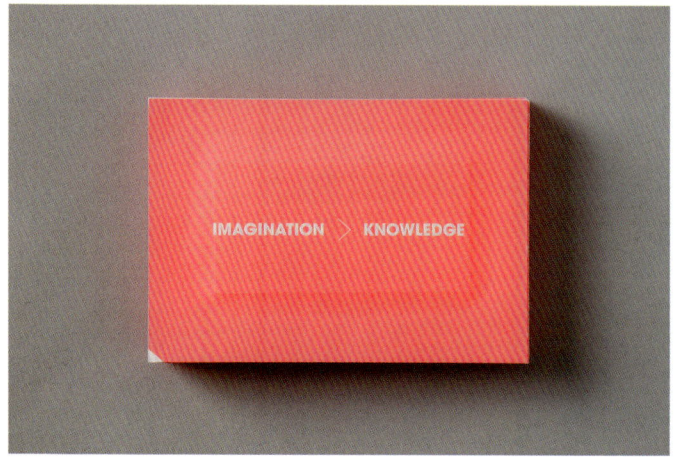

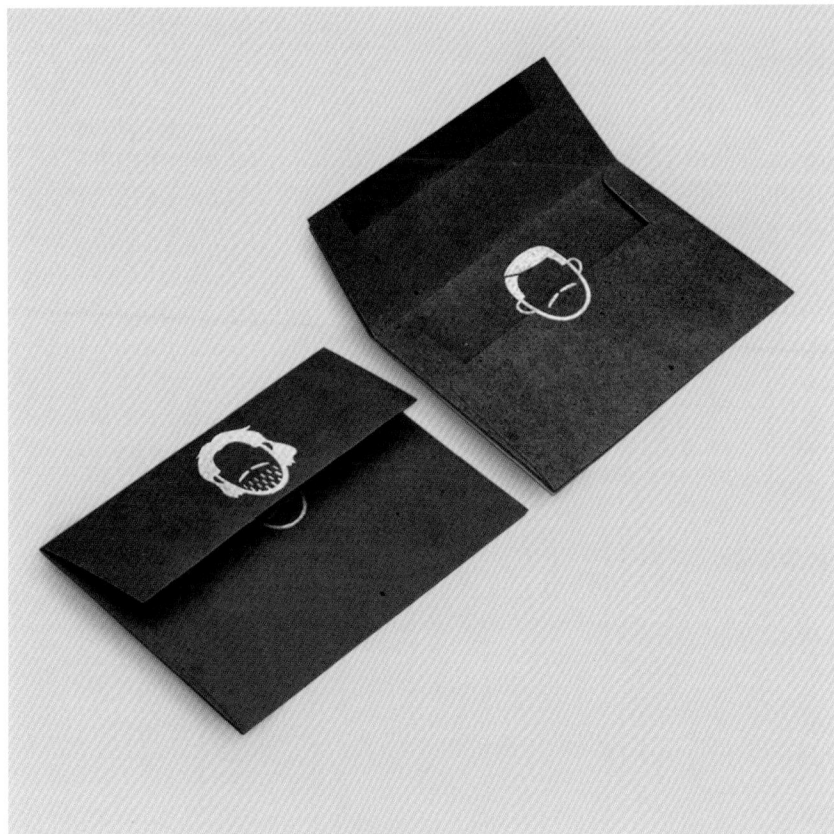

Giuliano Margheriti

Branding created for an Italian barber — Giuliano Margheriti. Their primary goal was to visually distinguish Giuliano Margheriti from the local barber competition. The ID was designed with elegance and minimalism in mind. Both classic and creative elements can be used in branding and advertising.

Design Agency / Cosa Nostra
Creative Director / Gracjan Wrząchol
Art Director / Magdalena Kapinos

Happy Tree

Commune's task was to incorporate the company's name "Happy Tree" into its identity to visualize the company's concept — "to be a tree which stands in the middle of everybody's happiness." The answer was very simple — use "tree of happiness" as the main concept. The pop up figure of the tree was created to cast a shadow that represents the balance embodied in all things. As Happy Tree mainly focuses on the cleaning industry, the white background was employed to bring a spotless and clean impression.

Design Agency / Commune
Designer / Ryo Ueda
Photographer / Kei Furuse
Printing Director / Manami Sato & Atsuhiro Kondo
Client / Happy Tree & Co., Ltd.

Filter Stationery

The Filter Business Cards are laser cut, perforated and white foil stamped on Black Keaykolour 450gsm Jet Black paper. At the base of the laser cut logo, the letterforms are perforated, which gives opportunity to the recipient to interact by folding, bending and tearing out sections of the card to become a simple way to offer creative expression.

Design Agency / Filter Studio
Designer / Claire Hamilton

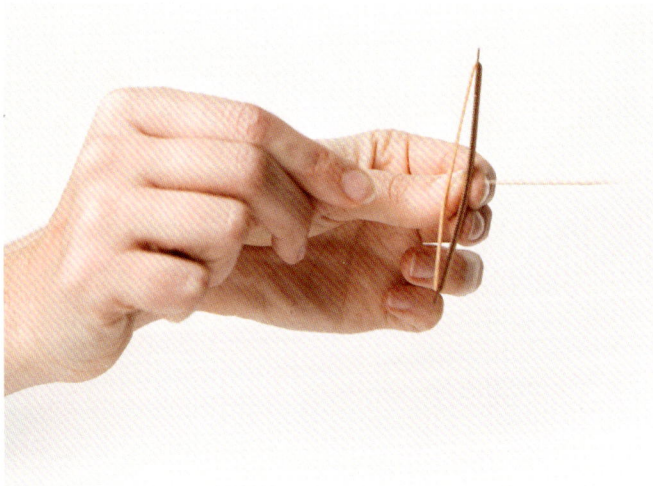

Longbow - Bow and Arrow Business Card

The Longbow cards are designed to connect with recipients by encouraging them to play with. They are laser cut and perforated 3 ply Mahogany. Snapping the card into three pieces, the top and the bottom of the card are almost identical apart from the slight curve remaining from the removal of the bow section. This allows the recipient to give away the contact information, while the remaining is the bow panel which converts into a completely functional bow when a rubber band is added to the forked ends. This makes it a playful and memorable greeting to the client.

Design Agency / Filter Studio
Designer / Claire Hamilton
Photographer / Bryan Crawford (Longbow)
Laser etch & cutting / Potato Press

&S Co.,Ltd New Year Card

The New Year Card was inspired by Hercules by Howard Hughes to deliver New Year's wish of growth. Each part of the paper plane on the card can be pushed out and assembled.

Design Agency / SAFARI Inc.
Designer / Tomoki Furukawa

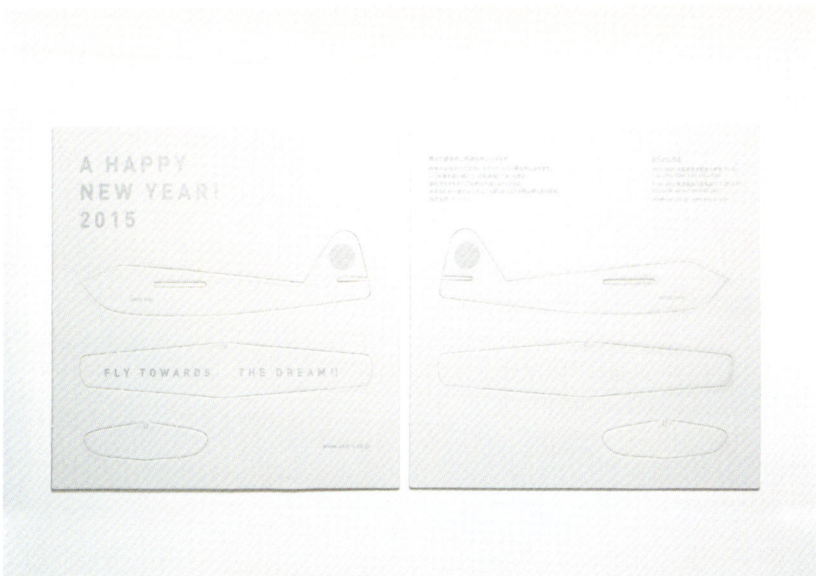

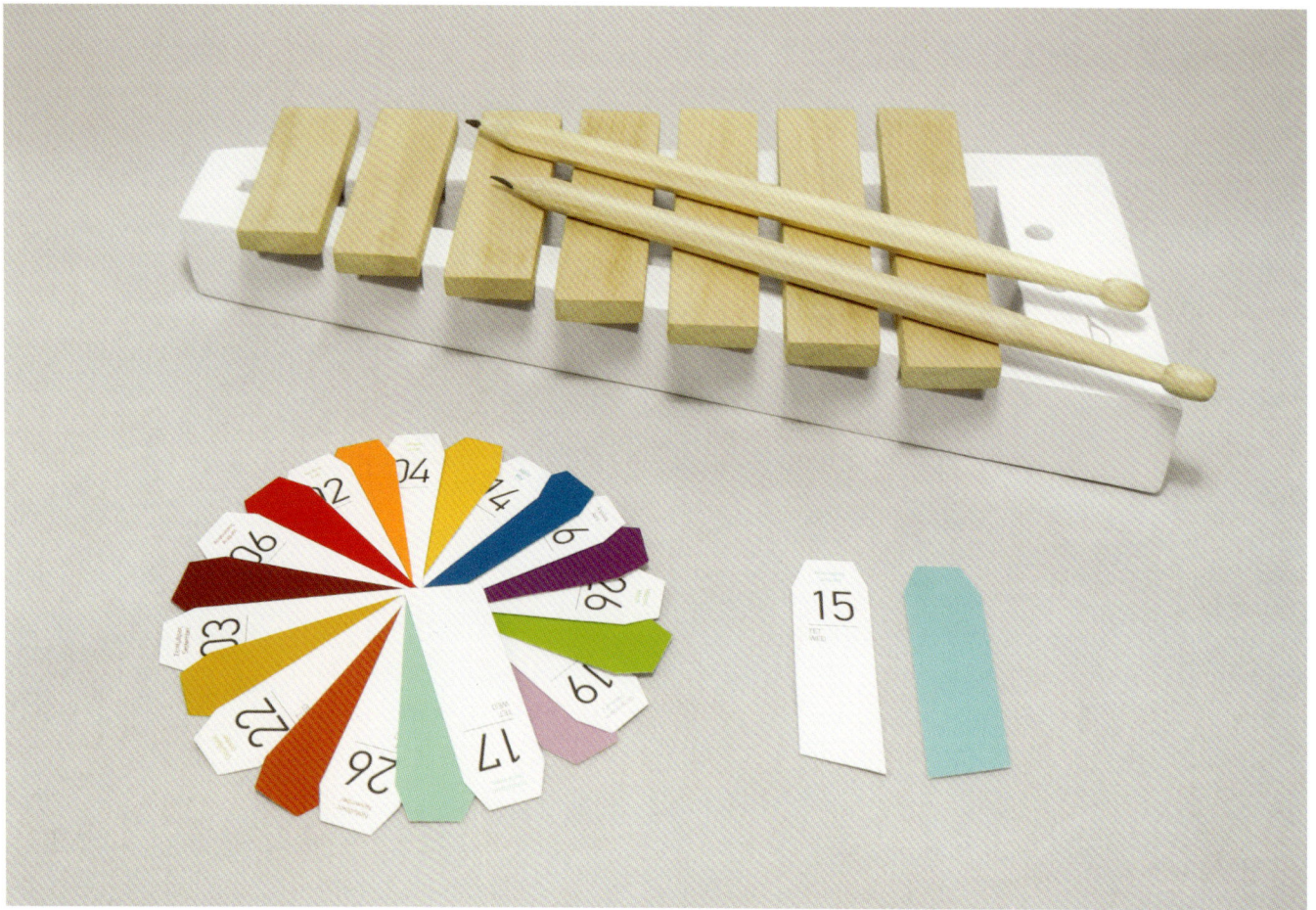

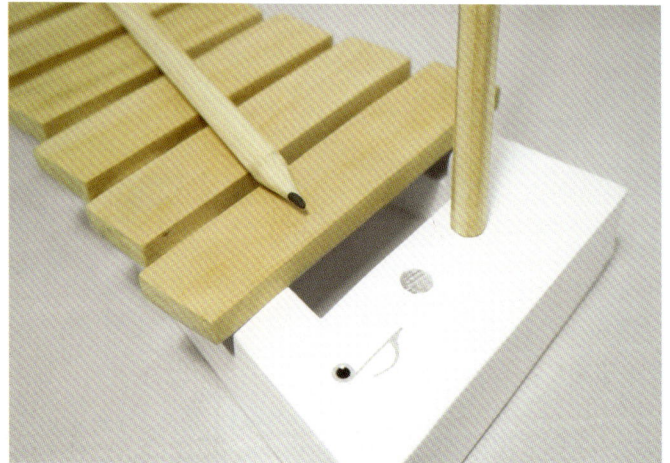

Eye Music

Eye Music explores the relationship between visual communication and music. The application of this program consists of a calendar, CD cases, and an invitation card.

As a said goes that I can see music through a colour book, each day of the week corresponds to one music note of the xylophone. Subsequently, the colours are associated with the CD cases which contain colourful cards with information about the Eye Music project. It can be easily opened and closed by using the magnets on its covers. Strings have been used as a basic stringed instrument in the invitation card. When you pluck each of them, sounds will be generated.

Designer / Tina Touli

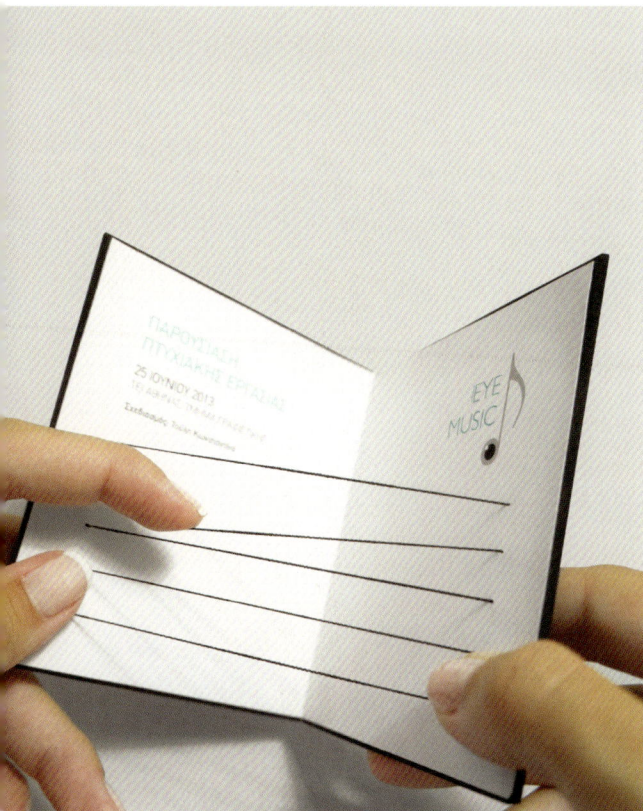

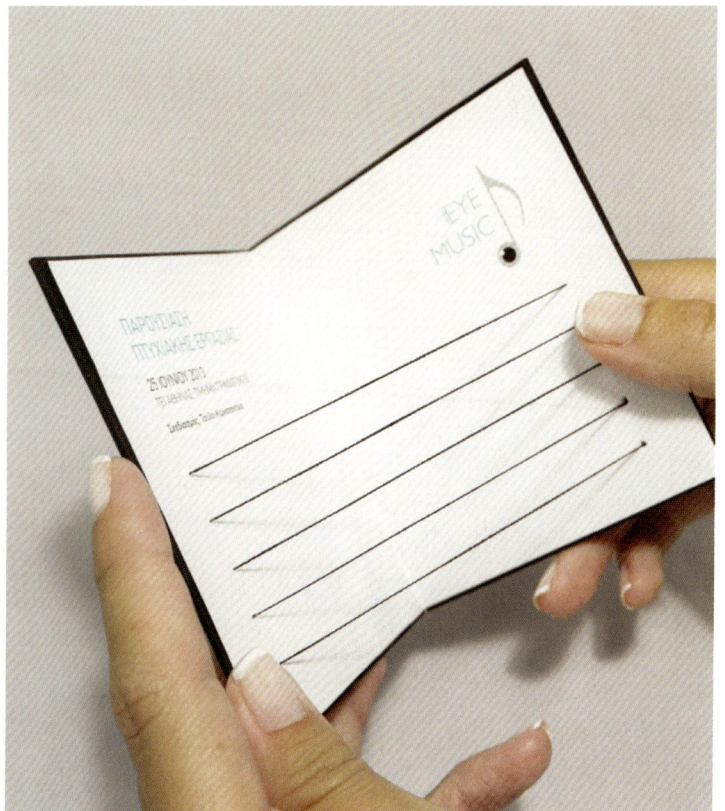

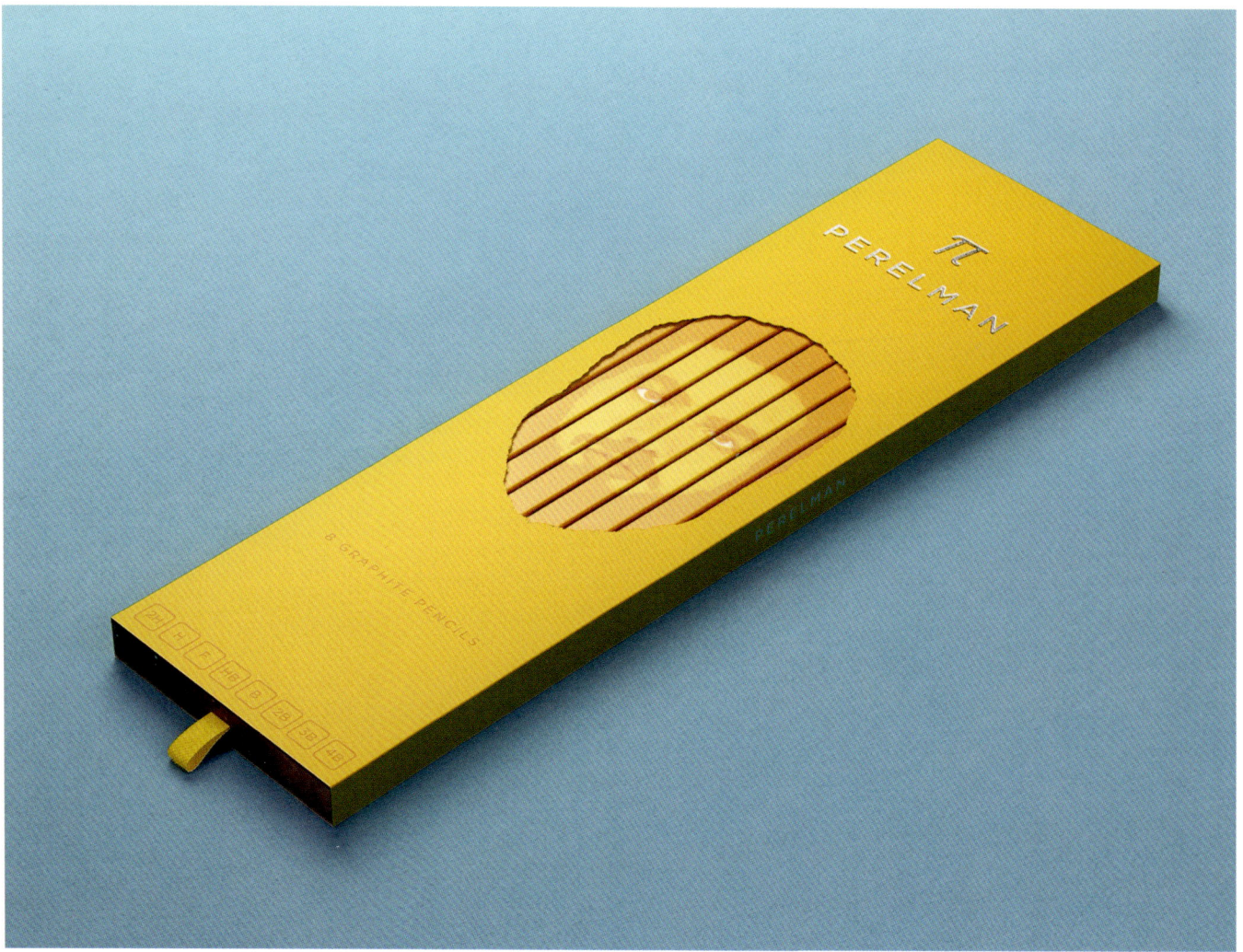

Perelman Pencils

Using a portrait of Russian mathematiciant Grigori Perelman by artist Jules Julien, designers Alan Temiraev and Volodenka Zotov created a beautifully designed pencil set. The packaging is designed with a die-cut window to enable the eight individually boxed graphite pencils make up the illustrated portrait. The interior of the box has a colour printed image of the universe.

Design Agency / The Bold Studio
Art Director / Alan Temiraev
Designer / Volodenka Zotov
Illustrators / Julien Jules & Philipp Gorbachev

Creative Collective Effect

Creative Collective Effect is a fashion show focusing on eco-conscious clothing. The key words of the identity were recycling, collaboration, engagement and creativity. This was emphasized on the poster by cropping the logotype to six different pieces and mixing them to create a graphical pattern. Along the lines of each piece, the paper was perforated so that the pieces could easily be ripped out and fit together to form the logotype. This calls for the previously mentioned creativity and symbolizes the act of collaboration and recycling. The perforation lines were set to resemble stitches on garments.

Design Agency / Lundgren+Lindqvist
Client / Creative Collective

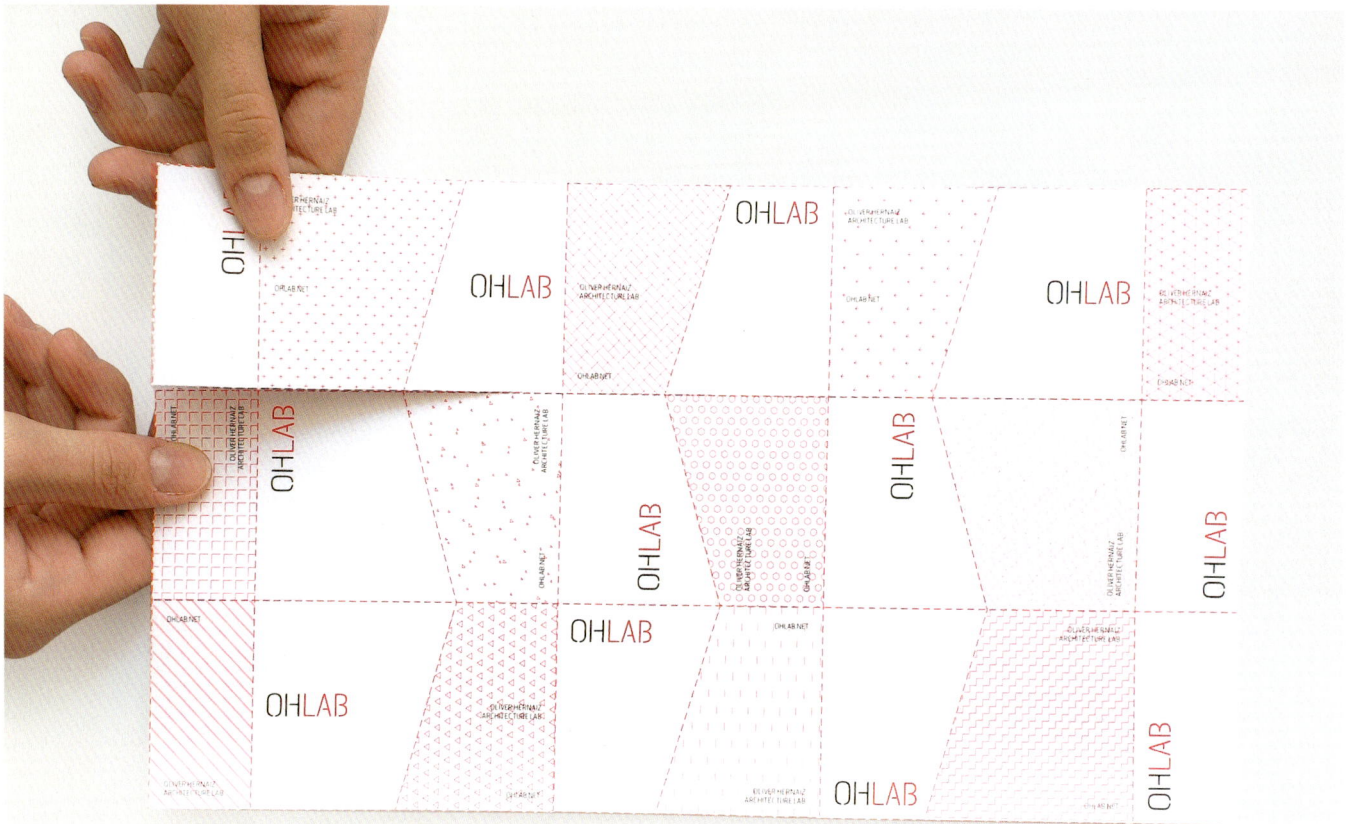

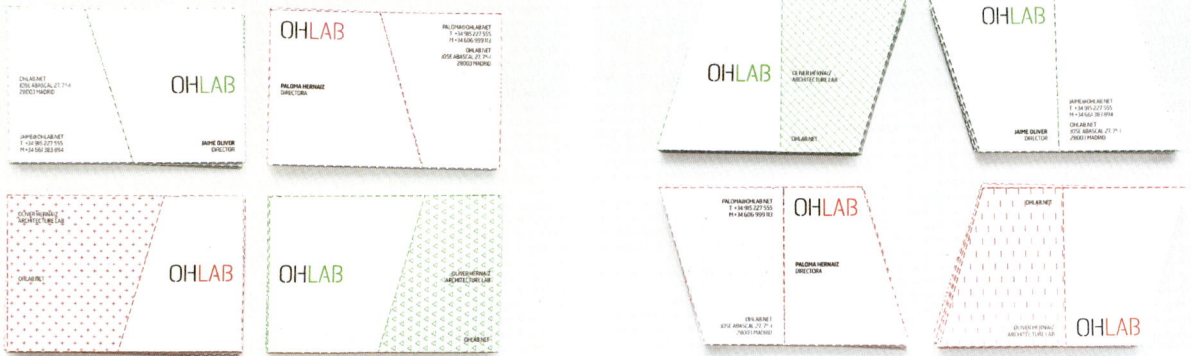

OHLAB Business Cards

Oliver Hernaiz Architecture Lab is an office devoted to urban analysis and cultural research of contemporary society through design, architectural practice and urban strategy. Regarding building is to join different shapes and materials, IS Creative created a card based on a completely opposite concept that you have to break, segment or deconstruct to use it. The cards have been perforated into different segments that represent the areas of an architectural drawing that can be segmented in different ways tailored to the needs in an efficient way.

Design Agency / IS Creative Studio
Designer / Richars Meza

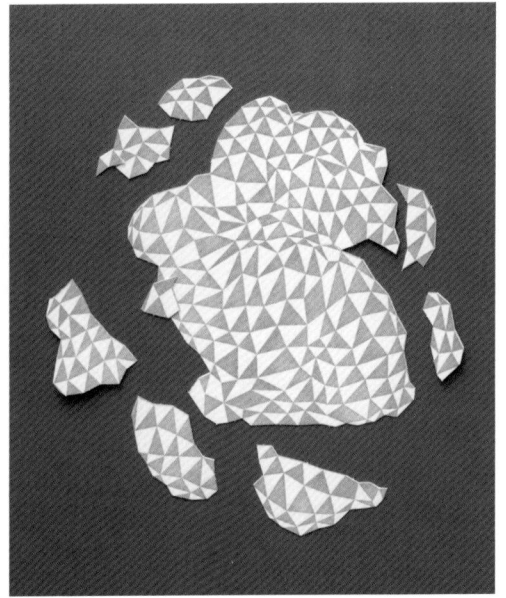

New Year's Card

This interesting card designed by Naonori Yago served as a greeting for the Year of Rabbit. When the card is broken apart slowly, a rabbit-like shape gradually emerges. In a subtle way, the card brings excitement and joy to recipients.

Designer / Naonori Yago

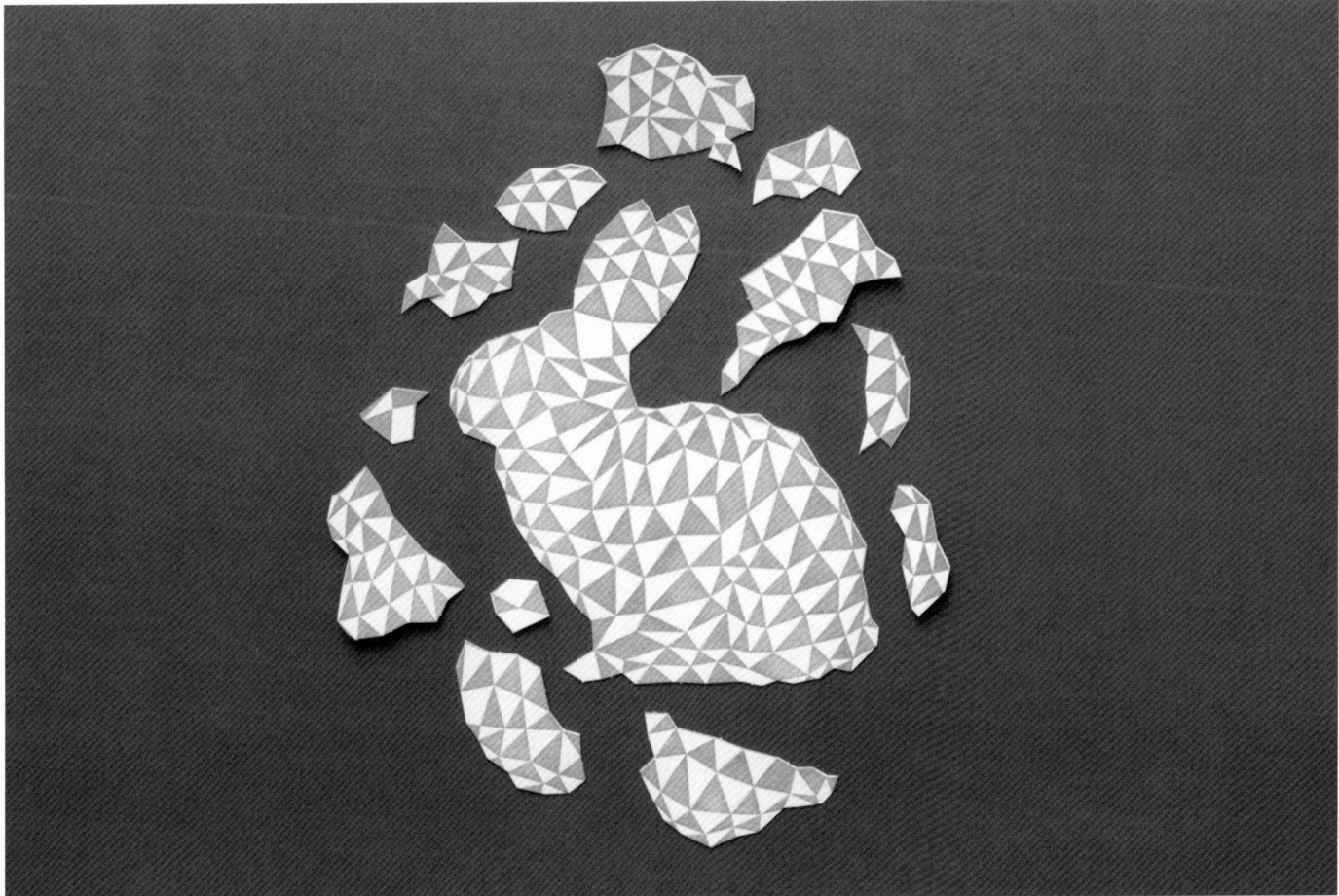

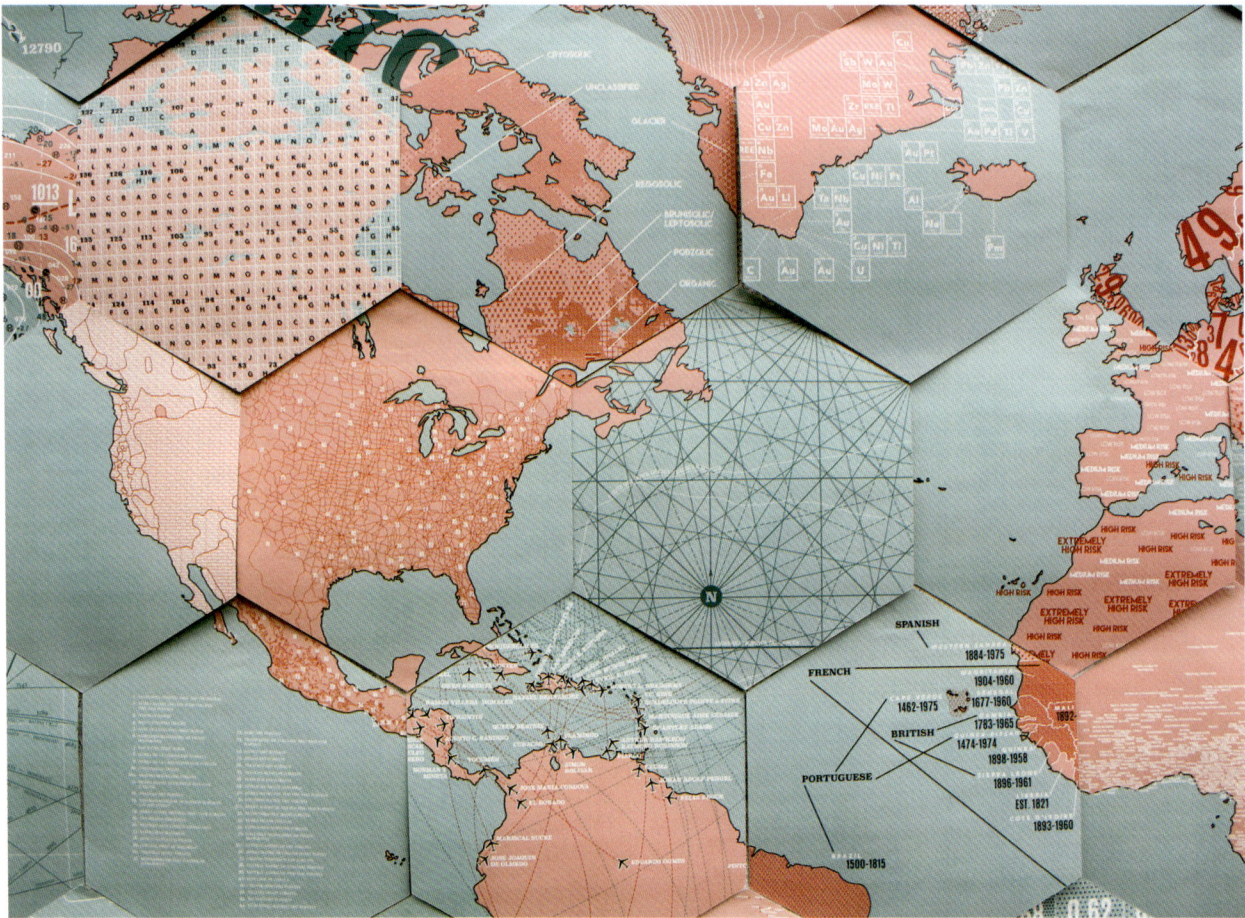

Earth to Everyone Map Book

"Earth to Everyone" is a hexagonal book documenting the history in mapping the world from the beginning of the time until present day. The book is perforated with a French fold. All 54 pages can be torn out to reveal typographic map tiles on the reverse side of the pages. Each tile displays a single type of information, emphasizing the diverse range of data that can be held on a map, but also the irrelevancy of each piece without further contextualization. The tiles can be reassembled into a wall-sized map of the world that can be organized with various cores and peripheries depending on one's world view.

Designer / Tree Abraham

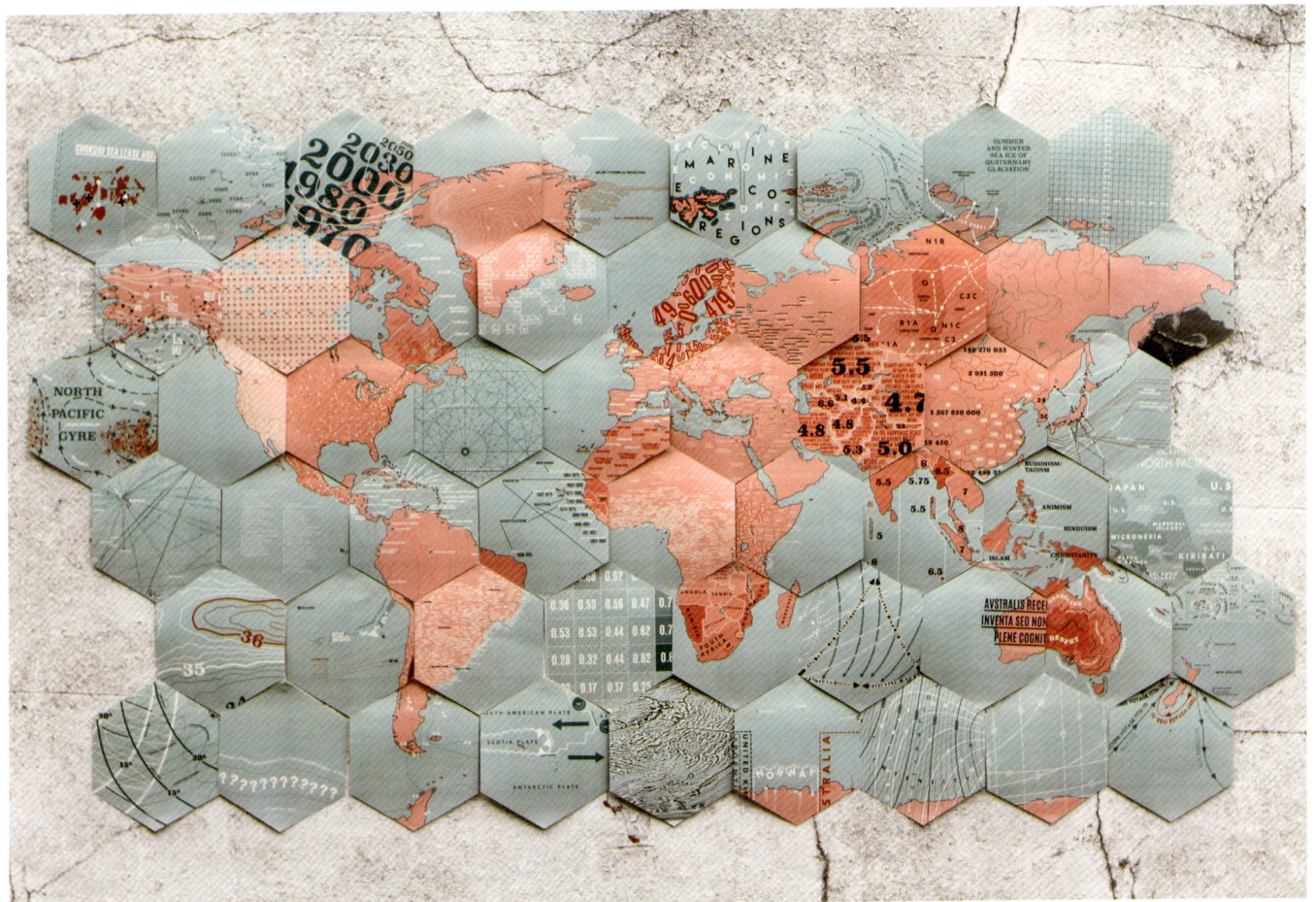

Sticker Calendar

Peeling away one sticker each day gradually reveals the scenery of the following season decorating the page, allowing you to feel the gradational changing of the seasons as each fades into the next. Peeling away stickers also reveals special illustrations on certain days like Valentine's Day or Christmas, and a whimsical cat can be found hidden somewhere on each page. Twists like these are interspersed throughout and make peeling away the stickers fun. The design breathes new life into the sticker backing, which would normally serve no purpose but to hold the stickers.

Design Agency / Nendo
Photographer / Akihiro Yoshida

Save Their Home

The number of endangered species has been tripled since 1989 due to environmental pollution and nature destruction. The Save Their Home calendar book seeks to promote awareness of endangered animals through the interaction of tearing off, by which symbolizing the animals' habitats which are disappearing day by day.

Designer / Yoonshin Kim

Polar Bear

Lorem ipsum dolor sit amet, consectetur adipiscing elit, sed do eiusmod tempor incididunt ut labore et dolore magna aliqua.

Lorem ipsum dolor sit amet, consectetur adipiscing elit, sed do eiusmod tempor incididunt ut labore et dolore magna aliqua.

SCIENTIFIC NAME	**POPULATION**
HABITATS	**WEIGHT**
CONSERVATION STATUS	**LENGTH**
THREATS	

二月

Galápagos Penguin

Lorem ipsum dolor sit amet, consectetur adipiscing elit, sed do eiusmod tempor incididunt ut labore et dolore magna aliqua.

SCIENTIFIC NAME	**POPULATION**
HABITATS	**WEIGHT**
CONSERVATION STATUS	**LENGTH**
THREATS	

三月

Giant Panda

Lorem ipsum dolor sit amet, consectetur adipiscing elit, sed do eiusmod tempor incididunt ut labore et dolore magna aliqua.

SCIENTIFIC NAME	**POPULATION**
	1,600
HABITATS	**WEIGHT**
	220-330 lb
CONSERVATION STATUS	**LENGTH**
Endangered	4-6 ft
THREATS	

四月

Manchurian Sika Deer

Lorem ipsum dolor sit amet, consectetur adipiscing elit, sed do eiusmod tempor incididunt ut labore et dolore magna aliqua.

SCIENTIFIC NAME	**POPULATION**
HABITATS	**WEIGHT**
CONSERVATION STATUS	**LENGTH**
THREATS	

九月

Riverine Rabbit

Lorem ipsum dolor sit amet, consectetur adipiscing elit, sed do eiusmod tempor incididunt ut labore et dolore magna aliqua.

SCIENTIFIC NAME	**POPULATION**
HABITATS	**WEIGHT**
CONSERVATION STATUS	**LENGTH**
THREATS	

十月

White Rhino

Lorem ipsum dolor sit amet, consectetur adipiscing elit, sed do eiusmod tempor incididunt ut labore et dolore magna aliqua.

SCIENTIFIC NAME	**POPULATION**
HABITATS	**WEIGHT**
CONSERVATION STATUS	**LENGTH**
THREATS	

十一月

Macaw

Lorem ipsum dolor sit amet, consectetur adipiscing elit, sed do eiusmod tempor incididunt ut labore et dolore magna aliqua.

SCIENTIFIC NAME	**POPULATION**
HABITATS	**WEIGHT**
CONSERVATION STATUS	**LENGTH**
THREATS	

十二月

Sea Lions

Lorem ipsum dolor sit amet, consectetur adipiscing elit, sed do eiusmod tempor incididunt ut labore et dolore magna aliqua.

SCIENTIFIC NAME	**POPULATION**
HABITATS	**WEIGHT**
CONSERVATION STATUS	**LENGTH**
THREATS	

Marunouchi Calendar 2015

Marunouchi Calendar 2015 is a desktop calendar for people who work in and visit Marunouchi area. This calendar consists of a case that evokes red bricks of Tokyo Station and Mitsubishi Ichigokan Museum, and a calendar winding round the red brick case. The calendar can be torn off month by month. It can also be used as a pen holder. The circle shape is inspired by maru of Marunouchi which means circle in Japanese.

Design Agency / UMA/design farm
Art Director / Yuma Harada
Designer / Yuka Tsuda
Illustrator / Yu Fukagawa
Photographer / Yoshiro Masuda

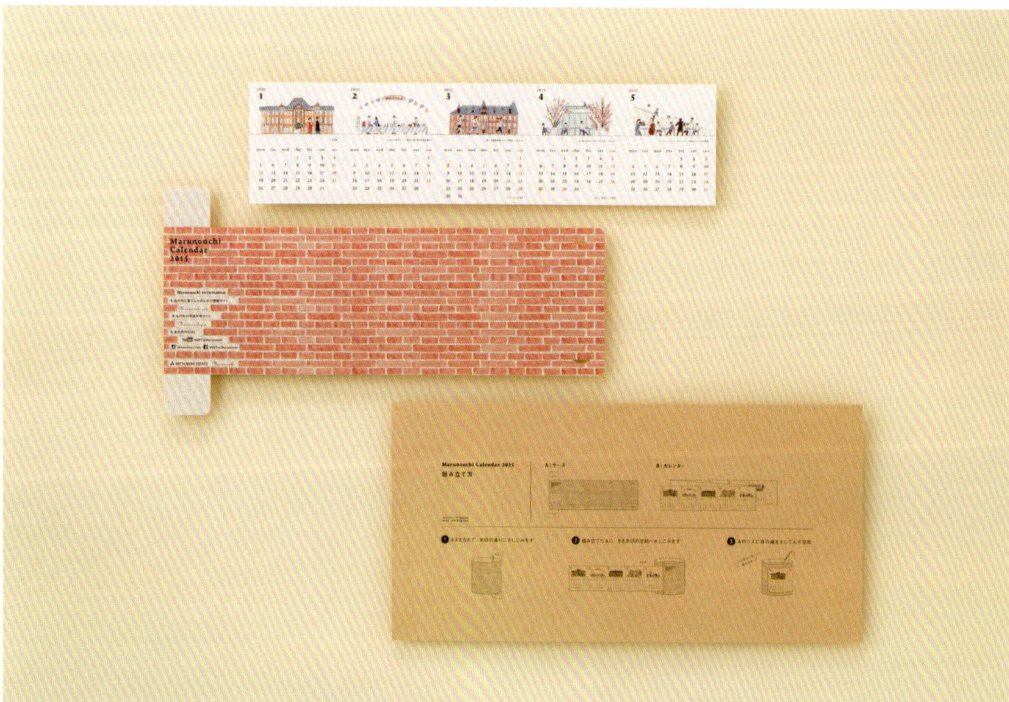

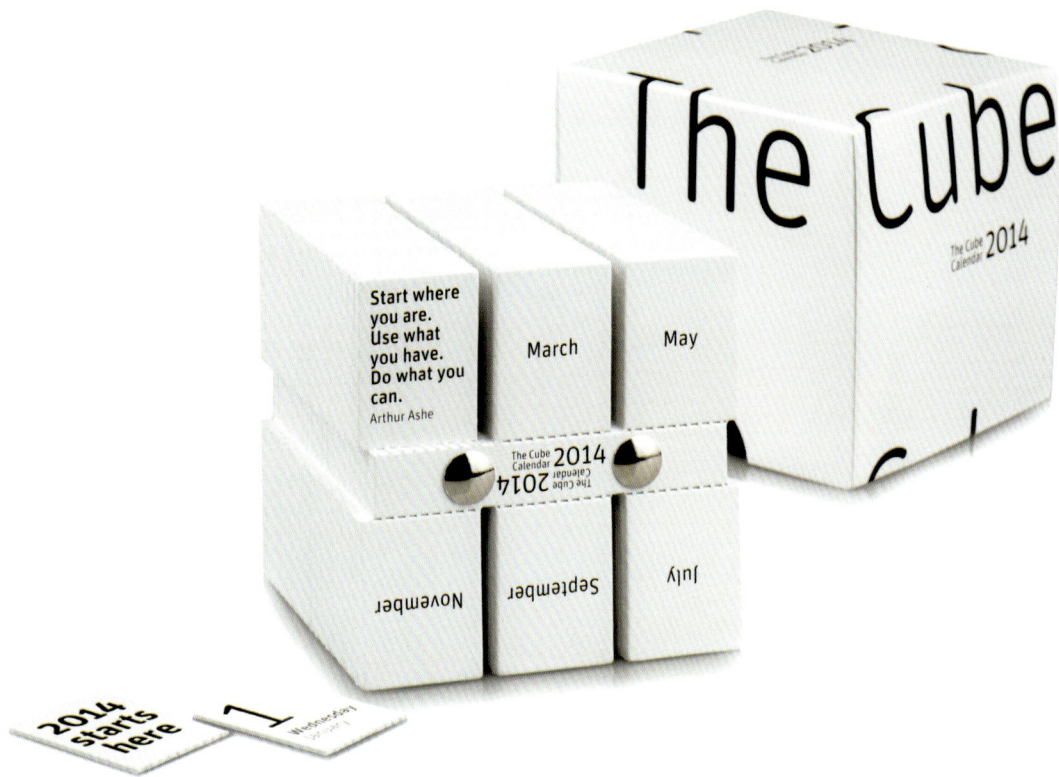

The Cube Calendar

With this beautifully designed calendar, Philip Stroomberg has added an innovative twist to the concept of the tear-off calendar. It is not a messy sheaf of paper hanging from a nail on your wall, but a compact object that subtly changes shape in your hands: by tearing off a card each day, you reveal the workings of time. Divided into six rows, hundreds of cardboard cards line up, and held together as a cube by two binding screws. There's a card for each day and, every few days, a card with a quote about time — a humorous observation or a philosophical aphorism.

Design Agency / Stroomberg
Designer / Philip Stroomberg

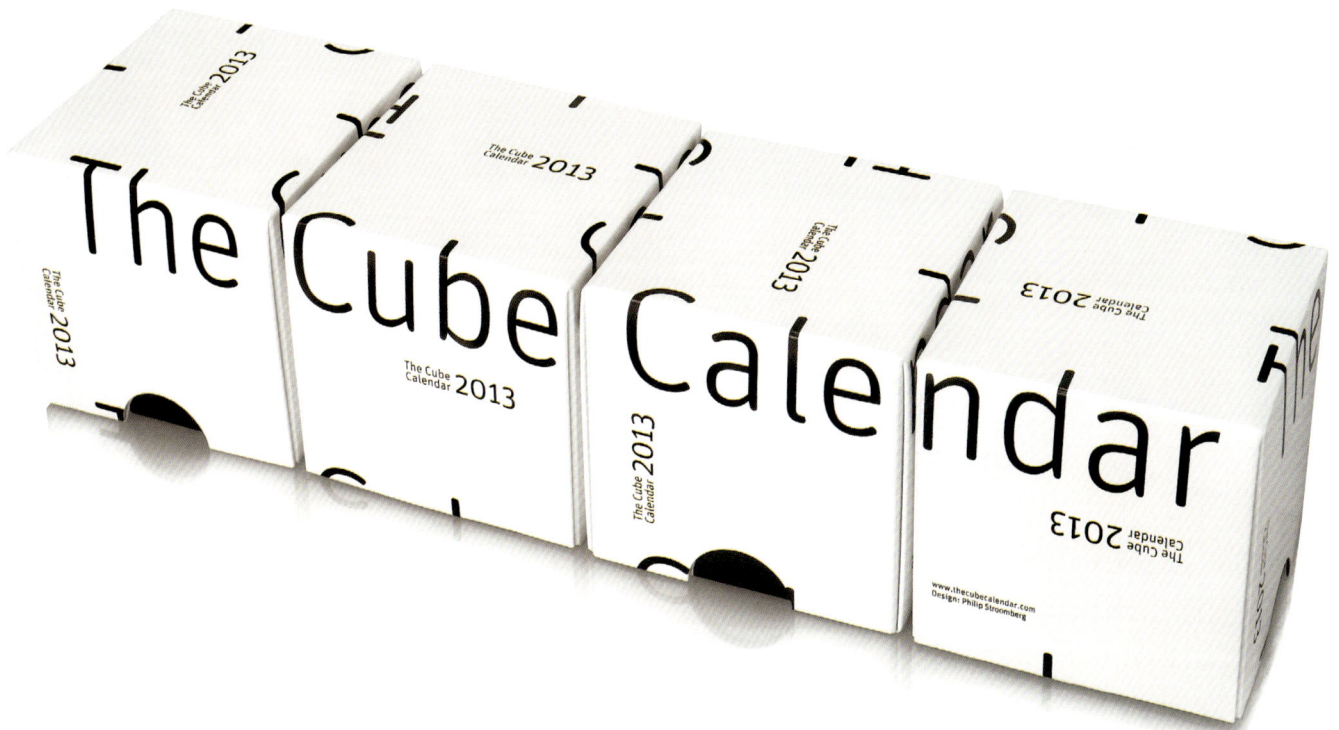

Underline

Underline is a dystopia about an undesirable information society. It criticizes how we access to information using new technologies. They promote immediacy, superficial data saturation, external storage or interruption, causing a lower knowledge and making us a superficial society.

The project is an analog information system divided in Consume, Store and Distribute. Information is the link between them, being contained in cards. Consume is a newspaper full of headlines, hyperlinks, timekeepers and tabbed browsing. Store is an archive that preserves forever the user information for not remembering it. Distribute allows sharing superficial data through mail subscriptions and in street walls.

Designer / René Miní Lázara

Un tercio de la población padece
memoria de pez.

Expertos de la O[...]
gobierno ameri[...]
los niños.

Las tabacaleras recomiendan el
humo del tabaco a los niños para
mayor capacidad pulmonar.

Hamburguesas
de la gran M,
premiadas con
tres estrellas
Michelines por
ser saludables.

Un estudio
demuestra que
cuanta más
información
consumes, más
adicto te vuelves.

Expertos de la OMS piden al
gobierno americano cebar más a
los niños.

la "cabeza hueca" es

underline⁻

Alter Edit : Identity Design

The Alter Edit identity focuses on a modern modular typeface used in a playful manner in traditional media. An animated business card was a result of this experiment that presented the power of interactive design while promoting the studio's approach.

Designer / Mark Wilson

Mystery Chocolate

The basic concept was to create a playful and clear chocolate package, which contains 3 different chocolates: white, black and milk.

The ingredients of the chocolates and all other information are shown on the paper stripe which bounds them together. The playfulness of the package resides in the fact that the type of the chocolate will be only visible when it is pulled out of the box. The letters appears and disappears one by one.

The basic mechanism corresponds to the barrier grid animation technique. This is an optical illusion generated by sliding two layers located over themselves.

Designer / Kevin Harald Campean

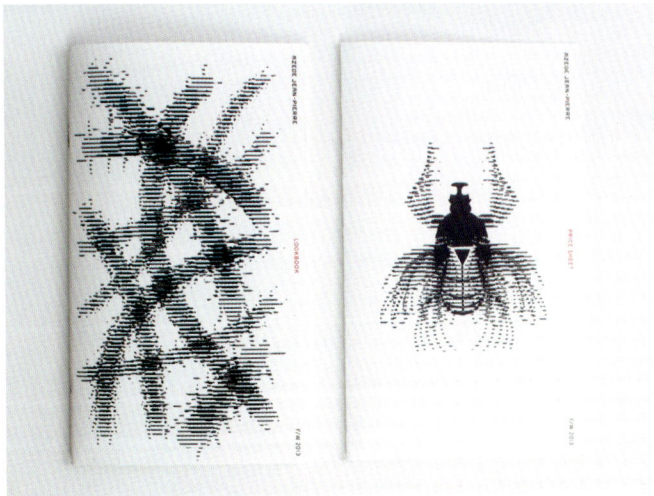

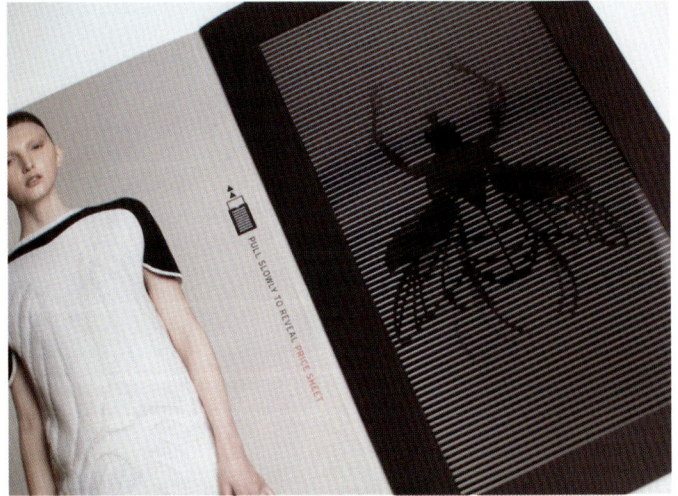

Azede Jean-Pierre FW13 Lookbook

This lookbook was created to promote the Azede Jean-Pierre Fall/Winter 2013 Collection. It was sent out to various stores and press. The prints in the collection featured a line screen animation which enabled the clothing to animate according to the movement of the wearer. Joseph Veazey duplicated this process in the lookbook, with the cover of the lookbook booklet and the price sheet animating as they pull out of their sleeves.

Designer / Joseph Veazey
Client / Azede Jean-Pierre

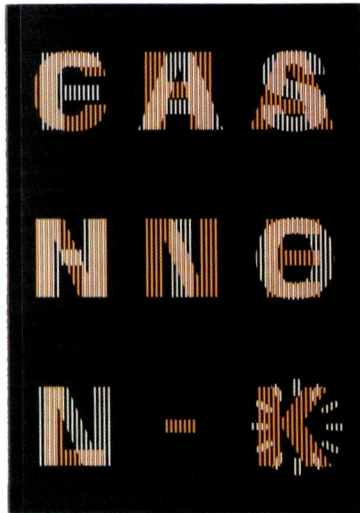

Changeable Type for Fashion Channel-K

This book is made for an annual fashion show. Wooksang Kwon made two different sets of words that make up of stripes on the book cover. The black striped case hides one set of the words and shows the other. Another set of words will alternatively show up when readers pull the book out of the case.

Designer / Wooksang Kwon

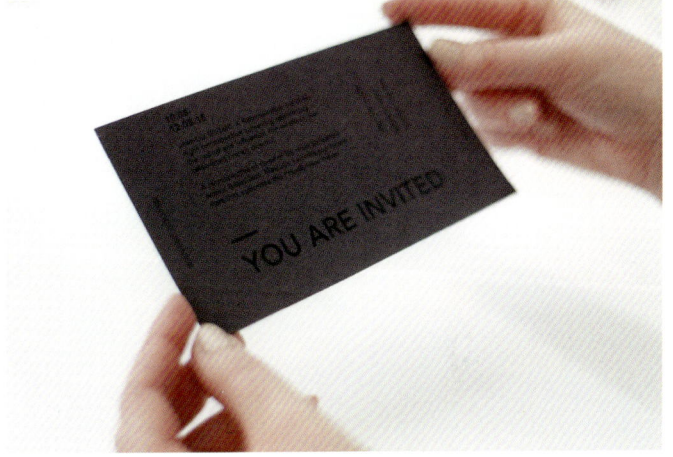

Jean-Luc Godard. A Retrospective

The basis for promoting a retrospective screening of French New Wave film director Jean-Luc Godard is his non-linear approach to film making. The concept of the design is a reflection on Godard's film style. The interactive poster is a stack of screen printed posters that are torn along a perforated edge. Each poster displays a different word; Debut, Milieu and Fin, which in French mean beginning, middle and end. They are arranged in no specific order and are revealed in a non-linear fashion when the public tear of the posters.

Designer / Stuart Lamont

An Exploration of Translation With Light and Shadow

With a complex structure and system of characters, Chinese make itself impossible for foreigners to understand. Qiang Fu explored a method to visually translate their meanings by the interaction of grid structure, movement and light.

It consists of two parts: a card with white dots and another one with pinholes. When light is projected through the pinholes and moved, the images transform from Chinese to English and finally to its symbolic meaning.

Designer / Qiang Fu

• 096 •

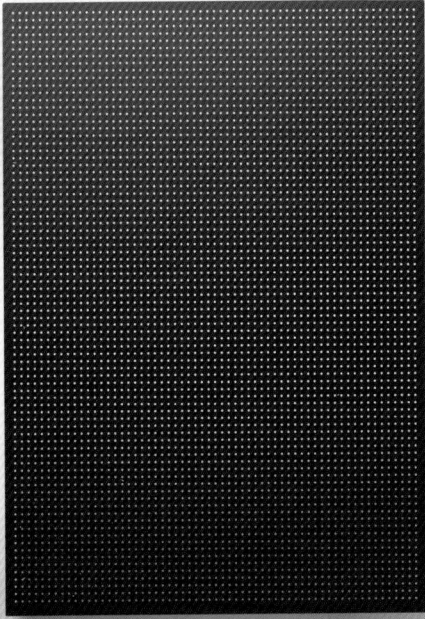

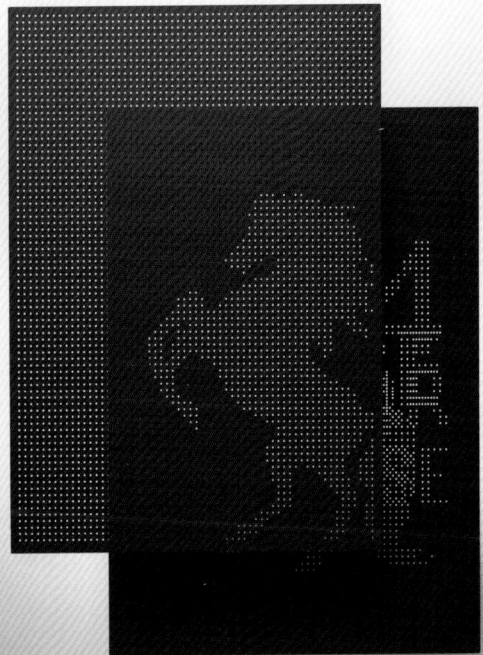

2014 The Year of Horse

This project is specially made for the year of the Horse, and this language translator kit explores the alteration of horse. The Horse symbolizes the zodiac of year 2014 in China and gives on a successful emblematic figure.

Designer / Qiang Fu

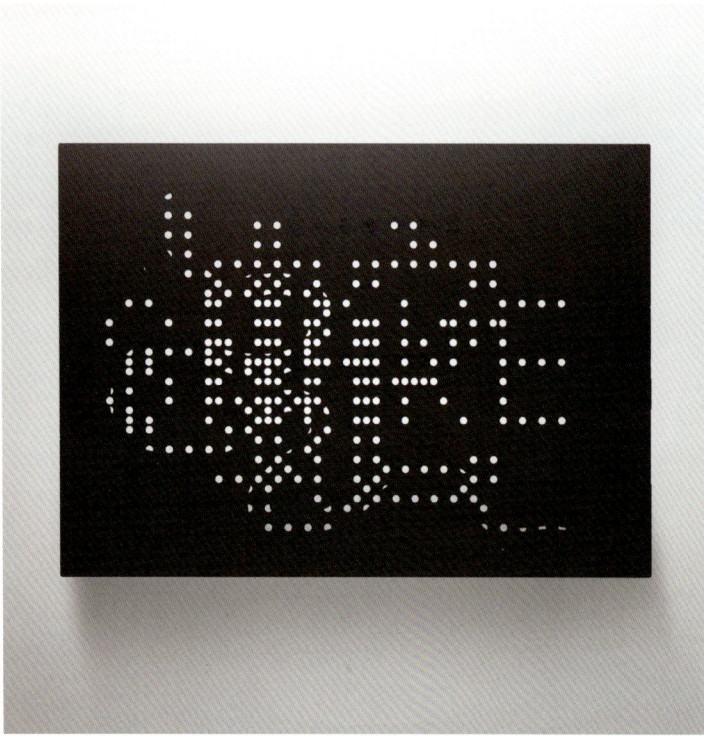

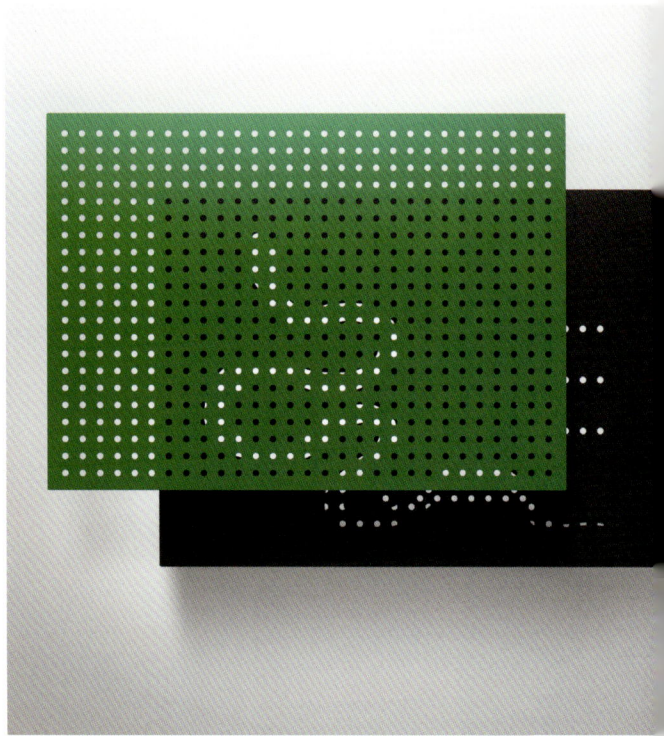

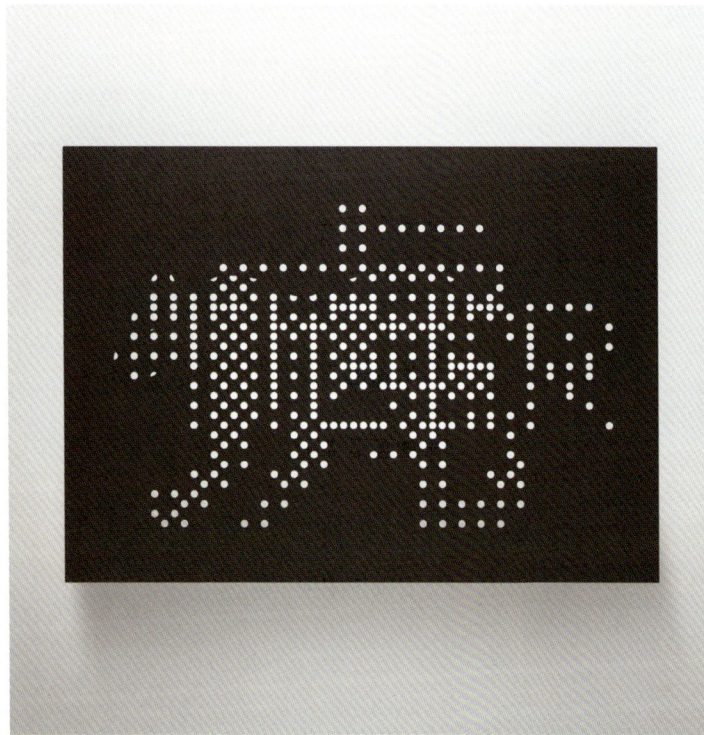

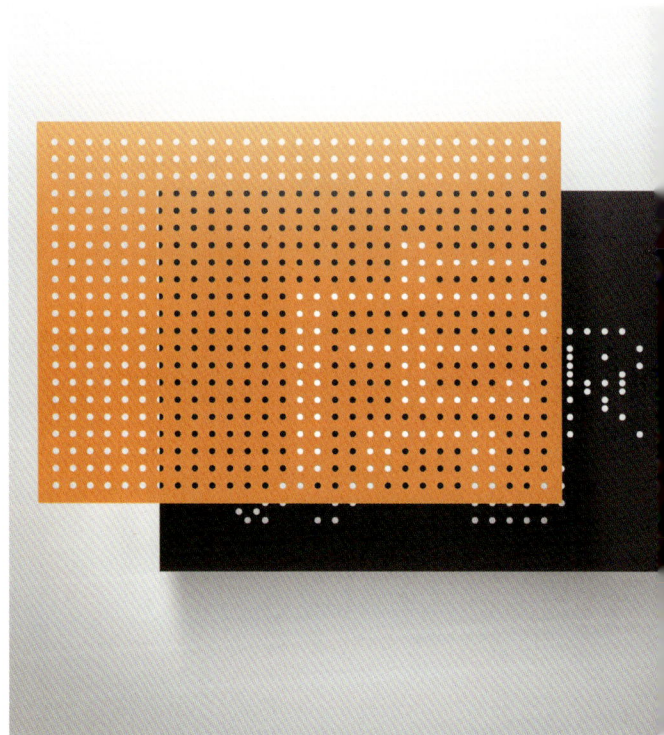

Chinese Zodiac

In this project, the experimental elements are the characters and images from 12 traditional Chinese zodiac animals.

Designer / Qiang Fu

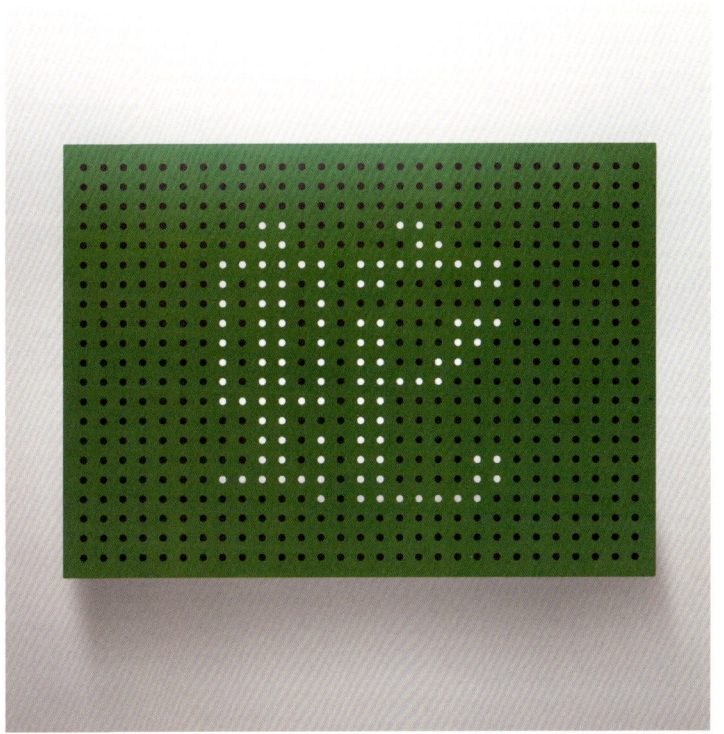

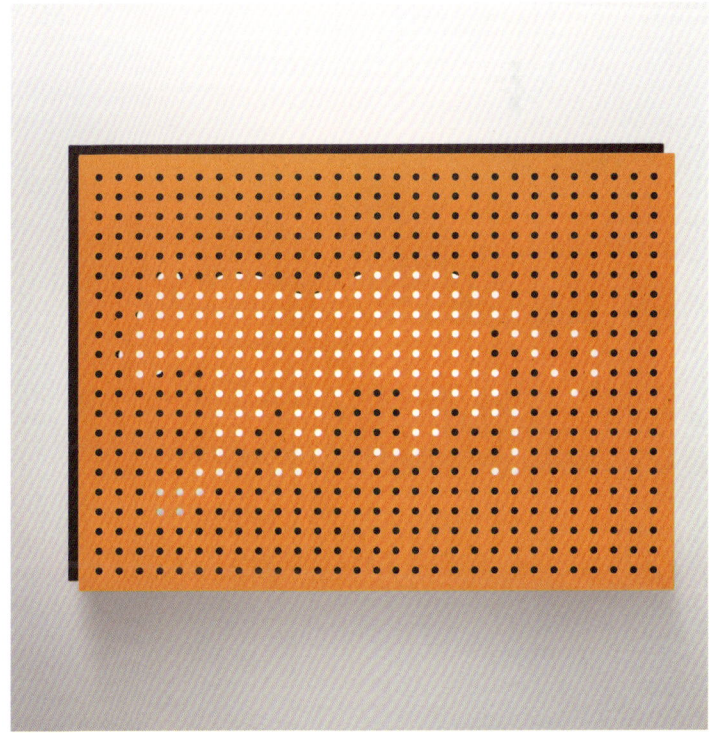

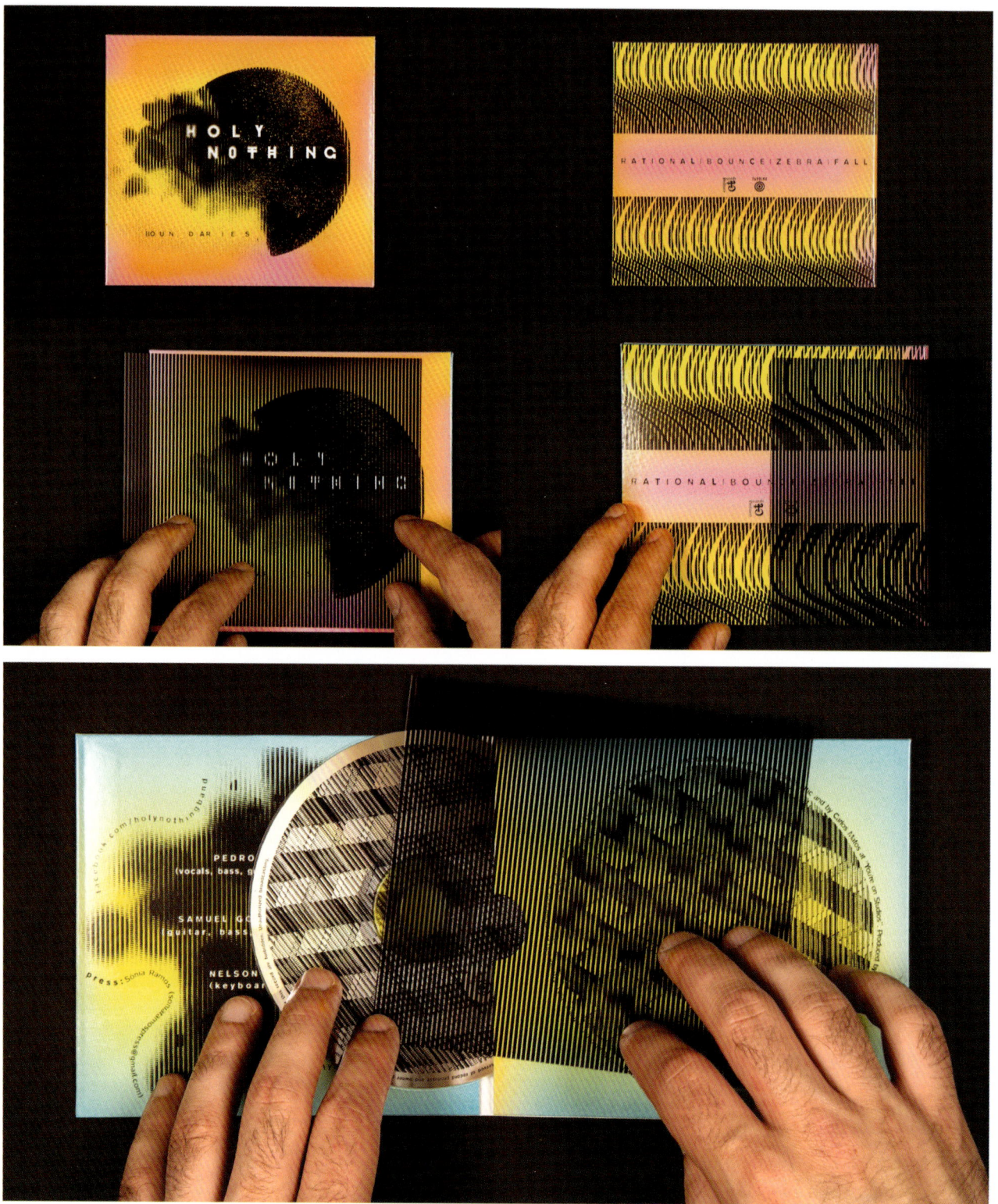

Holy Nothing - Boundaries

"Boundaries" is the first record of Holy Nothing, and it was released in the format of an extended play with four tracks. The images for this EP came directly out of the audio-visual project that Bruno Albuquerque developed with the band, throughout a sequence of visual narratives that are projected during their live performances.

The idea for this artwork emerges from the exercise of gathering four frames from four different animations of the mentioned live projections to define four different cd covers. This makes a proximity link between the physical object and the performance that define the band, the EP and the concerts.

Designer / Bruno Albuquerque
Photographer / Rui Pinheiro

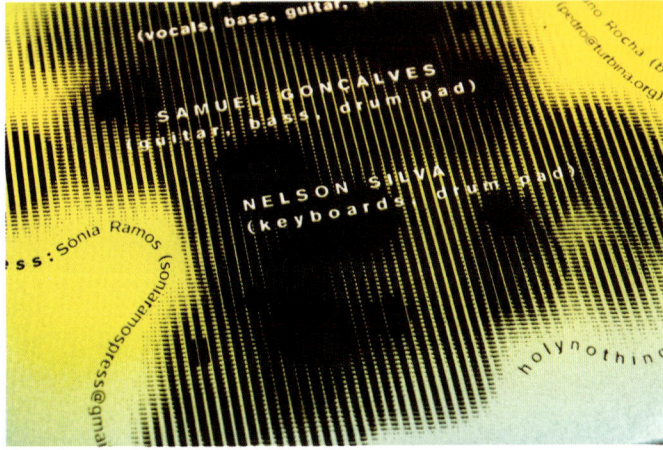

Album

This triple-vinyl is the first release of Leipzig based record label NYT. The design is based on two print layers: the top layer can be rubbed off with one's fingernail, thus revealing the second hidden layer.

Design Agency / Grabowski Böll
Photographer / Ralf Haunschild

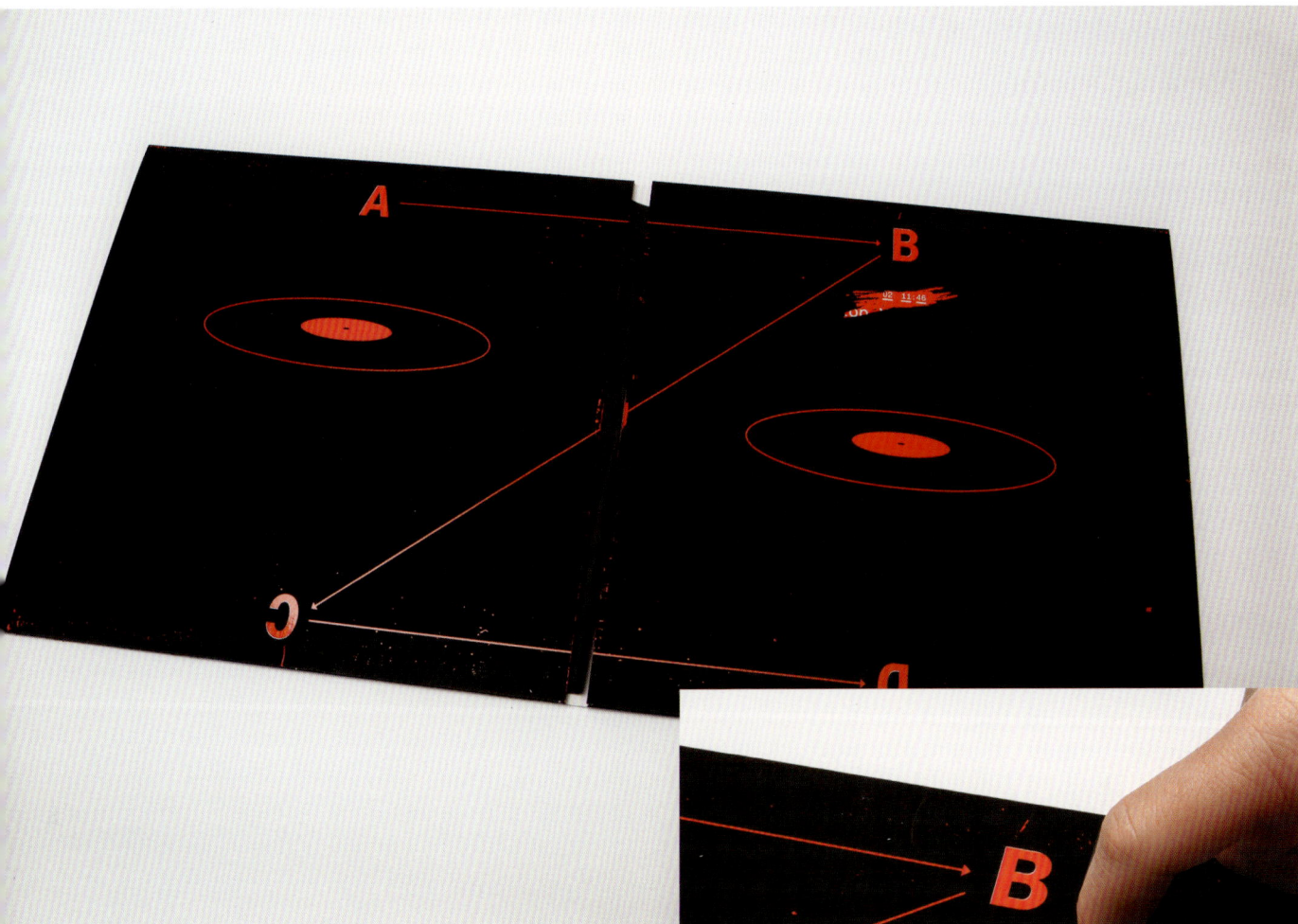
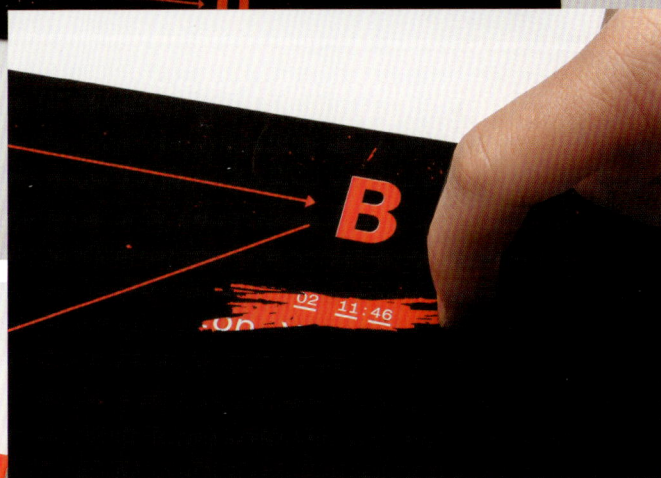

A

02 11:27
Rename The War

P.O.P.
05 05:32
We Got It All
04 03:04
We Take It Slow
03 10:48

C

B

02 11:46
Stop Your Drama

Pulchritudinous
06 08:41

D

Orchestra Baobab

Orchestra Baobab is an Afro-Cuban, Son, Wolof, and Pachanga band. This special edition LP was designed for the 15-year anniversary of the album release. The cover, inside, and back cover are all old photographs linking with an orchestra. The content of the photographs is covered with colours and patterns derived from textile patterns originating in the region of Africa where the band comes from. The pattern can then be scratched away with a coin to reveal the hidden texts.

Designer / Evan Pokrandt

Amnesty International

Enforced disappearance is a term that has not yet been familiar to the public. The chief purpose of the project was to call for awareness of illegal detentions across the world and to promote the convention against it. The man kidnapped and the truths are hidden until the frogs are clear off with a silver brand.

Designer / Vladimir Shlygin & Alina Kaspariants
Final production / Vladimir Shlygin
Tutors / Dmitri Karpov & Laura Parke

Amsterdam
Pays-Bas

Amsterdam
Pays-Bas

L'ours polaire
Famille des Ursidae

Le colibri
Famille des Trochilidae

Global Warming

This project aimed to raise awareness of global warming among people. The basic concept was to design projects that can disappear when people use or see them.

The set of cards, whose images can be erased easily with nails, represent animals or places threatened by total collapse and tell how fragile the environment is.

Designer / Chloé Heinis, Jonathan Kleinpeter & Lina Kahal

Tadashii Soutaiseiriron

These are the CD album and the Limited Edition Analog of a Japanese rock band "Soutaiseiriron (=Theory of Relativity)." A red and green check sheet, which is a familiar tool to Japanese students to enhance memorization, is attached to the jacket. Audiences will be able to feel the joy of "imagination" by attempting to read the studded mystery hiding in the analysis diagrams and lyrics. Through this playful approach, it has created a new value of experience in the jacket in this "downloading" era.

Design Agency / Spread
Designer / Haruna Yamada & Hirokazu Kobayahi
Drawing / Etsuko Yakushimaru (The singer)

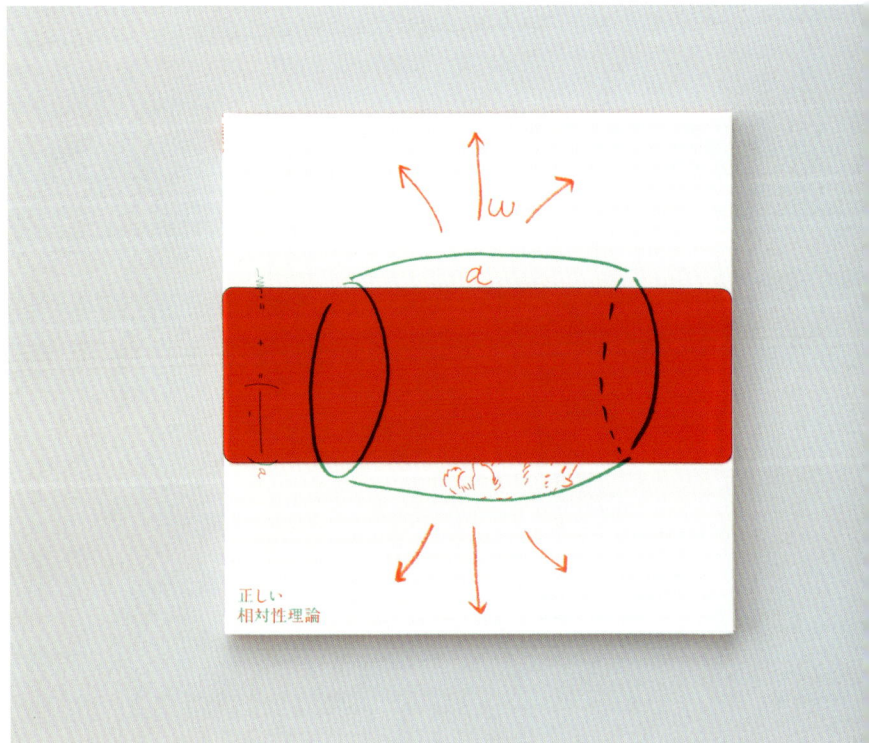

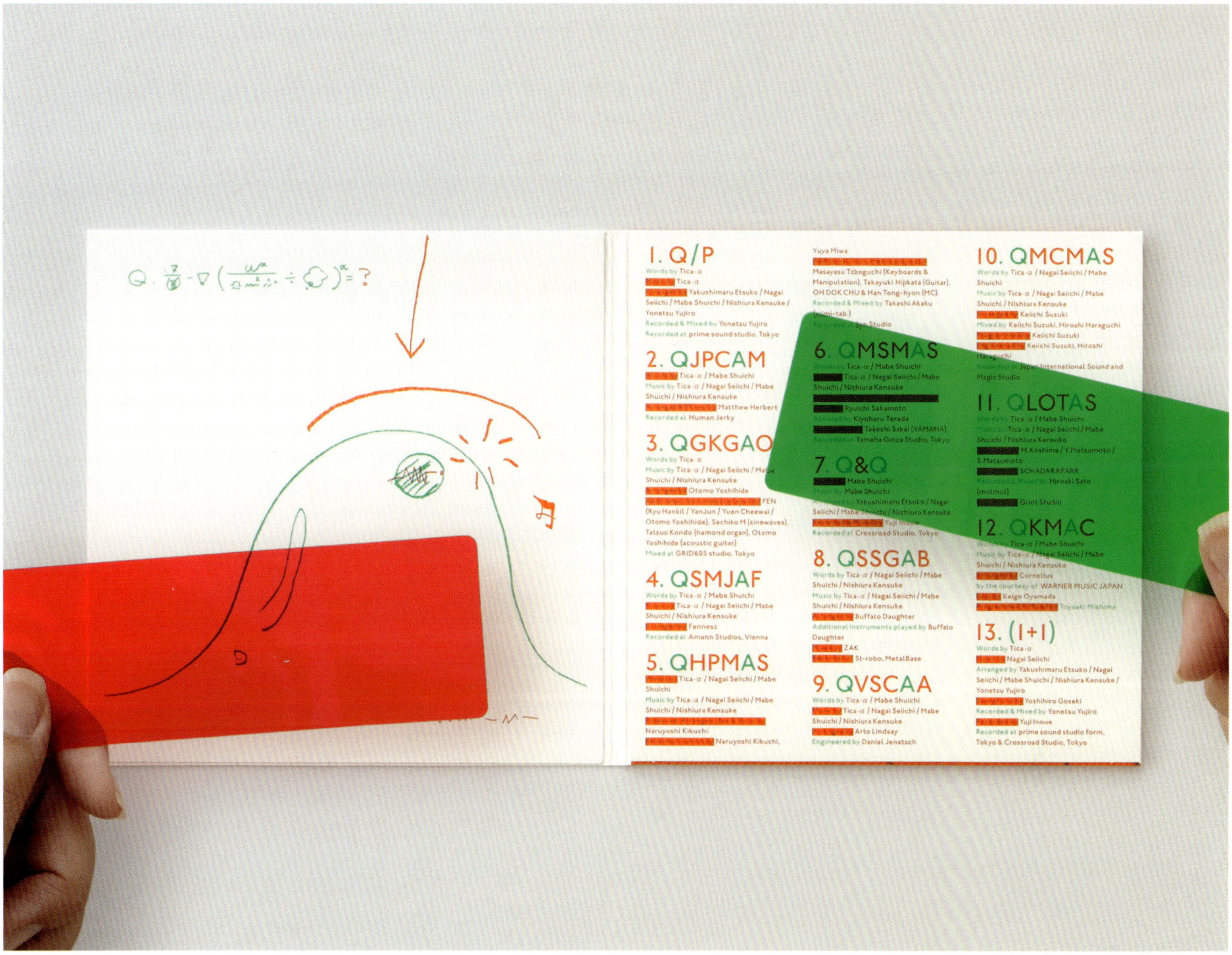
1. Q/P
2. QJPCAM
3. QGKGAO
4. QSMJAF
5. QHPMAS
6. QMSMAS
7. Q&Q
8. QSSGAB
9. QVSCAA
10. QMCMAS
11. QLOTAS
12. QKMAC
13. (I+I)

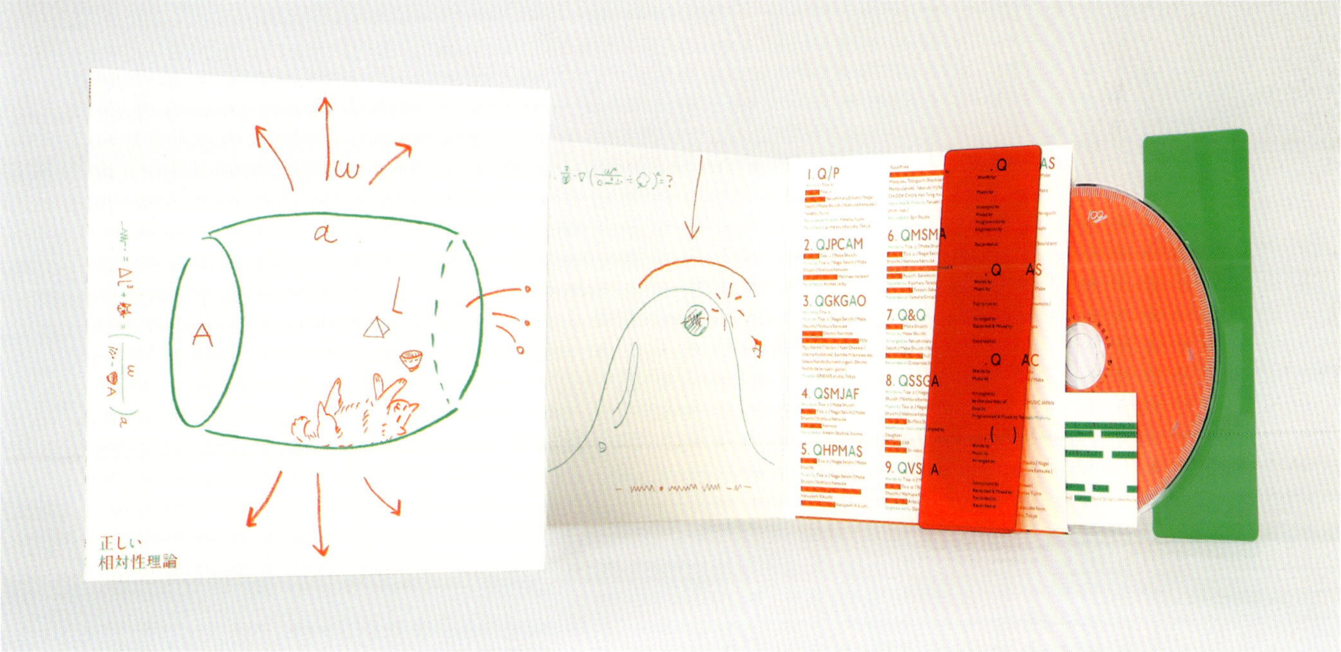
正しい
相対性理論

Photomagic

Dark room, developer, fixer, and the red light are symbols of the magic of photography. Saatchi & Saatchi Ukraine incorporated these elements into the design for a famous photographer Andrey Lobov. In order to bring back the magic in this digital world, they made the name only visible under red card, through red glasses, and under red light by using overlap technique.

Design Agency / Saatchi & Saatchi Ukraine
Director / Kirill Christyakov
Art Director / Schneider Kostiantyn
Designer / Alexander Litvin
Photographer / Andrey Lobov

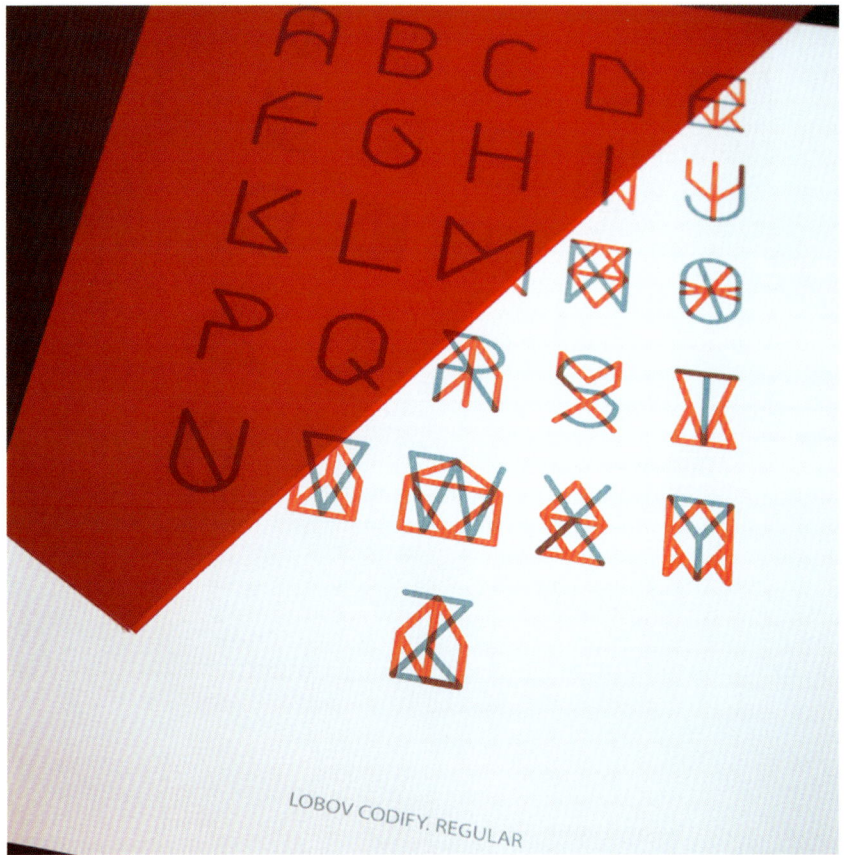

LOBOV CODIFY. REGULAR

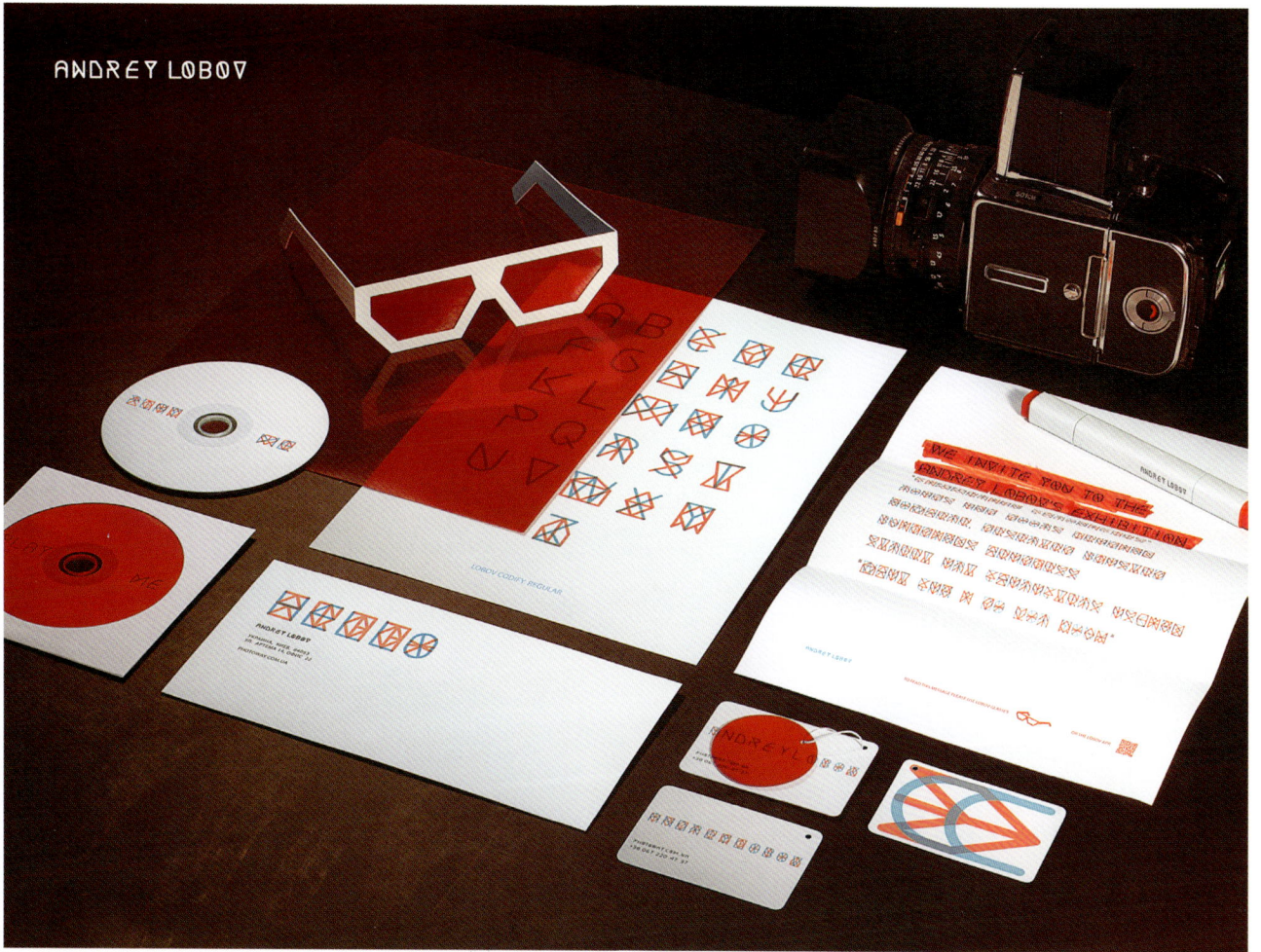

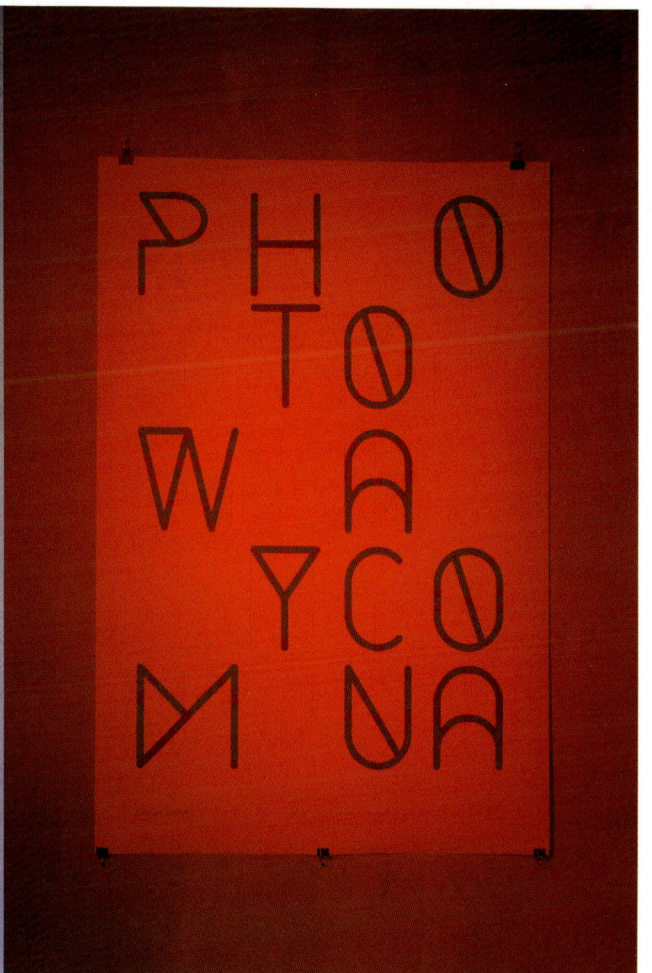

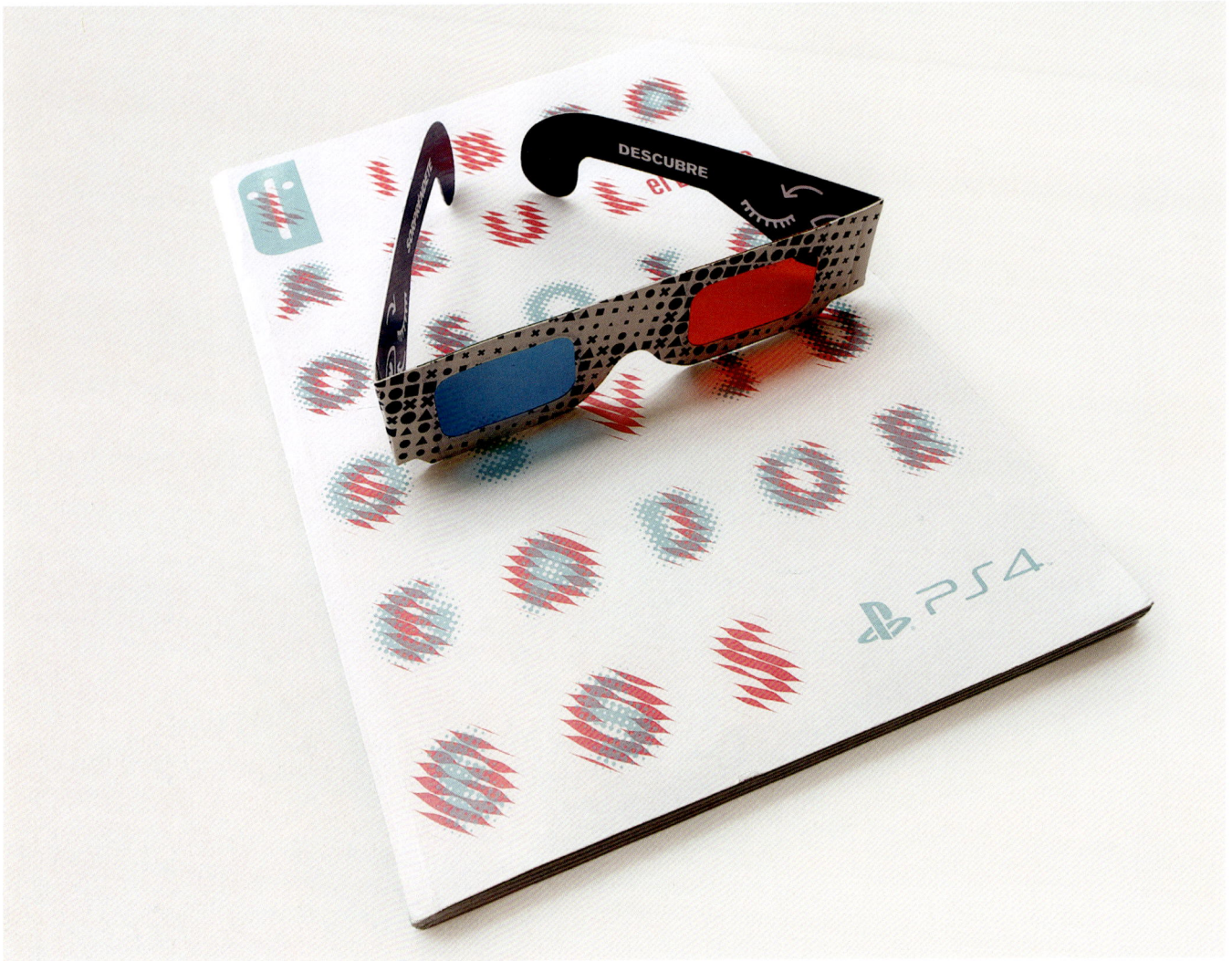

El Duende + PS 4

IS Creative designed the cover of the video game edition of "El Duende" magazine, with PS 4 as a sponsor for this issue. The cover needed to feature the brand and the product in a subtle way. For the typographic cover for the special issue of PS 4 they came up with a concept of overlapping the images and letters in red and blue, which are the colours of the buttons on PS 4 controllers.

Design Agency / IS Creative Studio
Designer / Richars Meza

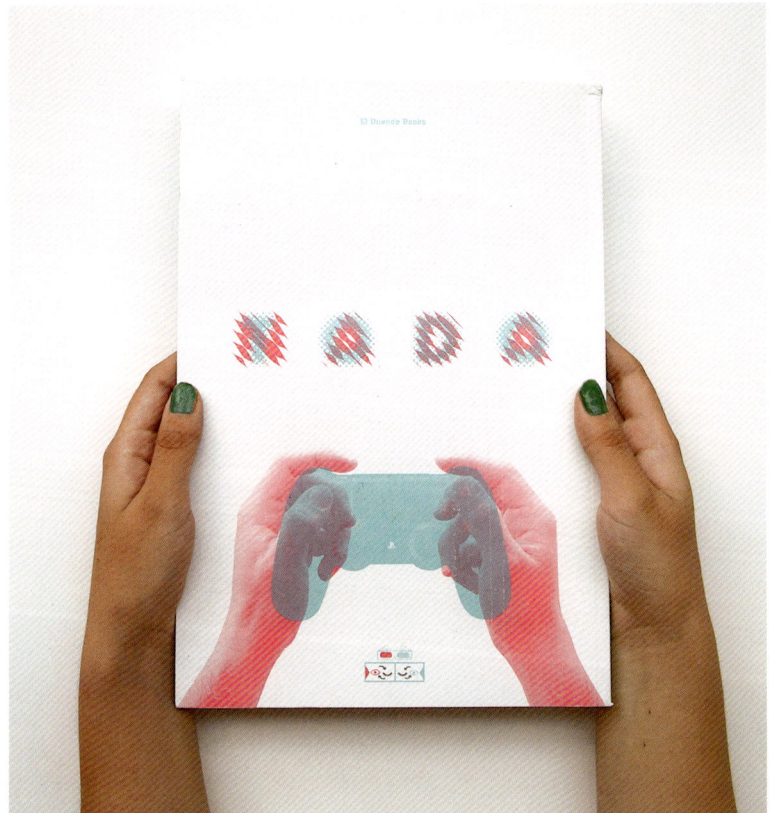

COMEDIA EN VIÑETAS
CHEMA GARCÍA

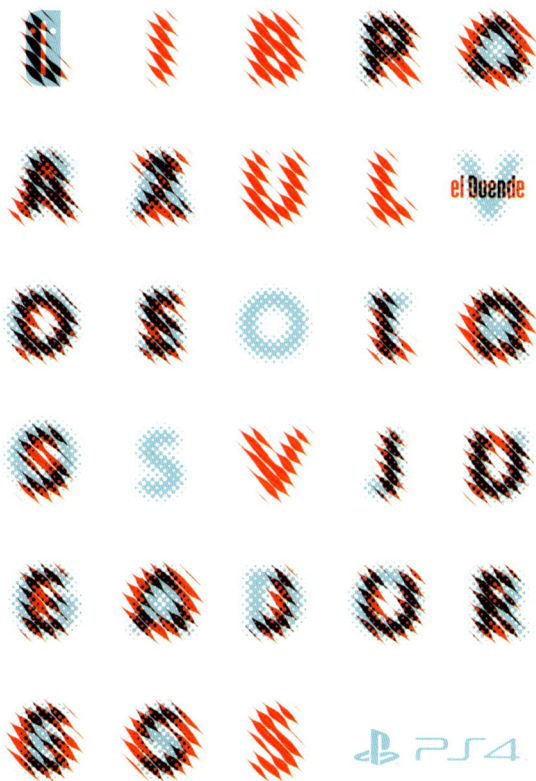

Unleash Your Inner Animal

The theme of this project comes from the experience one has at nightclub, which is converted to the combination of mixed animal-human images.

When the blue acetate sleeve is removed, it reveals a hidden wild side of the girl. It unfolds to show some brief information about the club. It unfolds again to reveal a calendar of upcoming events. It finally unfolds into a large poster of the original image. The poster glows in the dark and reveals secret illustrations. It reminds the viewers to unleash their inner animal and go to the club. The interactivity makes it special and fun to play with.

Designer / Ana Curbelo
Model / Franchesca Butler

TaoTie is an extremely legendary
evil beast, known to be so cruel
it will even consume its own body,
meaning usually it is only seen as
a head without a body.

(3310 – 2250 BCE).[5]

Intersect Origins

"Intersect Origins" has been envisioned and
designed to act as a portal, providing a new
aesthetic view of the ancient world. The
designers have implemented a highly modernist
screen transforming the thousand year old
Chinese cultural relics into objects which can
now be seen in an entire novel form.

Designer / Chén Fan & Maxim Cormier
Photographer / Chén Fan

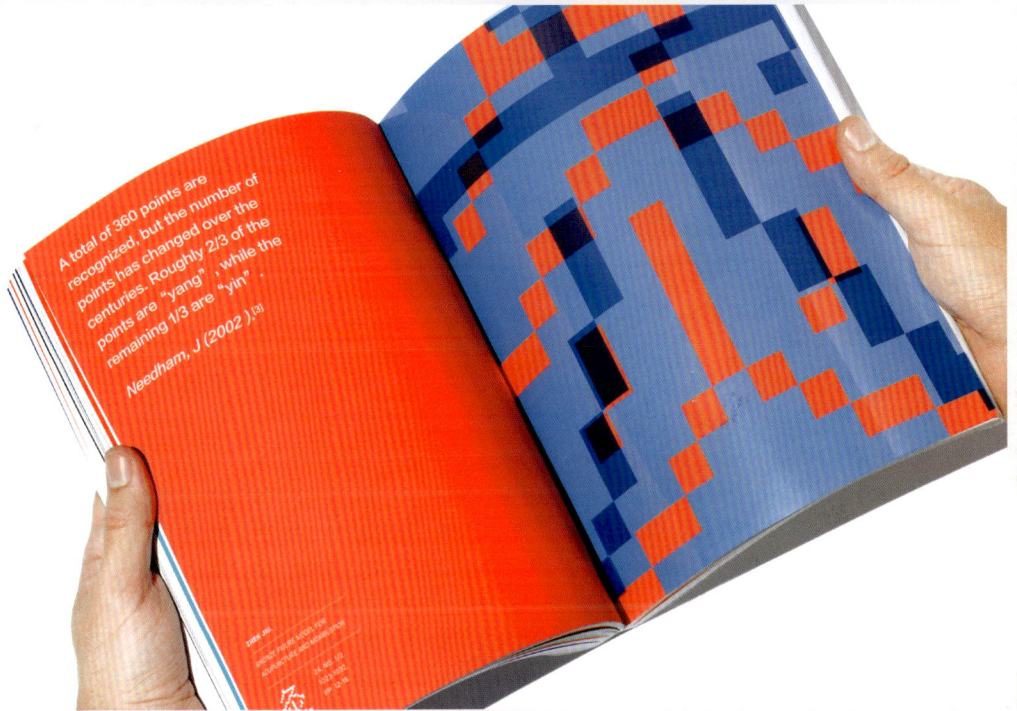

Laforet Private Party 2013 AW

Laforet Harajuku is a fashion mall in Tokyo asking for a direct mail as an invitation for a party held there called "Private Party." The theme of the party was "Pattern," which was a fashion trend of 2013. This unique direct mail is composed of four pieces of transparent sheets that a variety of patterns are printed on so that the interaction creates countless new patterns. It represents that the "Private Party" becomes a place where new culture and imagination emerge by blending and mixing different fashion cultures.

Designer / Naonori Yago

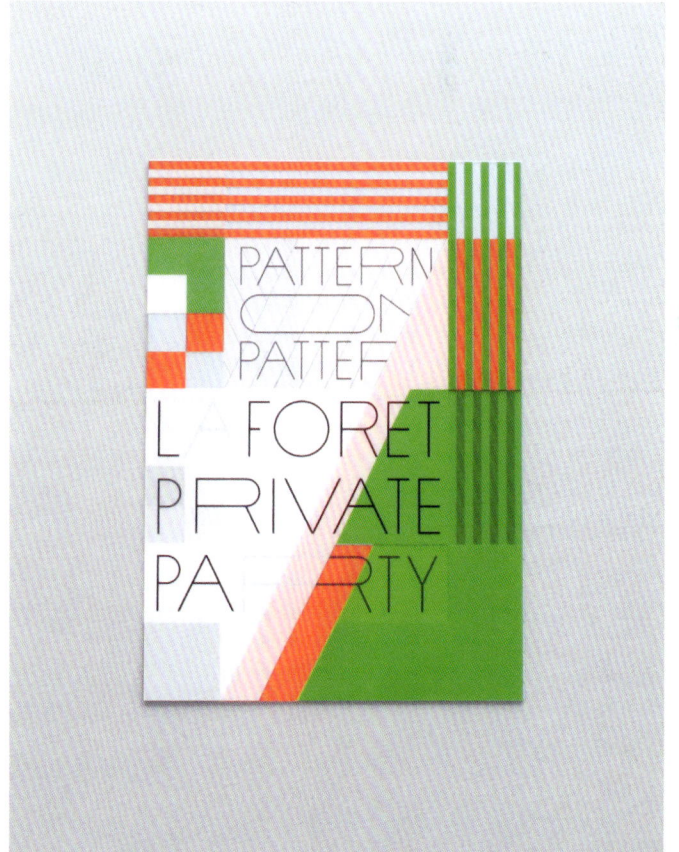

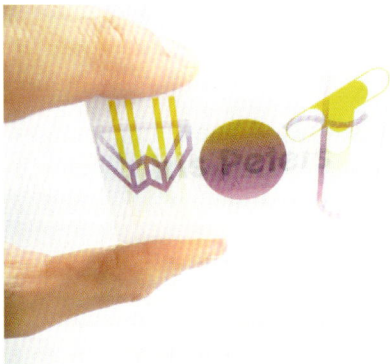

Wave of Tomorrow (WOT) Identity

Wave of Tomorrow shows developments in art, (digital) culture and society with an emphasis on play, interaction and game design. The images on the identity cards are changeable when you see from different angles.

Designer / Stephan Lerou

KATSUYA ISHIDA

This is business card for Mr. Ishida who is a visual producer centered on video production. The target is to create a long-lasting impression to the recipient. To convey the idea that video is a piece of information about light and time, Commune used a special material that can storage light and become luminescent in the dark.

Design Agency / Commune
Art Director / Ryo Ueda
Printing Director / Manami Sato
Client / Katsuya Ishida

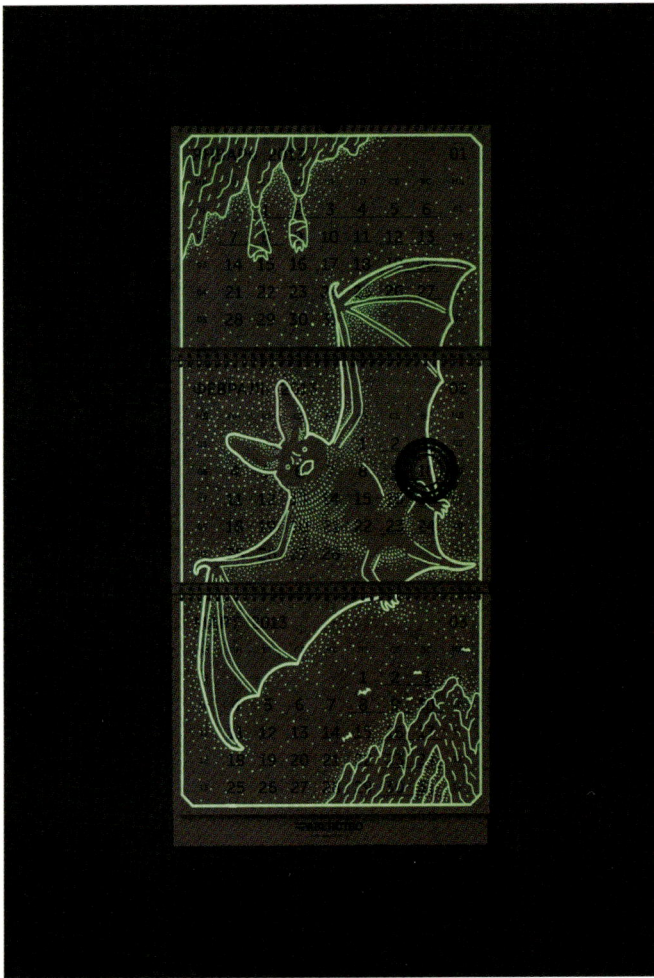

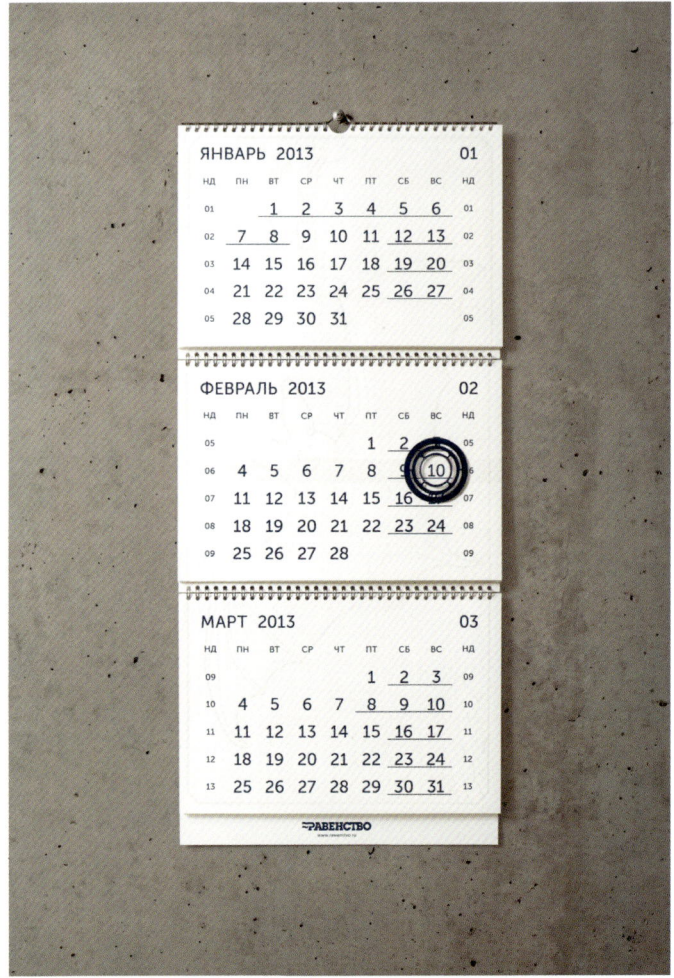

ЯНВАРЬ 2013								01
НД	ПН	ВТ	СР	ЧТ	ПТ	СБ	ВС	НД
01		1	2	3	4	5	6	01
02	7	8	9	10	11	12	13	02
03	14	15	16	17	18	19	20	03
04	21	22	23	24	25	26	27	04
05	28	29	30	31				05

ФЕВРАЛЬ 2013								02
НД	ПН	ВТ	СР	ЧТ	ПТ	СБ	ВС	НД
05					1	2		05
06	4	5	6	7	8	9	10	06
07	11	12	13	14	15	16		07
08	18	19	20	21	22	23	24	08
09	25	26	27	28				09

МАРТ 2013								03
НД	ПН	ВТ	СР	ЧТ	ПТ	СБ	ВС	НД
09					1	2	3	09
10	4	5	6	7	8	9	10	10
11	11	12	13	14	15	16	17	11
12	18	19	20	21	22	23	24	12
13	25	26	27	28	29	30	31	13

РАВЕНСТВО
www.ravenstvo.ru

Glowing Calendar

The calendar should be traditional, practical and understandable for conservative users. Ukrainian designer Yurko Gutsulyak turned it into a special and desired present based on illustrations printed with luminescent material.

Designer / Yurko Gutsulyak
Illustrator / IC4design
Client / JSC Rawenstvo

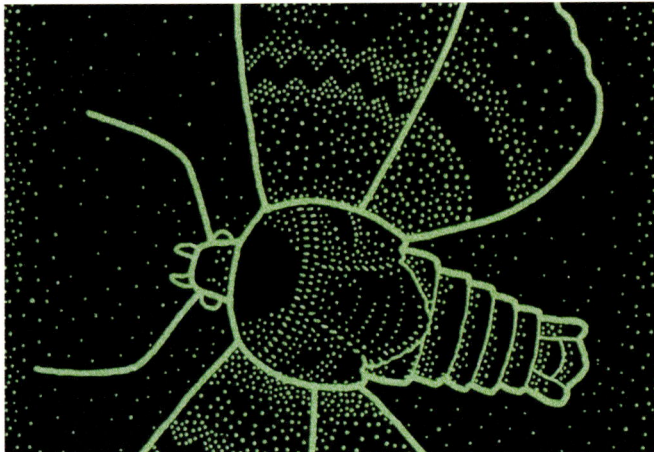

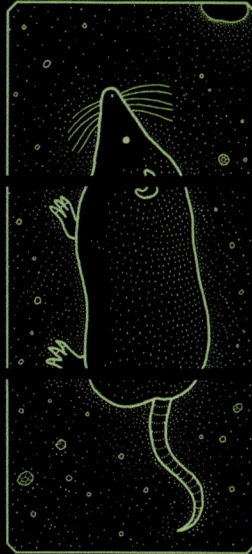

ЛЕТУЧАЯ МЫШЬ
Microchiroptera

Большинство летучих мышей ведут ночной образ жизни. В условиях ограниченной видимости они ориентируются в пространстве, испуская неслышимые для человека звуки и улавливая их эхо, отраженное от предметов.

Сравнивая посылаемый импульс с вызванным эхом, мозговая и слуховая нервная система воспроизводит детализированные изображение окружающ... ...зволяет летучим мышам обнару... ...делять точное местоположе... жение ... ...фицировать свою добычу в полной ... во время полёта летучие мыши поют песни, используя сложные сочетания слогов, которые служат не только для ухаживания, но также для опознавания друг друга, обозначения социального статуса а также определения территориальных границ.

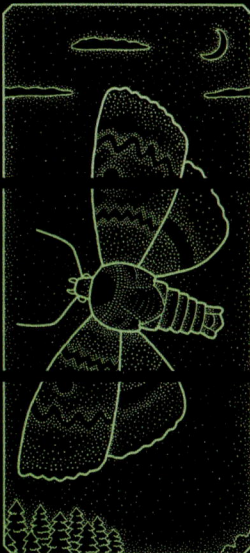

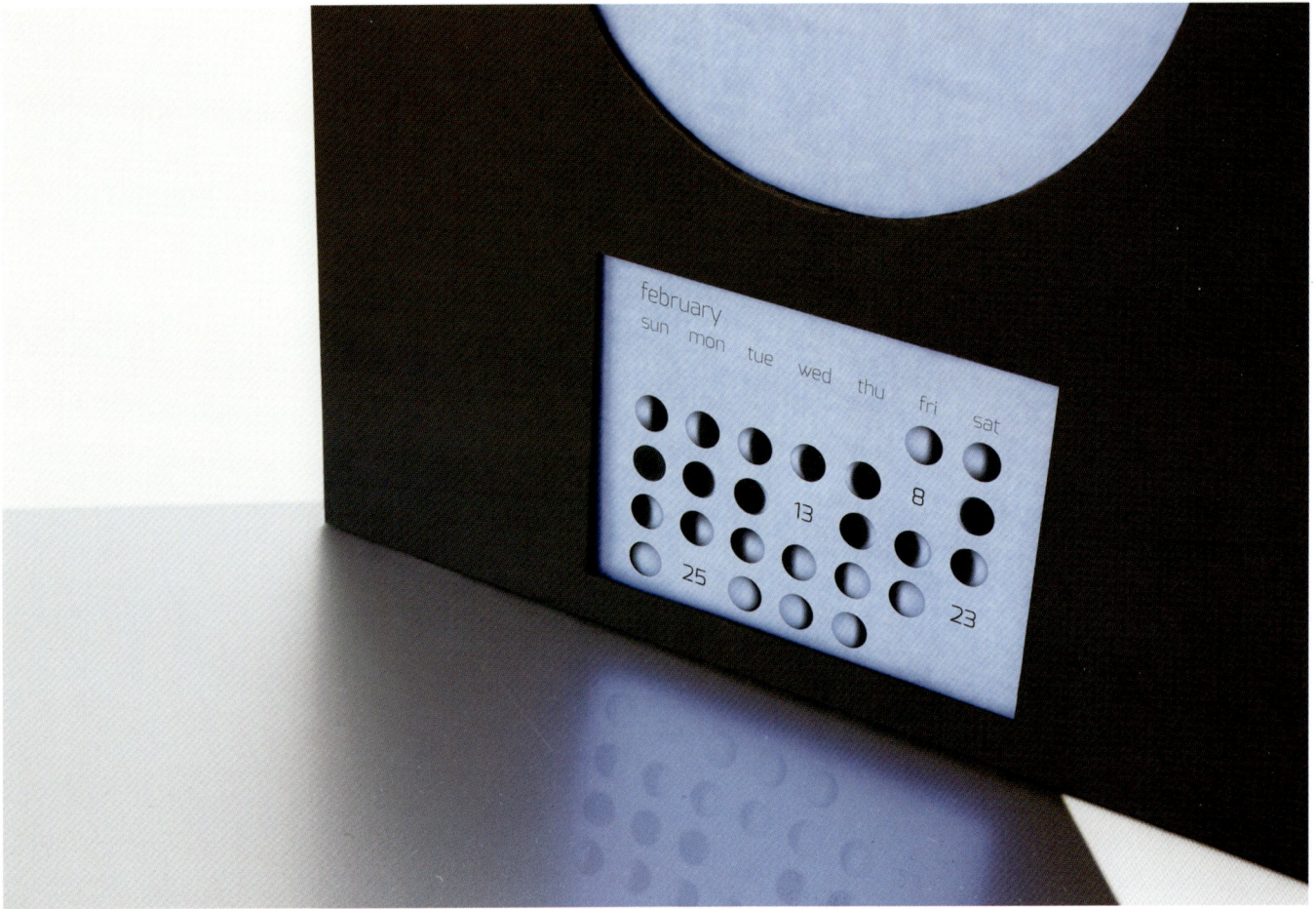

Planet Calendar

Designer Szani Mészáros used different papers for each month and a special case which could be opened as needed for this calendar. As time went by, users could remove the old paper and replace it with the current month. This calendar indicated only some days of a given month, from which users could track the rest of the days as needed.

Designer / Szani Mészáros

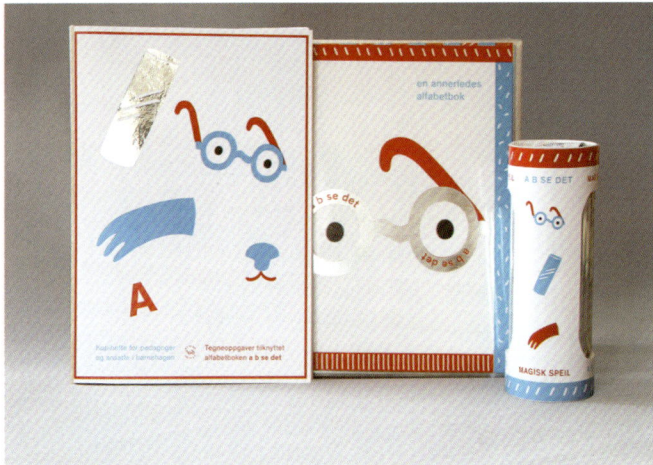

AbSeDet

AbSeDet, which means "a b see that," is a game designed to introduce alphabet to children. Each letter has its own personality, which is visualized by an animal character. With a cylindrical mirror, the image revolves around the optical illusion anamorphosis, which invites the observer to participate in revealing the hidden picture.

Designer / Mille Windfeldt

Figula Wine Label

The multi-layered label symbolizes the layers of earth and the image of grape hills because of its shape, and by being slightly three dimensional, the bottle looks unique. The top layer is rotatable and therefore playful. Using the basic pattern with different typographies or by adding different graphics, it is possible to create a design for a whole family of wines, which gives the tasty beverage a standard but also diverse look.

Designer / Cecília Pletser

Dűlő Selection Sóskút 1st Version

Inspired by the wine's origin that the village are very rich of mineral salt, Agnes Herr created a wine label that consists of three layers, which symbolize the layer of earth.

Designer / Agnes Herr

Mari – the Musical Bottle

If you blow into a bottle, a tone will sound —
but which tone exactly? After experiments with
a bottle with different volumes of water, a label
with a chromatic tuner is created which tells you
exactly the note being played. The coasters are
instructions to play a song.

Designer / Judith Kroisleitner & Christina Hosiner

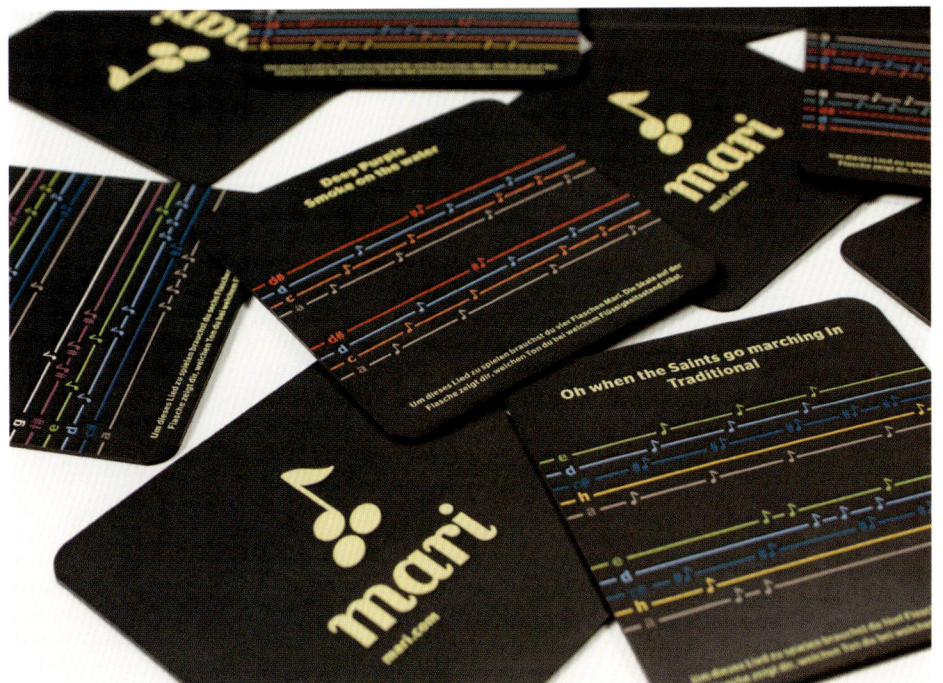

Pinto Punto Wine Label

The fundamental theme of the client was to connect with different companies to do business. Based on this idea, Xisco Barceló visualizes the network with numeral dots on the label, and allows consumers to contribute to the final image by connecting them.

Designer / Xisco Barceló
Photographer / Mónica Serra & Manuel Barrientos

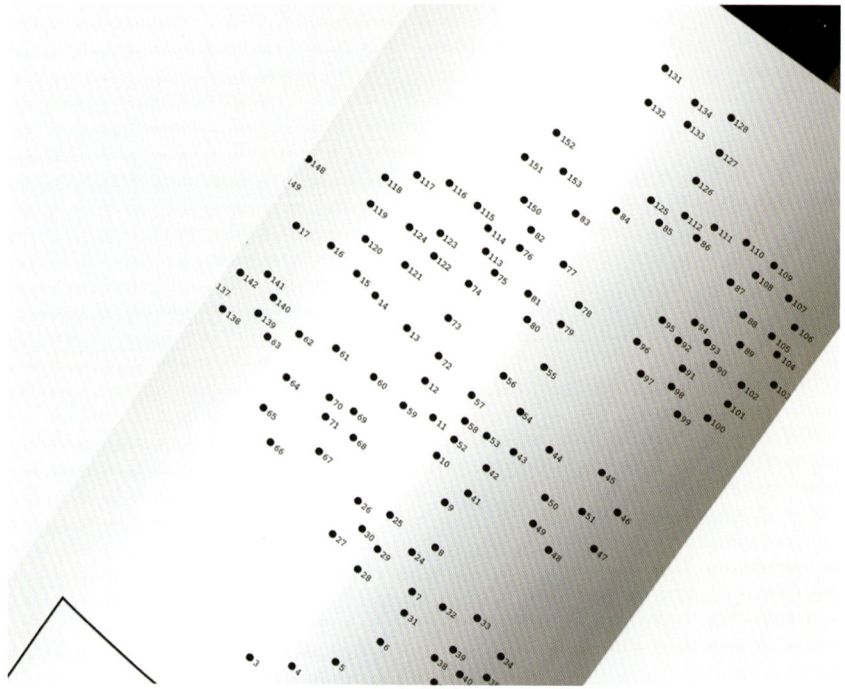

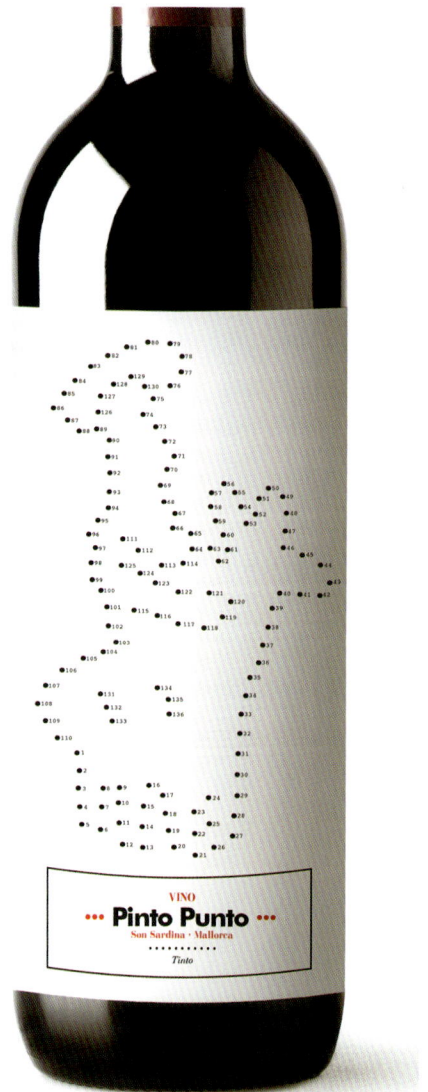

"Point After Point" Wine Bottles

Conceptually, the solution needed to make a strong connection to red wine and dogs/cats. "Point After Point" was the direction taken as it connected the positive points offered by Empyreal 75. Point after point, when you add up all the benefits, it forms a clear picture of its value as a protein additive for any pet food. Bottles were adorned with white grease pencils that allowed the prospects to connect the "points" to create either a cat or a dog.

Design Agency / Bailey Lauerman
Creative Director / RonSack
Designer / Brandon Oltmani
Illustrator / Greg Paprocki

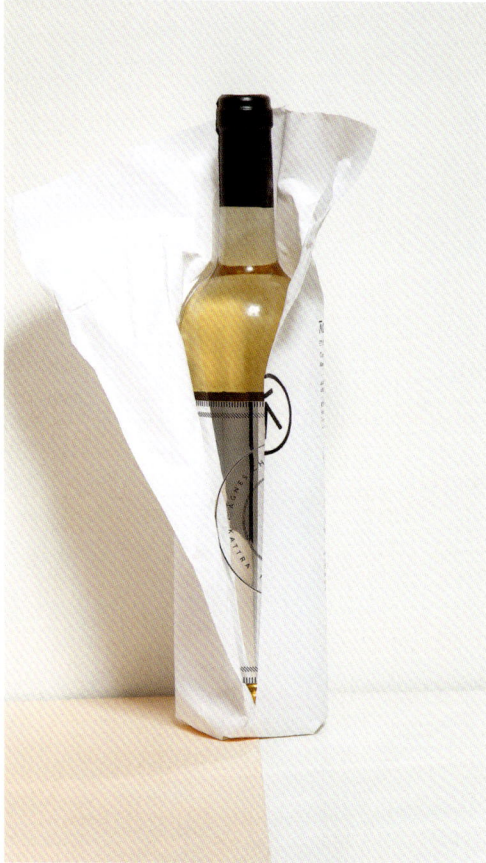

Ágnes Chardonnay

Kristóf Kőmíves worked with Kinga Nyoszoli to design the logo and label for Ágnes Chardonnay. Based on the principle that the rounded pattern plays a significant role in this brand, while they also wanted to utilize it as an advertising tool, they made a round shaped drop stop that may be popped out from label and fits the image of the wine cellar. The Ágnes Chardonnay is a true quality wine, matured in barrels. The special mirror-like material of the drop stop foil symbolizes the oily feature of the wine. The pattern running on the side of the label refers to the barrel.

Art Director / Kristóf Kőmíves
Designer / Kinga Nyoszoli
Photographer / Mate Moro

Dűlő selection Sóskút 2nd Version

Taking the fact that this wine is very high of acidity into consideration, a test paper is inserted in the label so that the consumer can examine the scale of acidity which is related with taste by their own.

Designer / Agnes Herr

Tubu-tubu

Sube-sube

Zara-zara

Toge-toge

Goro-goro

Fuwa-fuwa

Poki-poki

Suka-suka

Zaku-zaku

Chocolate Texture

In coming with a new chocolate concept, Nendo turned out attention not to general factors that determine the taste, instead they thought about "shape." The 9 different types of chocolate are made within the same size, but feature varied appearances. Although they used identical ingredients, the distinctive textures create totally distinct tastes.

Design Agency / Nendo
Photographer / Akihiro Yoshida

Okawa Conserve

This design is intended to make a proposal of a new lifestyle with its fusion of "Eat" and "Tree." As more and more people gather around the table, the single tree becomes woods, and the woods become forest.

Design Agency / Tetusin Design Office
Designer / Takayuki Senzaki
Photographer / Hiromasa Otsuka

The Hälssen & Lyon Tea Calendar

The Hälssen & Lyon Tea Calendar is the first ever calendar to feature days made from tea leaves. The 365 exquisitely flavoured and thinly pressed calendar days can be individually detached and steeped in hot water. The tea calendar was sent to a select group of Hälssen & Lyon's business partners, highlighting the company's role as an innovative trendsetter.

Design Agency / Kolle Rebbe
Art Director / Patrick Schröder
Executive Creative Director / Sascha Hanke
Production / Martin Lühe

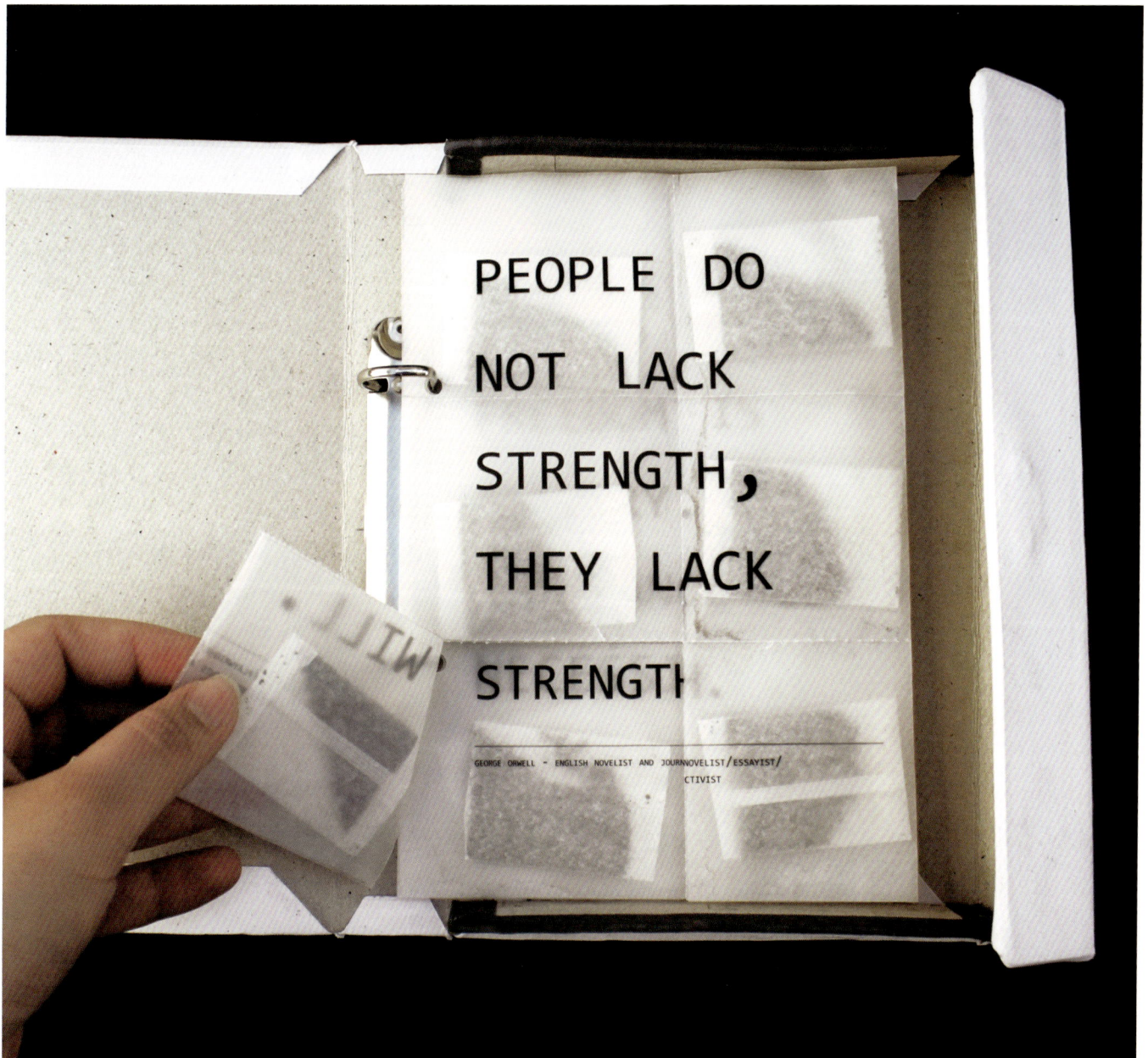

PEOPLE DO
NOT LACK
STRENGTH,
THEY LACK
STRENGTH

GEORGE ORWELL - ENGLISH NOVELIST AND JOURNOVELIST/ESSAYIST/
CTIVIST

Shrubs Tea Package

This tea package, which is especially targeted the people at work as well as young people, is designed as a reusable notebook. It contains 6 packs of tea for a week which are comprised of a quote. It aims to bring a relaxing moment during the routine.

Design Agency / A Patent Design

| Philosophie

Brainfood

Exhibition furniture and media to explain and to experience the root of the German language.

Design Agency / Morphoria Design Collective
Director / Daniela Herweg

Griechisch
indoeuropäisch/hellenisch

Medizin I

Biologie

Religion

Medizin II

Philosophie

Latein
indoeuropäisch/italisch

Biologie

Medizin

Physik   Religion

Andere
afroasiatisch, romanisch...

Religion

Naturwiss.

Linguistik

| Biologie | Religion

| Philosophie

| Religion

| Medizin

| Naturwiss.

"The Dalkey Archive" - a Visual Book

"The Dalkey Archive," which is about self-growth, has been recreated as an evidences' collection about the development of the main character's self-awareness. The novel is bound as a manuscript (made of waste paper, such as old engravings and maps) in order to suggest that the protagonist wrote himself the story. The paper evidences are symbols of circumstances in which he behaved negligently and naively. On the contrary, the pictures (by Francis Bacon) represent situations of progress. Indeed, while the first ones are unconnected and disorganized, the second ones can actually be used as pieces of a puzzle and recreate the original engraving of an Irish city.

Designer / Alice Scalfi

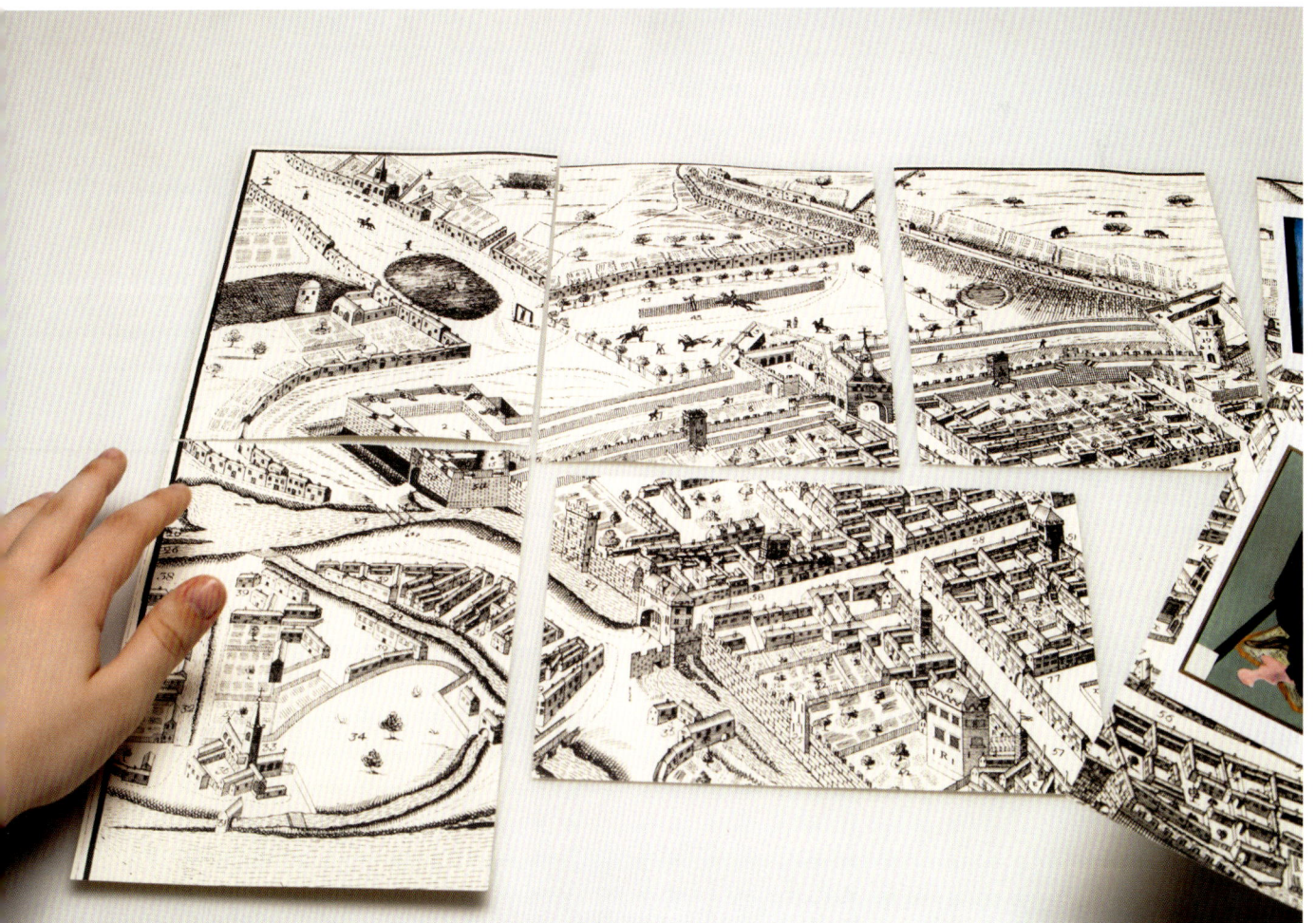

Gabriel García Márquez Book Design Series

Gabriel García Márquez's stories are so evolved and eloquent that Melodie Eve Pisciotti designed the origami covers to show that the hidden meanings are behind the surface. By unfolding the origami with key words summarizing the novel, the concept and theme will be revealed.

Designer / Melodie Eve Pisciotti

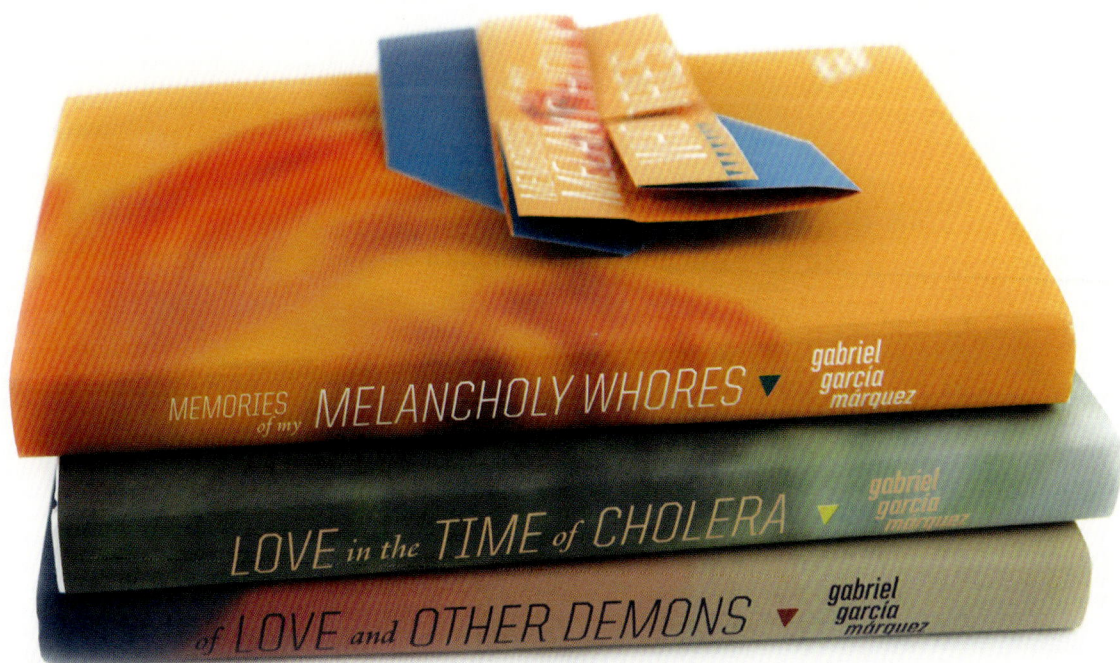

Amaze

This book aims to explore the word 'maze' in both as concept and content. Conceptually Pedro Veneziano used the state of being lost as a starting point for the material structure: it consists of three different books, in which the main one is folded in a non-linear way, allowing the user to go through the whole material. He also explored the word as a visual queue for the sleeve and the books and as a theme for the main book, which contains all the imagery and texts in one side and a giant maze that can be recombined and played in an infinite way on the other.

Designer / Pedro Veneziano

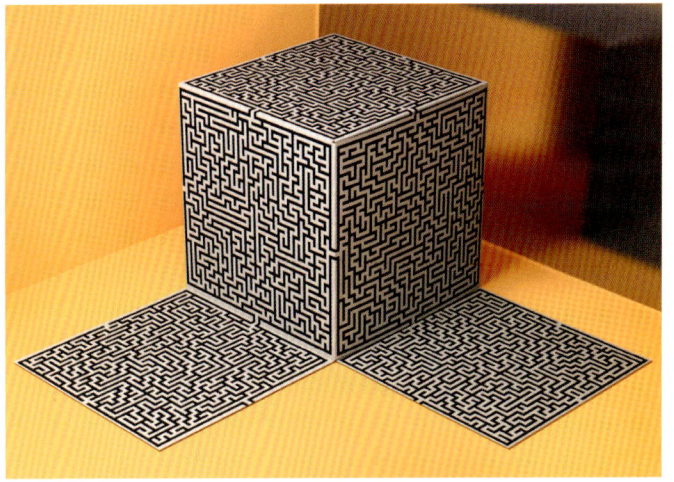

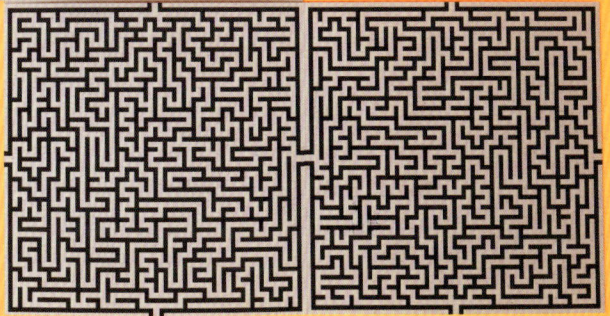
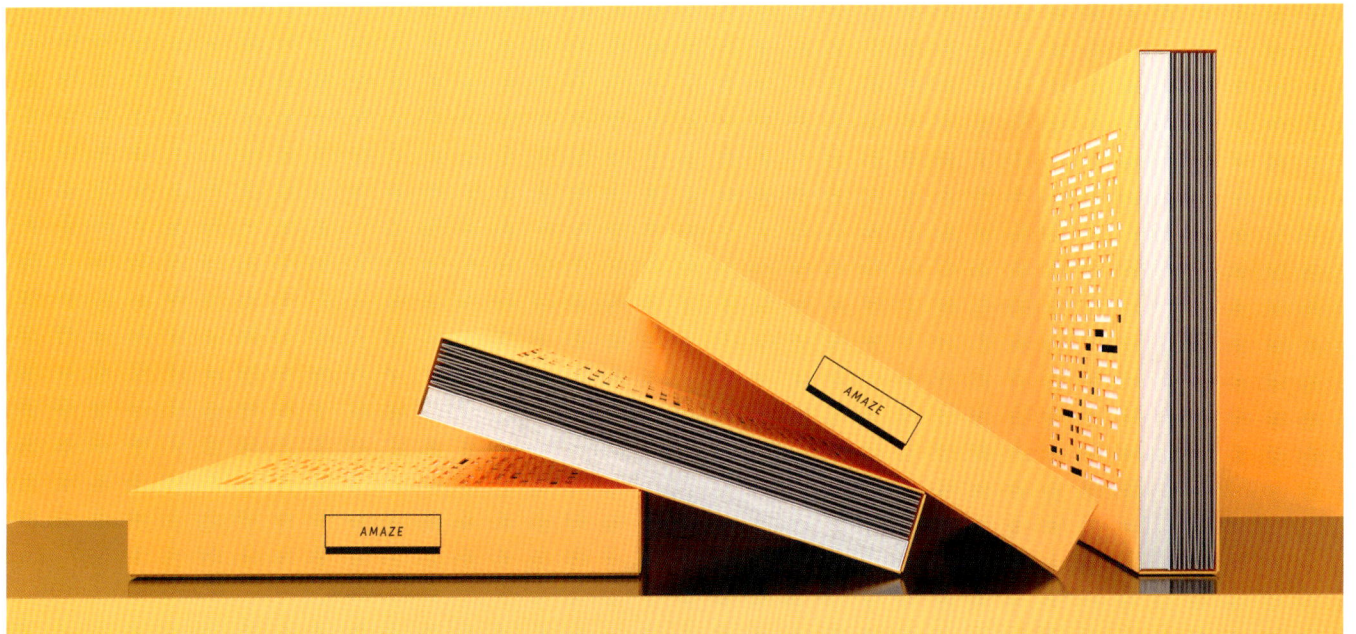

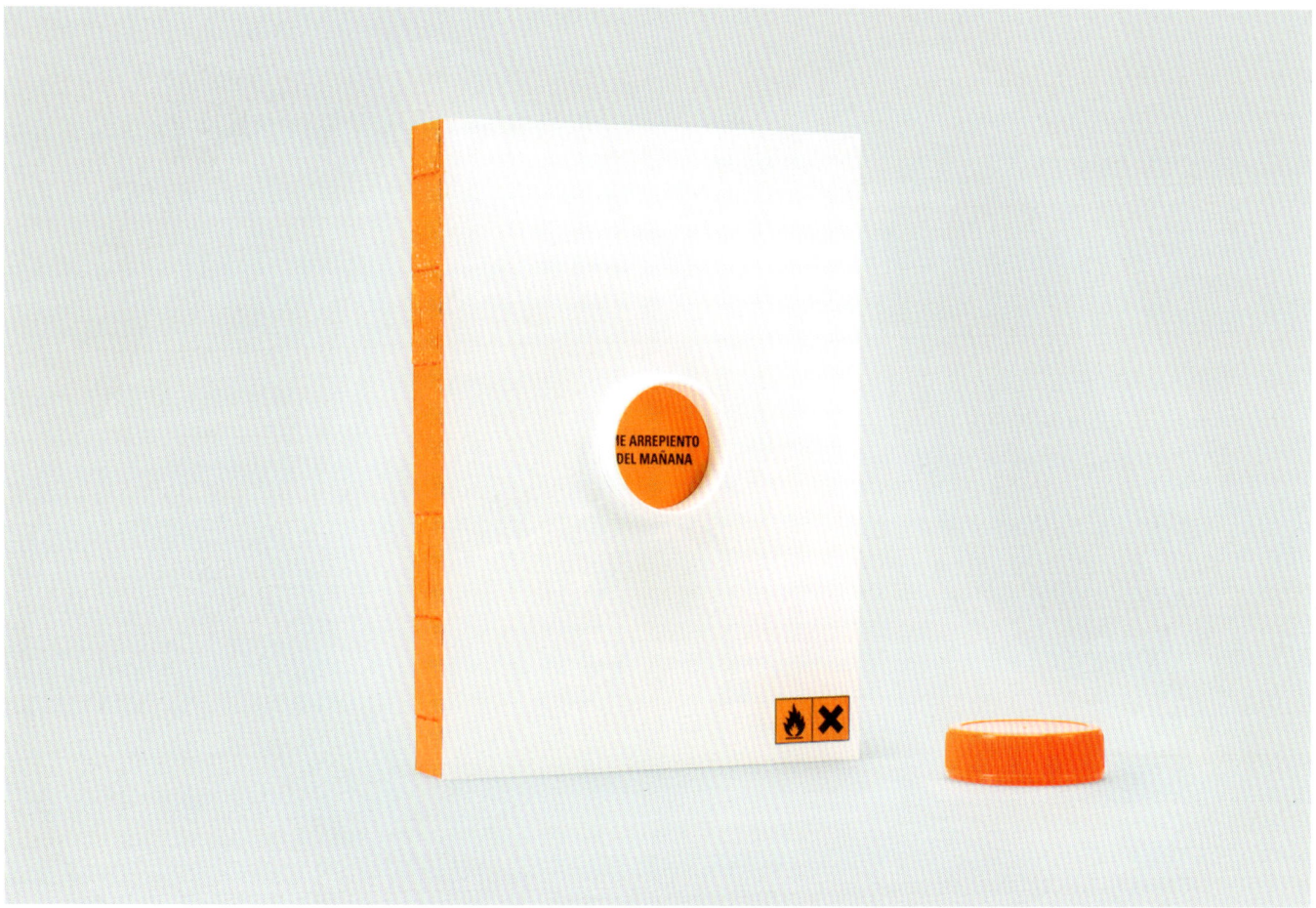

I Regret of Tomorrow

The writer Enrique Rubio was looking for something that he could not find in the editorial world: the complete fusion between the content and the form of his work. The strength, simplicity, and causticity of the texts, sometimes truly corrosive and incendiary, led to the idea of a bottle of the most toxic and poisonous product so that the form and content would merge in a way that was indissoluble.

Design Agency / Rubio & Del Amo
Designer / Guillermo Rubio
Photographer / Julián Garnés
Binding / Belmonte Encuadernaciones

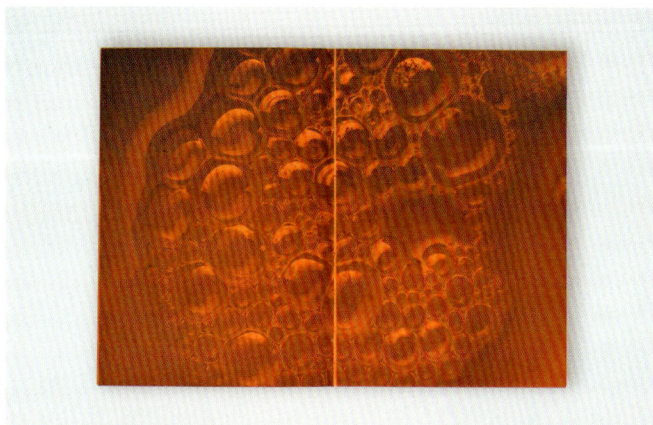

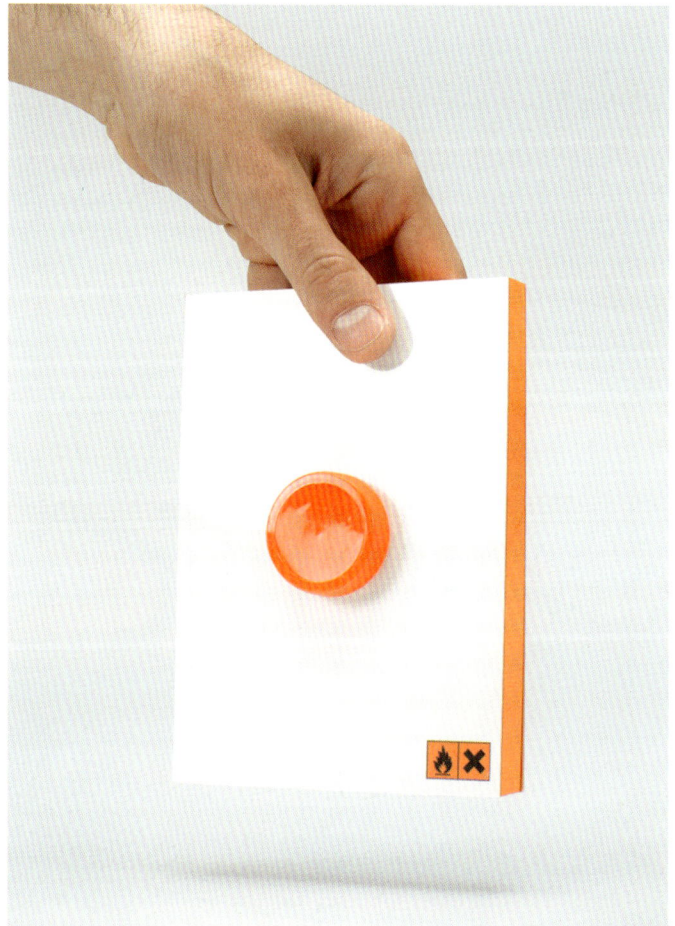

Typoberlin

Using a basic black colour ink on the brown paper with bright lithography colour, Yoonshin Kim created a logo for the brochure in the form of alphabet S based on the theme "shift." When the brochure opened, the black circle on the front can be changed to the logo. Inside the brochure, there is a 3-day schedule with a logo which are divided in day and night so that user can check the schedule efficiently.

Designer / Yooshin Kim

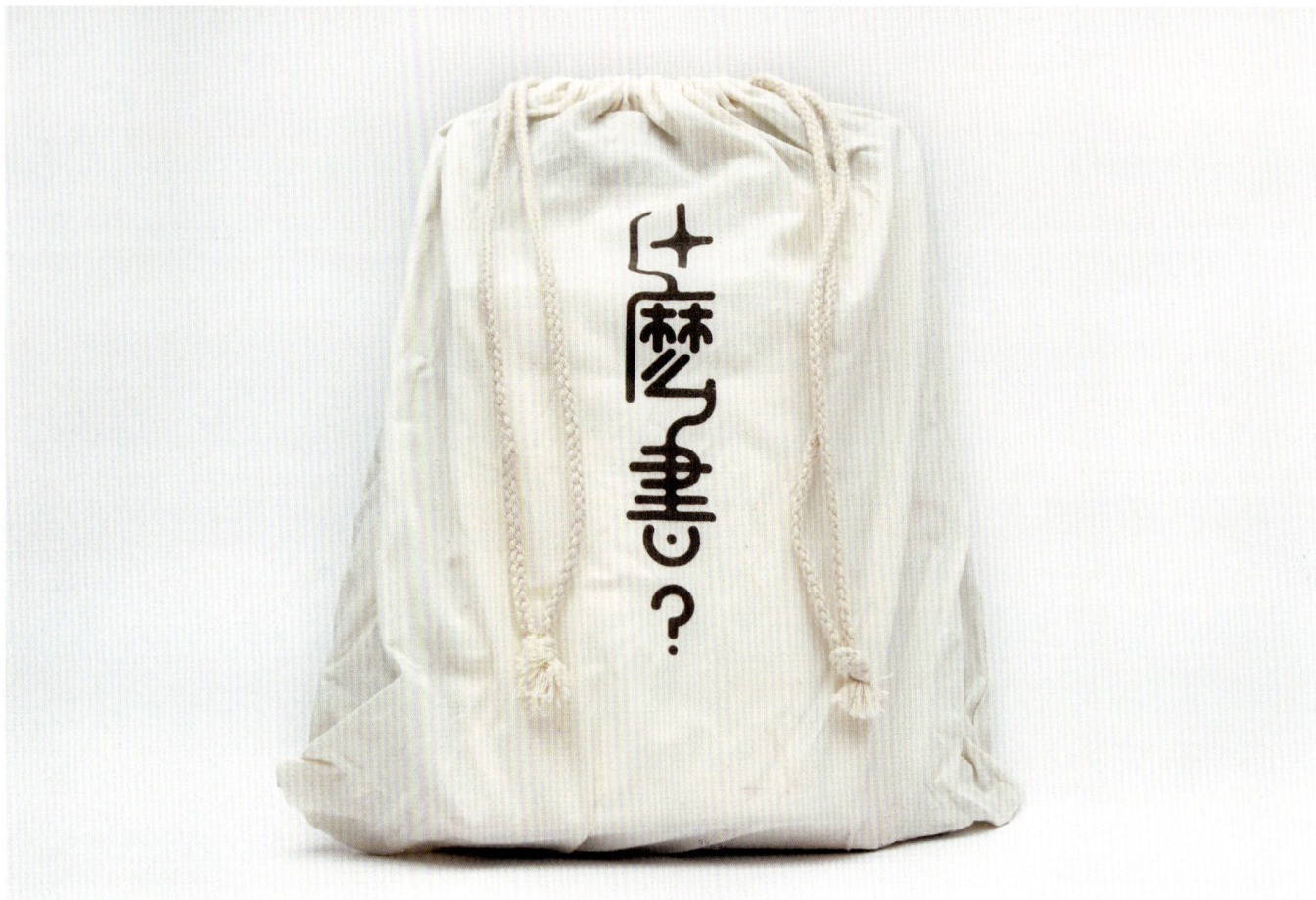

What's the Book?

With the title, Gong Xinyu expects readers would curious about its content before opening the package, such as "What is the book about" or "Is it a paper book or a digital one." This project aims to explore the interaction and emotional exchange between a paper book and its readers. The pack consists of four books, in which three are presented here, compiled based on four strong emotions: family letter, love letter, blood note, and suicide note.

Designer / Gong Xinyu

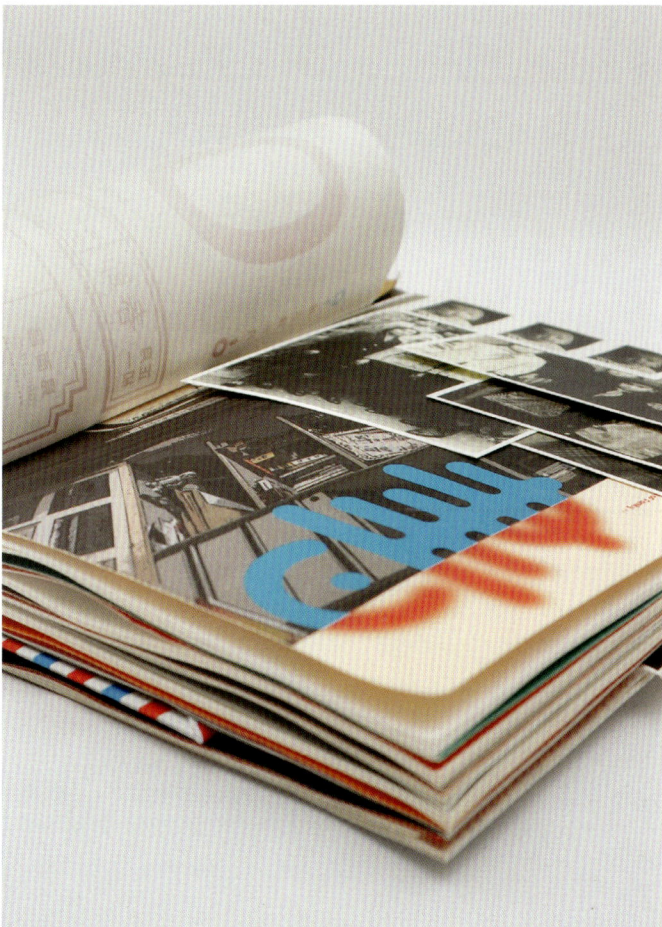

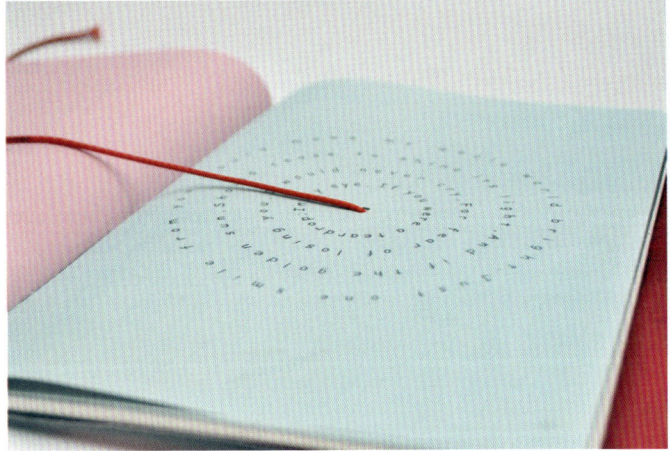

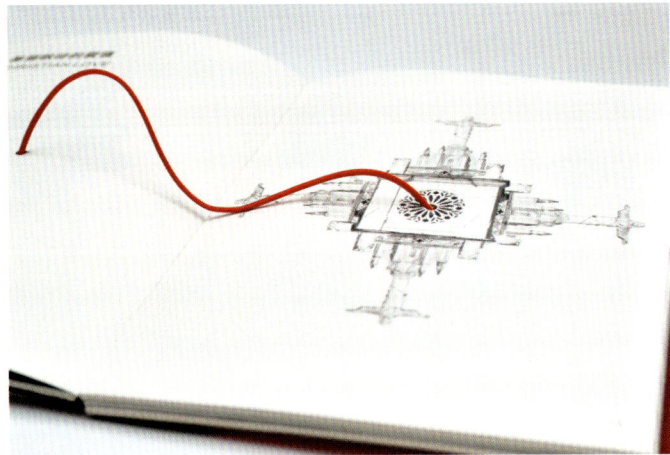

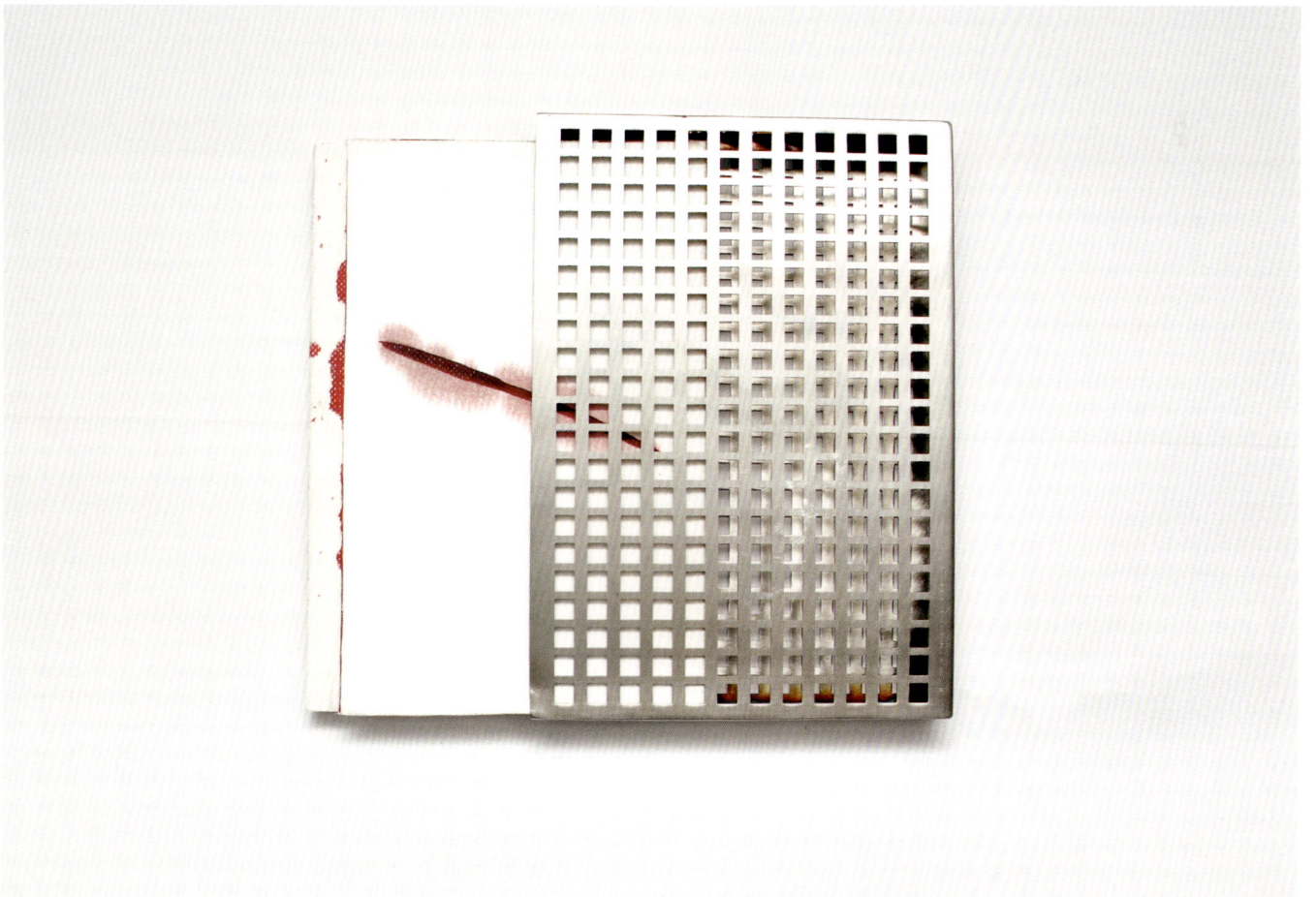

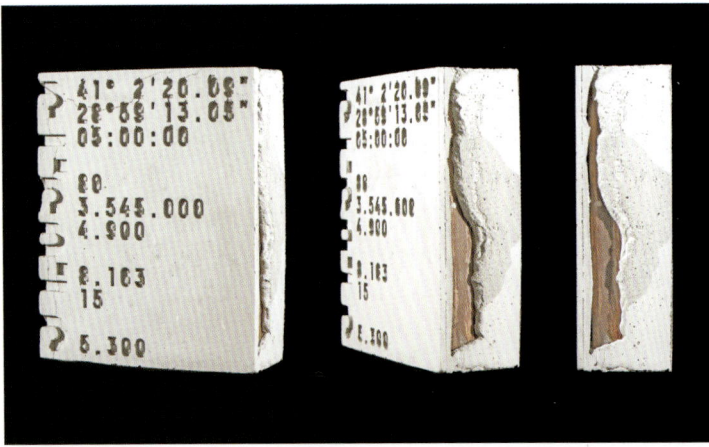

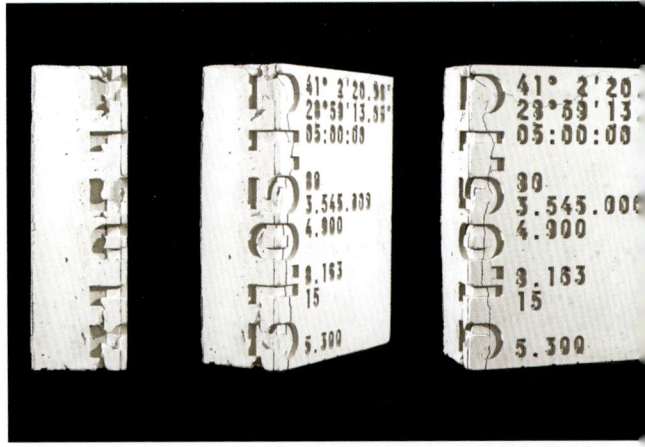

31.05.13

"31.05.13" is a book about the first 15 days of Gezi Park protests in Istanbul, Turkey which began in May, 2013. Encompassing the personal experiences of the author with visual-audio archives, it serves as an object of physical interaction. With an emphasis on storytelling, the book also aims to expand the limits of print by offering a personal experience.

Designer / Ali Emre Doğramacı
Advisor / Ahmet Atıf Akın

Biblia: a Book Within a Book

The word bible comes from the Greek word Biblia, which means books. Biblia is the Holy Bible Red Letter Edition in which words spoken by Jesus are printed in red ink. This project is a series of packages containing an earlier chapter inside the bible so one can find a unique binding of it: it contains a book in which contains another book. It has seven books in total: six container shaped books and one final book, Genesis, which is the first book of the Bible that is the origin of other books. Number six represents the number of days that God worked when He created the world while number seven represents the day when God rested after his works of creation. The ribbon pieces are used in order to pull out the books easily, but they also indicate the order of the books. The colour goes lighter as the reader reaches toward the core of Biblia: Genesis.

Designer / Ji Yun Kim

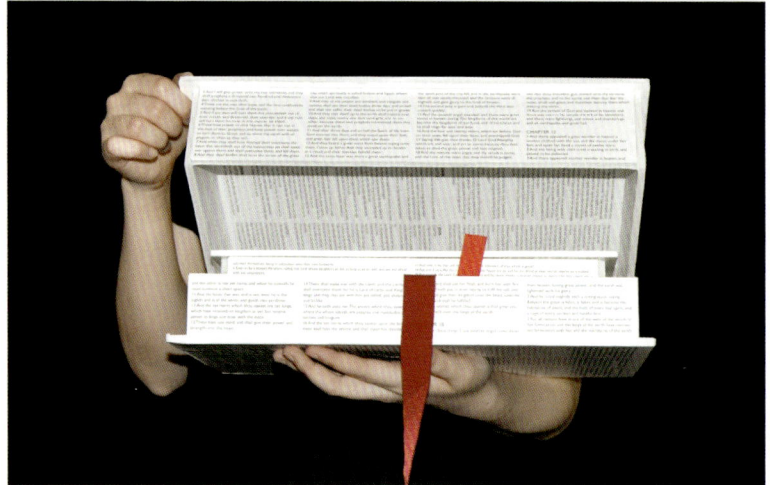

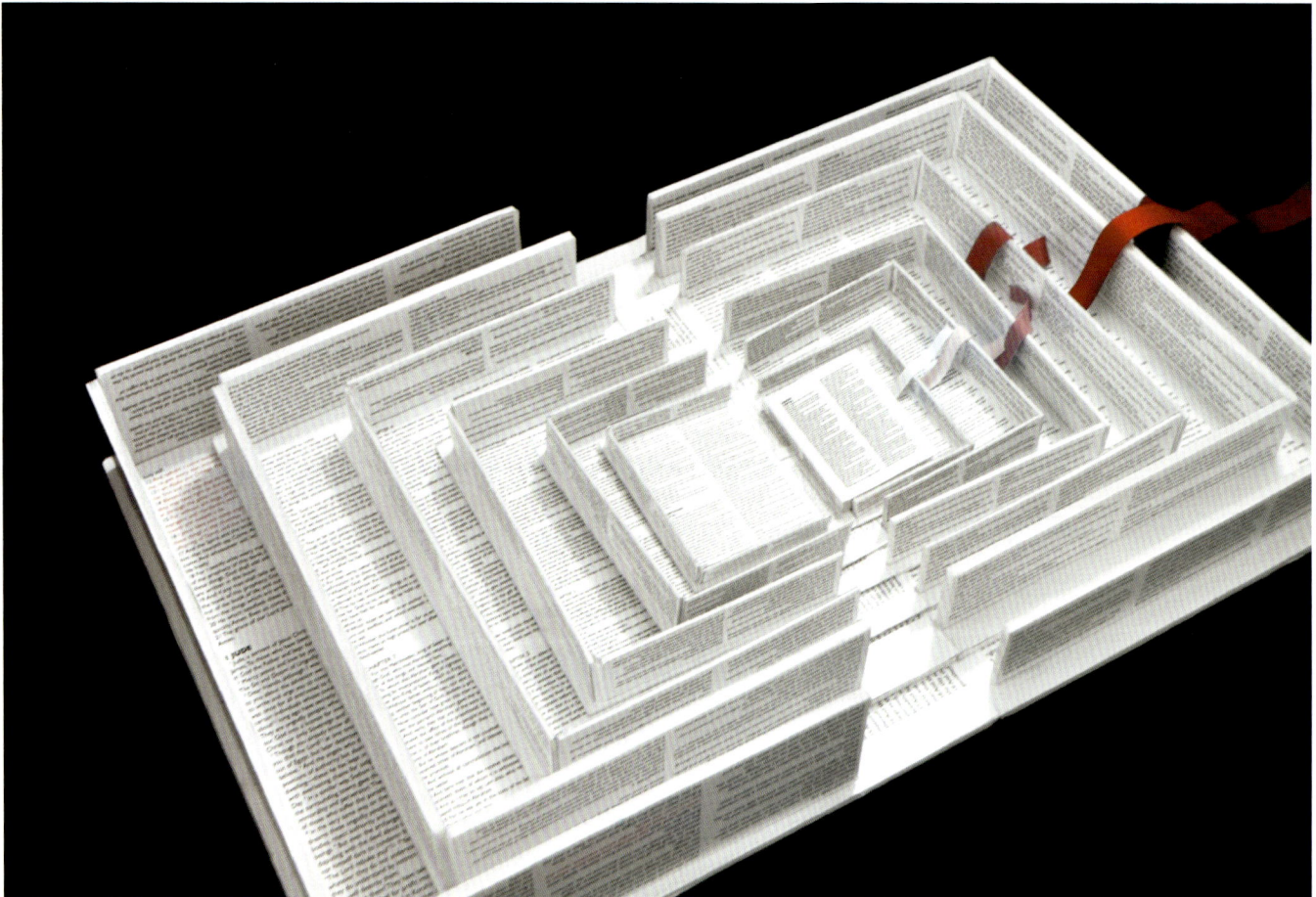

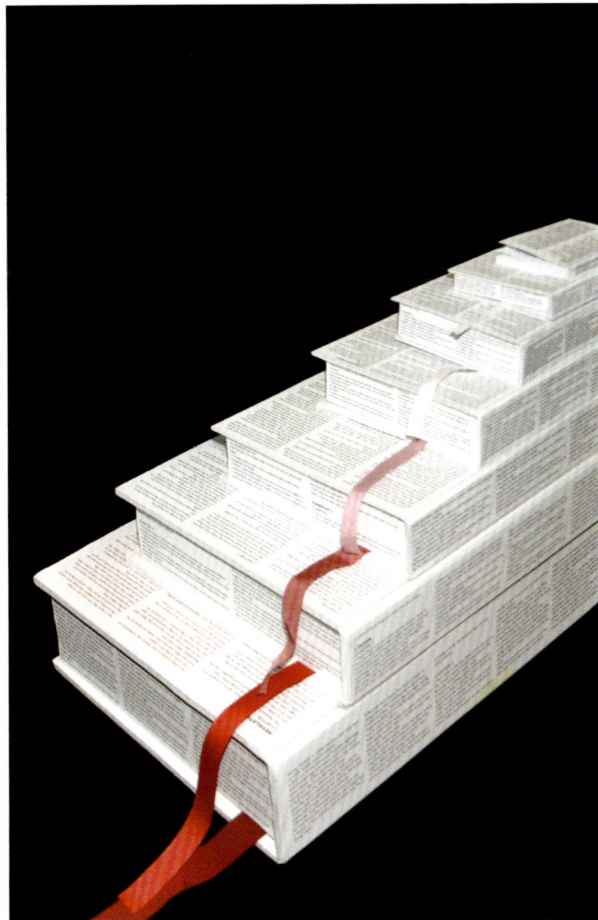

Ways of Seeing

Ways of Seeing is a campaign project to reveal unheard stories from the homeless and to raise awareness on how stereotyping can keep us from seeing the full picture. Juyeon Lee and Hyunseo Yoo transcribed the stories of the homeless into patterns and hid true facts about them, representing how stereotypes block us from seeing them as an equal human being.

Designer / Juyeon Lee & Hyunseo Yoo

WAYS
OF
~~SEEING~~

WAYS
OF
~~SEEING~~

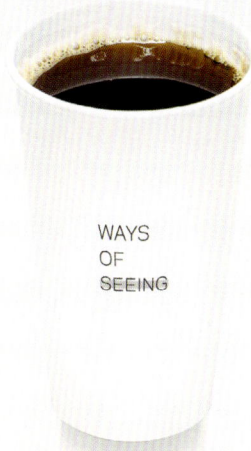
WAYS
OF
SEEING

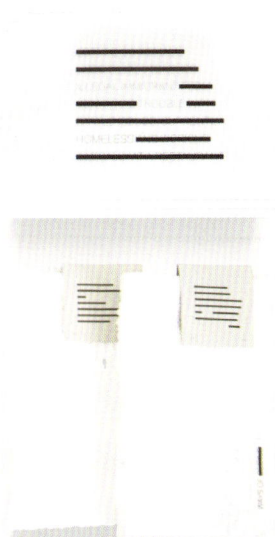

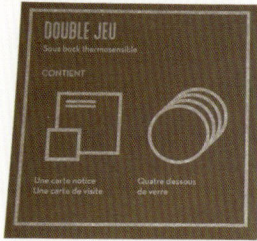

Double Jeu -
Thermic Coasters

Double jeu is a series of double-sided objects. Each coaster is heat sensitive, allowing the ink to become transparent and reveal a second message. When the hiddden words appear, the meaning of the sentences turns from positive into negative.

Designer / Mona Leu-Leu

Designers Anonymous Identity

Designers Anonymous created an interactive and playful identity for themselves. It was distinctive, fun, yet flexible enough to communicate various messages and demonstrate their creative flair. The stationery features a range of expressive silhouette icons that hide their name with heat sensitive ink or repositionable stickers.

Design Agency / Designers Anonymous
Designer / Darren Barber & Christian Eager
Photographer / Darren Barber

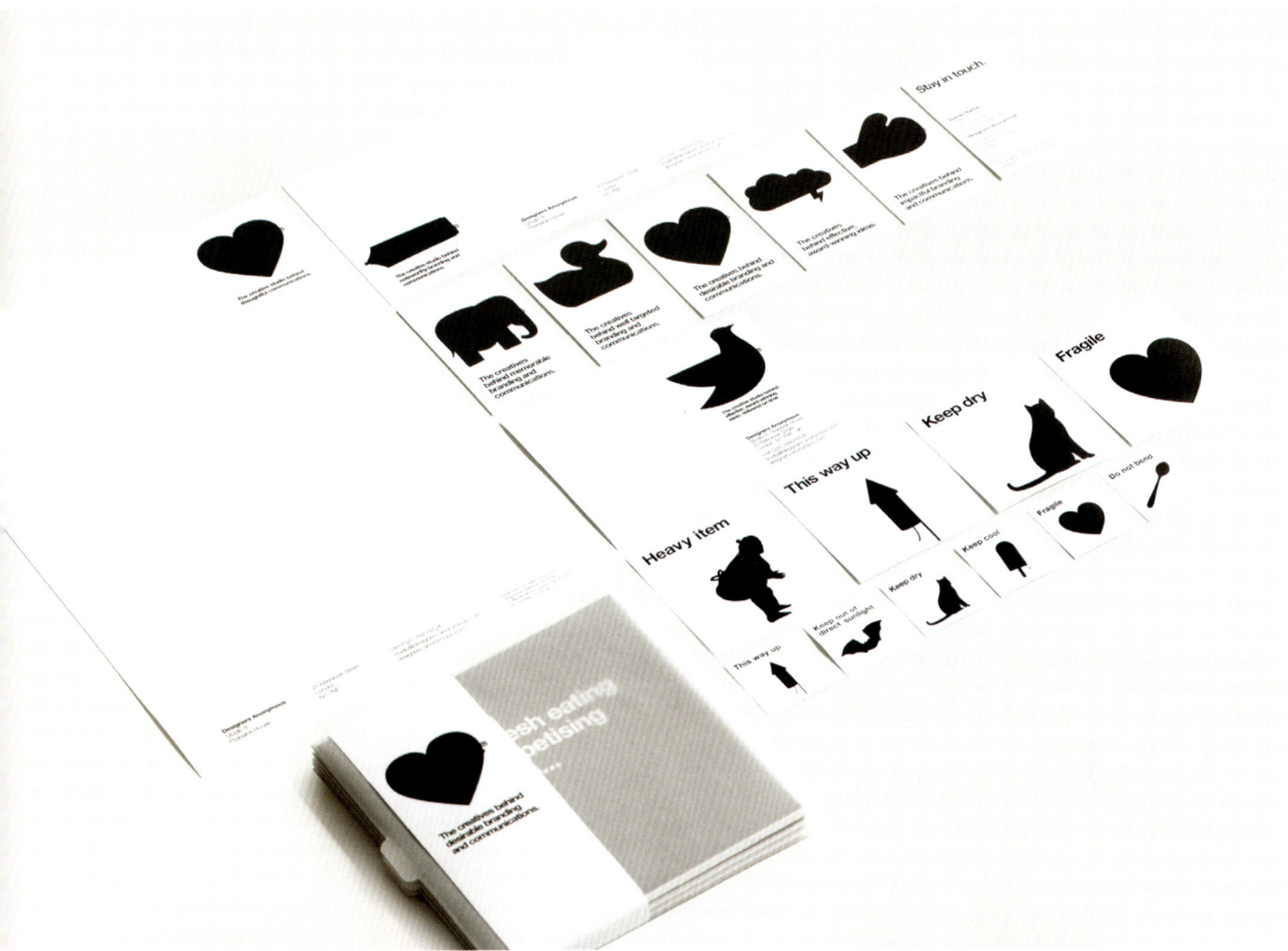

N. Daniels

This is the stationery design for N. Daniels, a rep
and photo producer in Vienna. It's simple, cool
and thermo-sensitive. The black colour of the
varnish fades at body temperature — as soon
as you hold it in your hands you literally produce
an image by yourself. It's a dynamic and living
design — the business cards are little polaroids
with a constantly changing surface. All these
cards might start looking similar, but with your
personal "touch," you brand them individually.

Design Agency / Bureau Rabensteiner

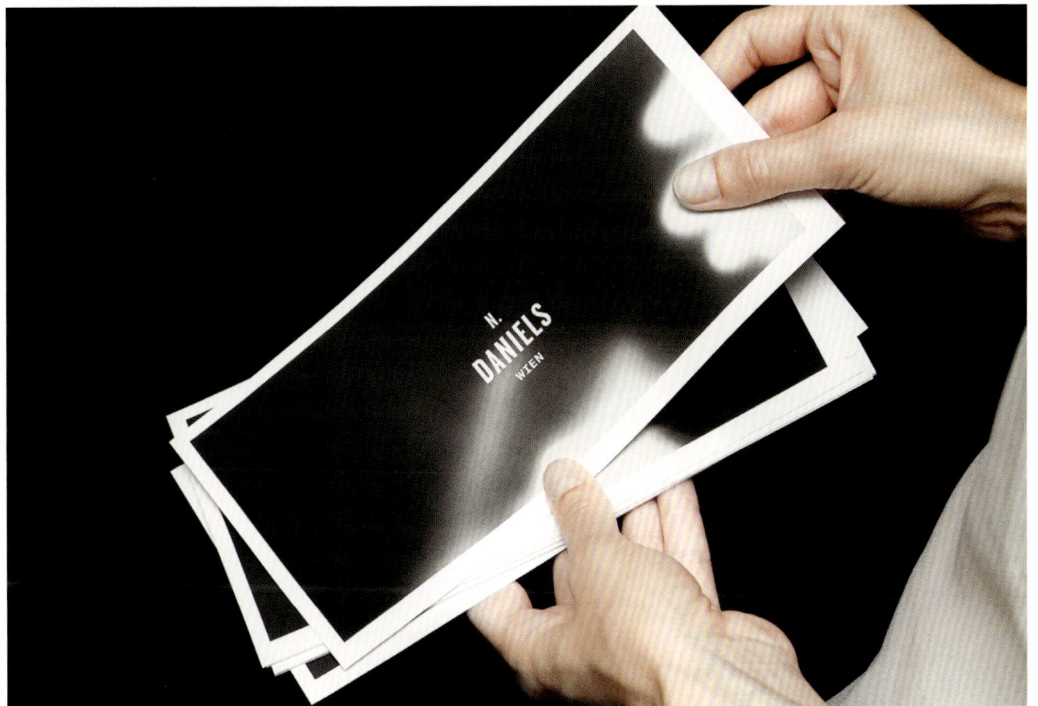
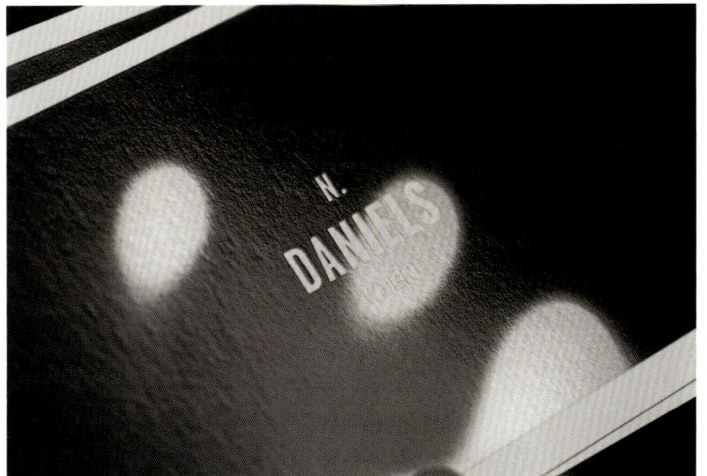

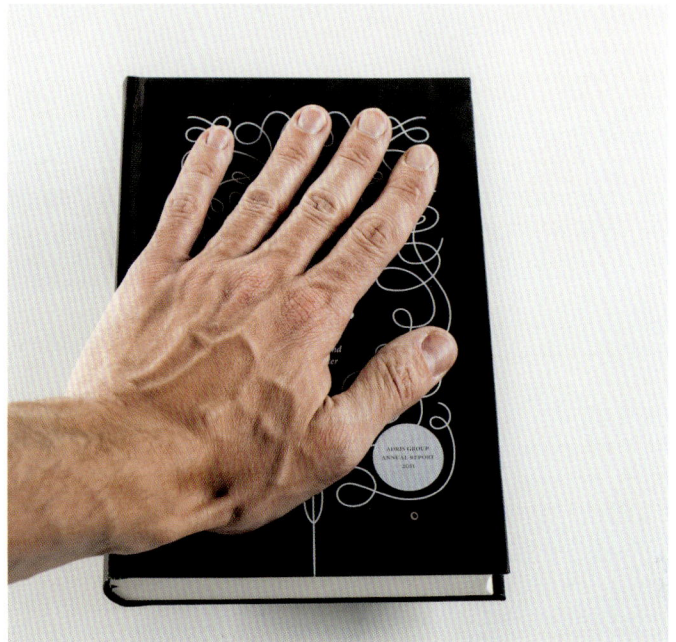

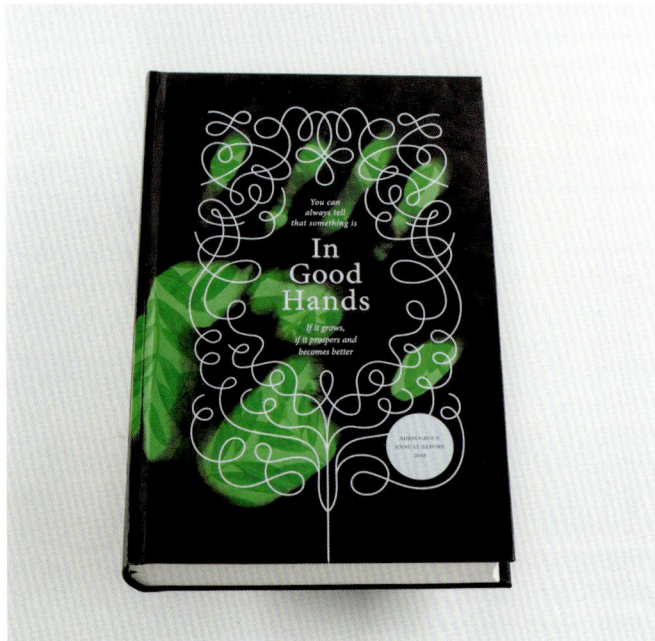

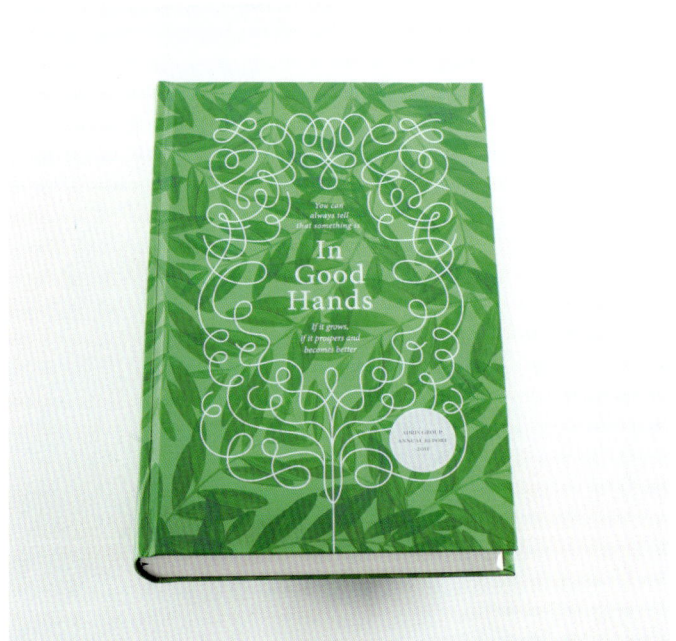

In Good Hands

Adris group's annual report entitled "In Good Hands" reveals floral details when heated by the palms of the hands, metaphorically illustrating hands can achieve anything. The same especially calibrated thermo colour as on the covers was used for the inside illustrations, and the concept of the annual report is also evoked by the short stories where workers and stockholders share their personal view to the past, future and influence of Adris group on their lives.

Design Agency / Bruketa&Zinic OM
Print / Cerovski Print Boutique, Stegatisak
Thermo Colour Printing / Knepsen
Binding and Blind Folding / Knjigoveznica First

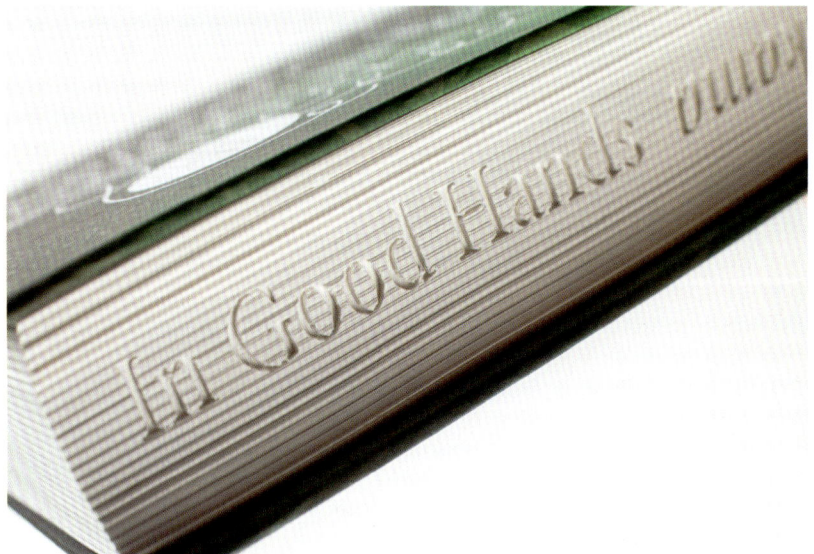

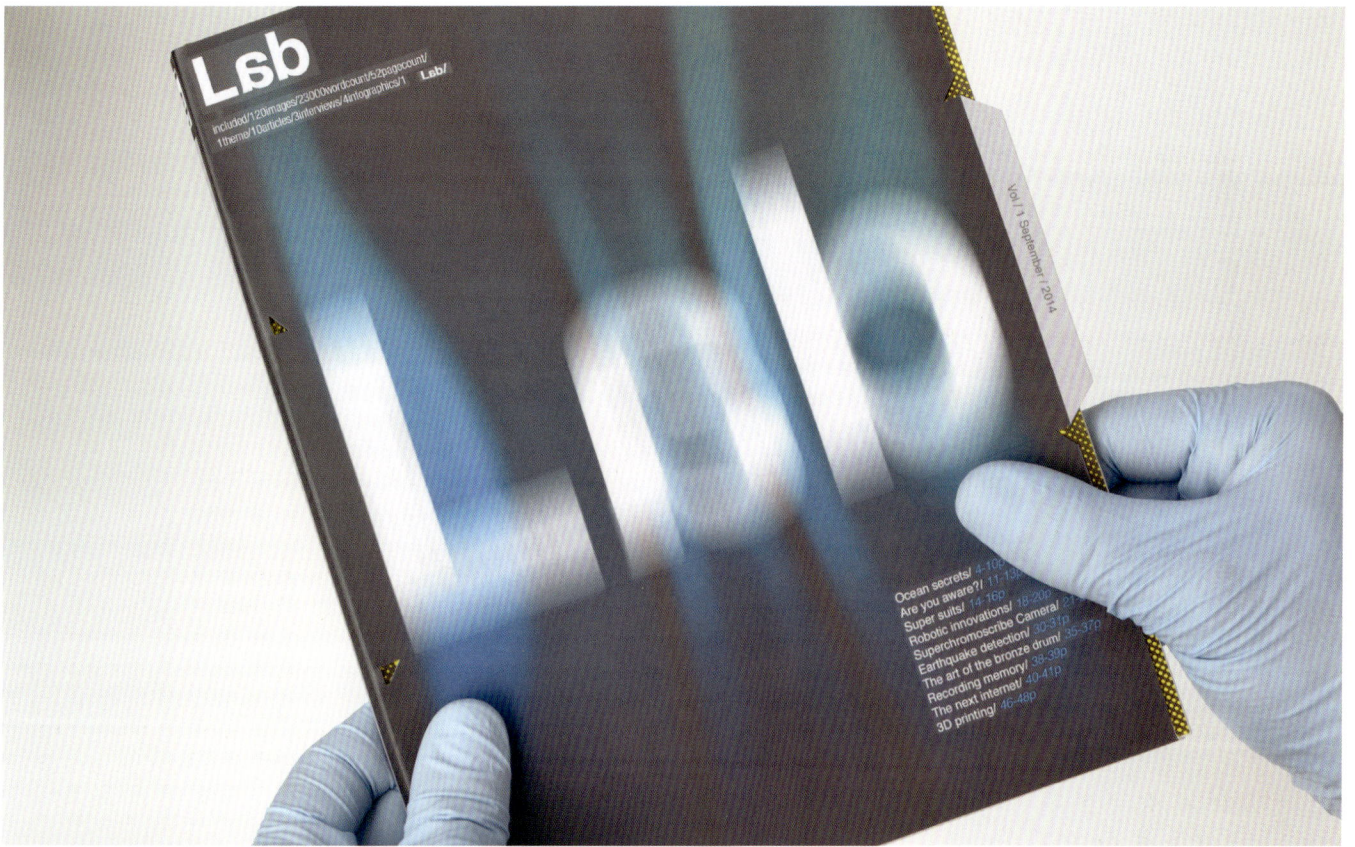

Lab Periodical

The project is a biannual publication with a focus on science, technology and travel.

Designer / Chén Fan & Maxim Cormier
Photographer / Chén Fan

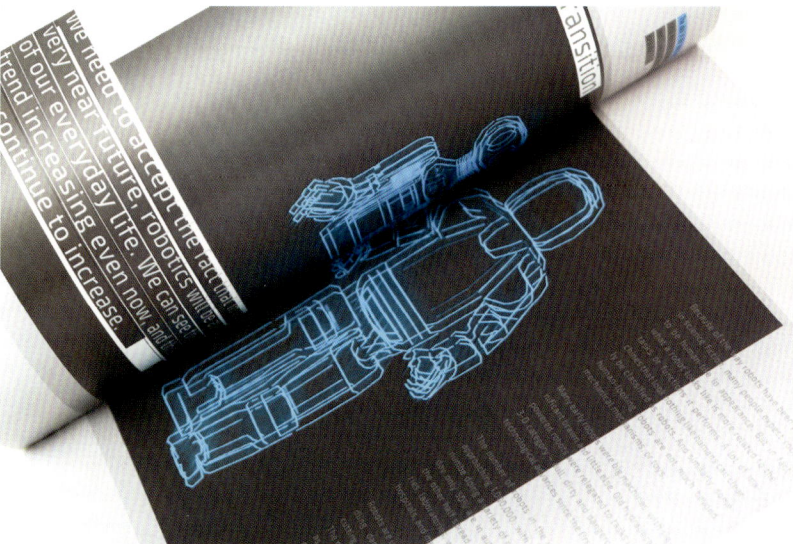

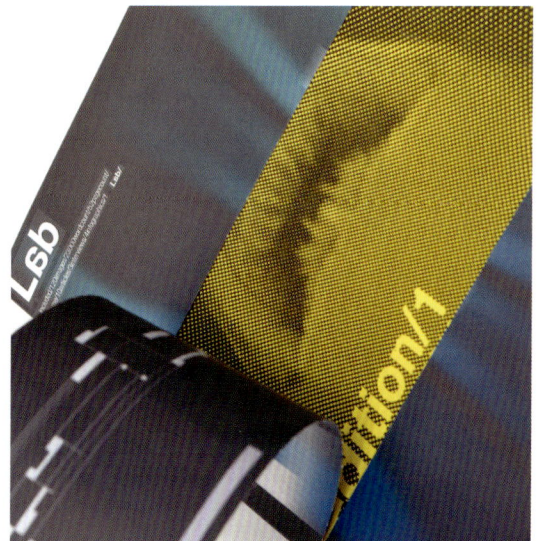

Thermo

Thermo is a series of thermo-sensitive business cards. The ink changes its aspect when exposed to body warmth. This object that goes from one hand to another becomes sublimated by this human contact reacting process.

Design Agency / Murmure
Designer / Julien Alirol & Paul Ressencourt

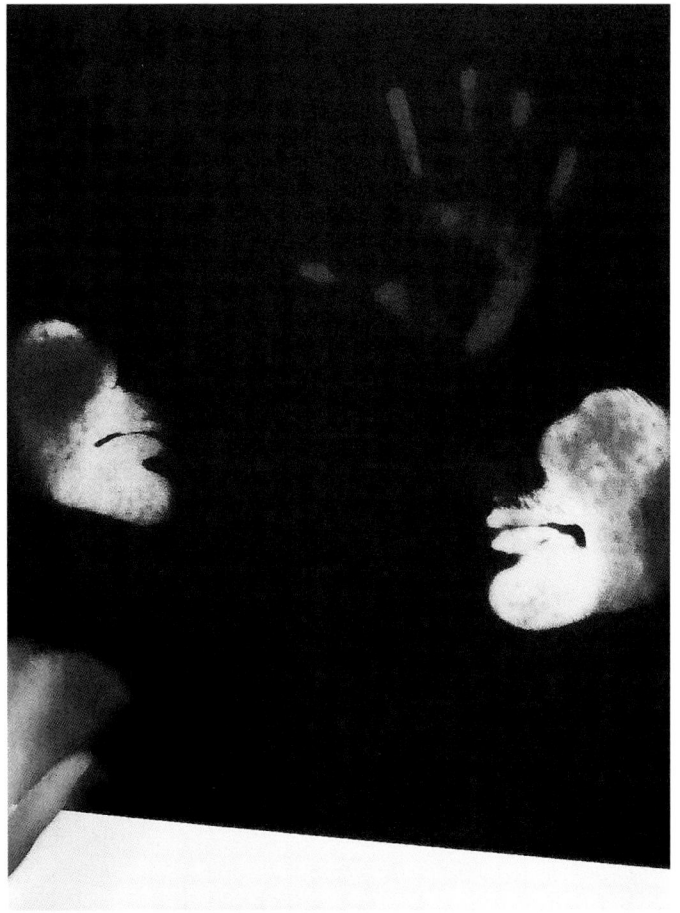

COPYCOPYCOPYSHOP

These posters were part of contribution to Go Visible initiated by Letterproeftuin and Grafisch Atelier Den Bosch.

COPYCOPYCOPYSHOP was about experiment, wonder, tactility and authenticity. It was about the human touch in analogue reproductions. The posters were made of heat sensitive ink, inviting to be touched to create something magical. They challenge to experiment and play.

The goal was to surprise the visitors and give them a more enticing and unique experience by touching a physically printed piece.

Thanks must go to Grafisch Atelier Den Bosch for their collaboration.

Concept & Designer / Stephan Lerou

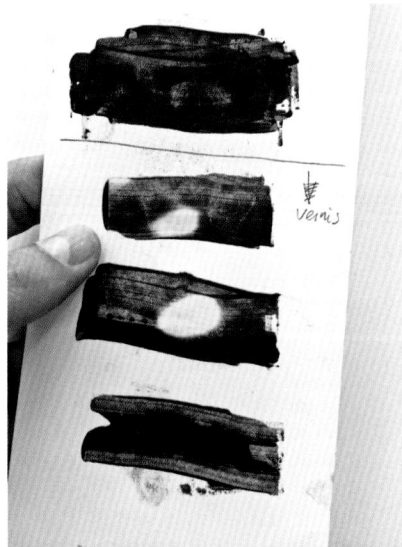

PRESS HANDS AGAINST POSTER

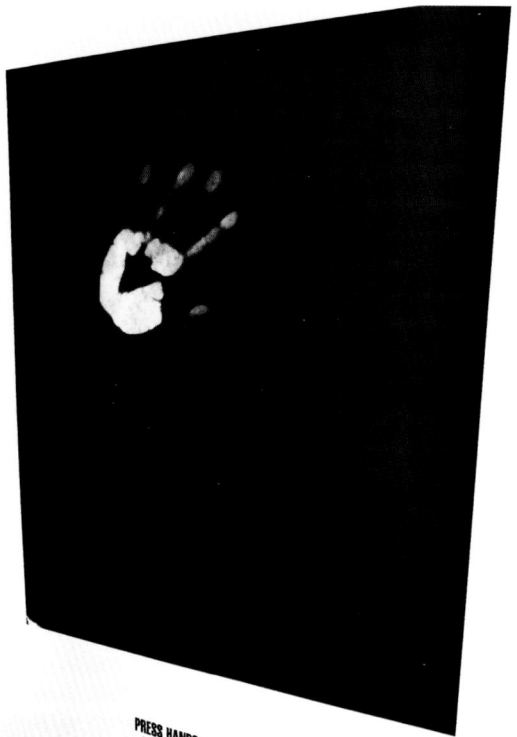

PRESS HANDS AGAINST POSTER

PRESS HANDS AGAINST POSTER

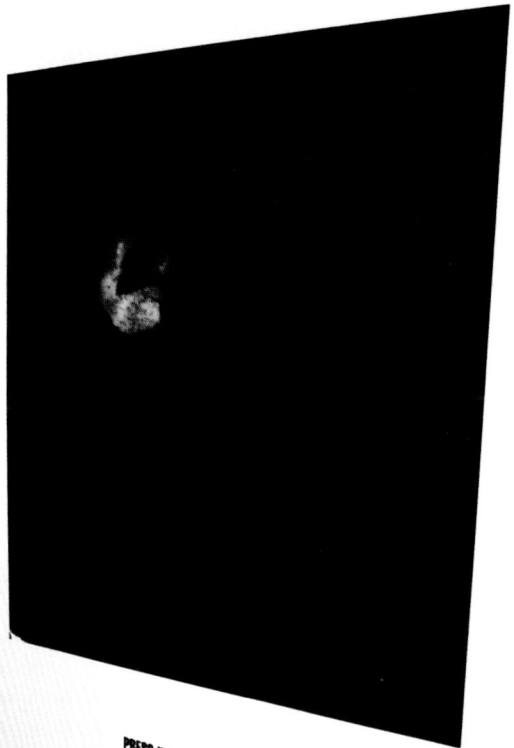

PRESS HANDS AGAINST POSTER

Le Guerre des Tranchées

Alexia Roux imagined an olfactory-visual device for an exhibition about the trenches, where the smell, the trace, the imprint were a special justification in the World War I. Research has allowed her to see that in this war, the smell had been used as a political subject, and it was also the symbol of the occupant.

The smell is a medium little used in graphic design, largely due to its difficulties to be put in work. However, it differs from other types of sensory messages, and has the power to make people surprise.

Designer / Alexia Roux

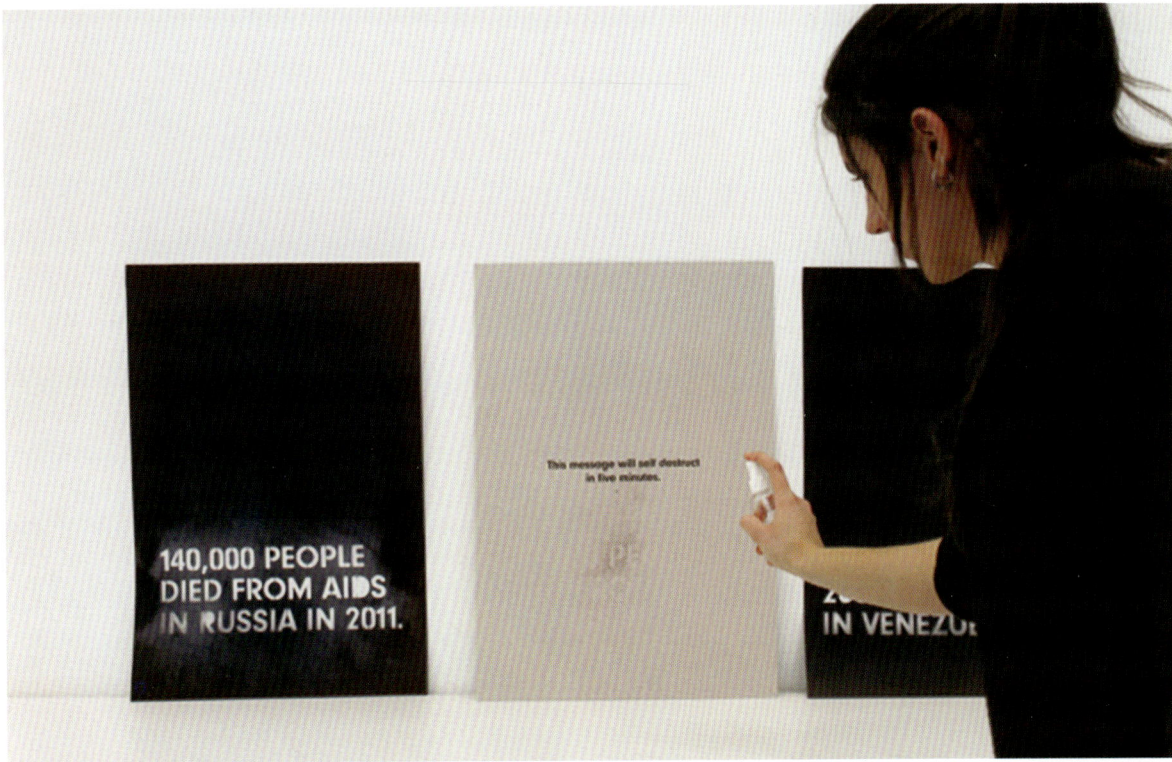

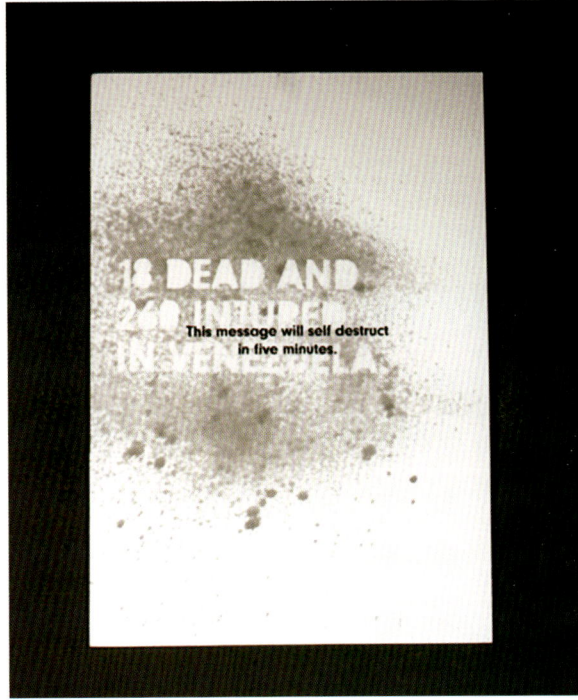

Blink Ignorance is Bliss

Based on the acknowledgement that we receive mass information everyday, while most of them make no sense to us, not even the important ones, these interactive posters with ephemeral messages were created. A strong message appears and disappears in a few minutes with just a spray of water, leaving the person wanting more and realizing the importance of understanding strong messages around us.

Design Agency / Blink
Designer / Jade de Robles, Andrea Maresch, Adria Serran & Maria Boixed

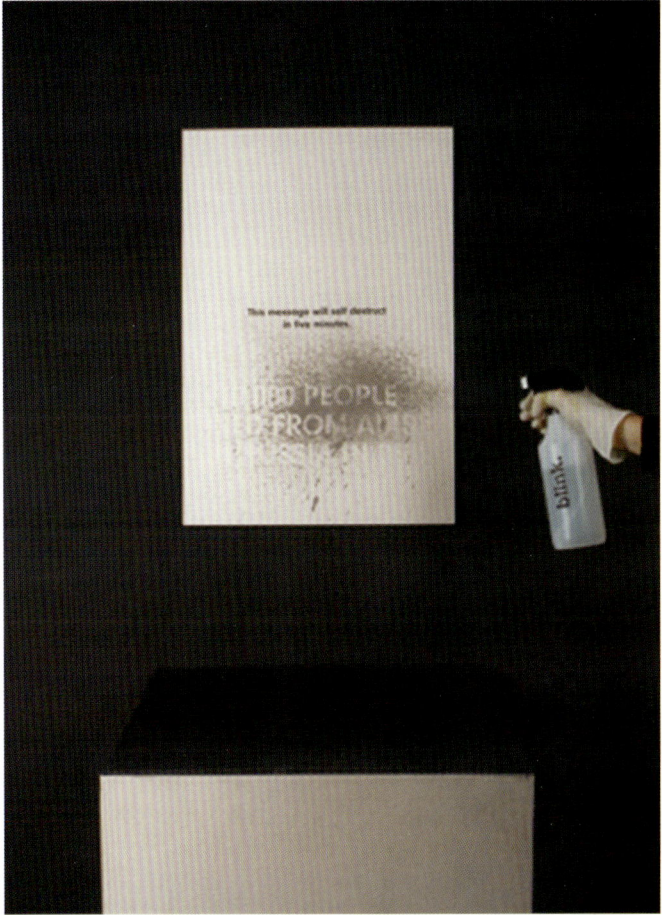

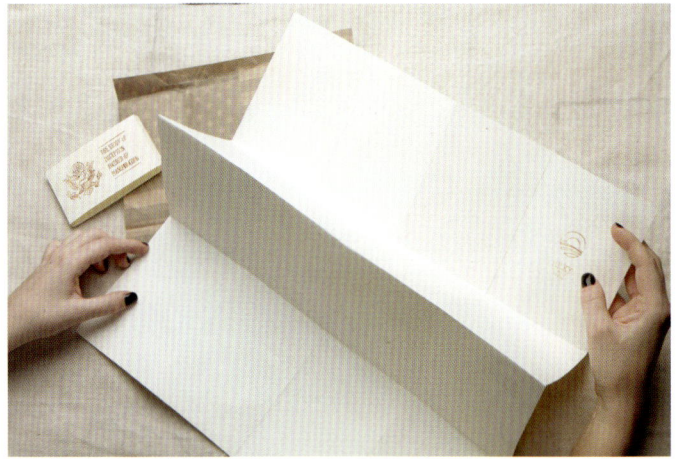

Milky Way

This poster is an imaginary scenario on the theme: "What if milk were forbidden in USA." Based on this idea, this poster is created with milk which makes the messages invisible until the paper is heated up to 150 of Celsius.

Illustrator / Kir Rostovsky
Production / Kir Rostovsky

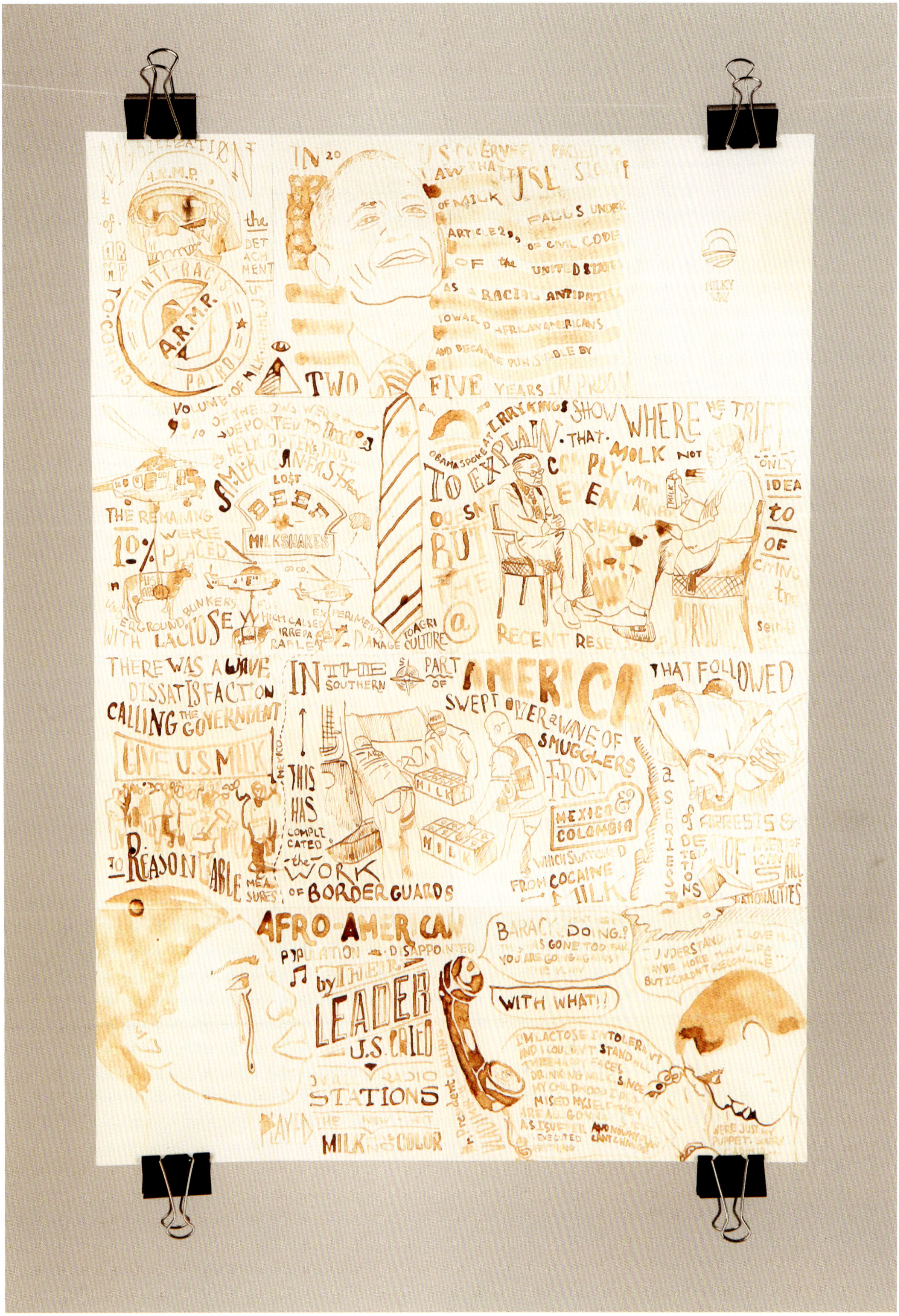

the worst
is yet to come

NO YOU
i will have kids
WON'T

NO YOU
i will succeed
WON'T

NO YOU
i will get a job
WON'T

NO YOU
i will be free
WON'T

NO YOU
i will meet someone

NO YOU
i will love
WON'T

i will be fine
i will find a wife
i will make new friends
i will be happy
i will meet someone
i will be

The Worst Is yet to Come

This project used a specialized electrical wire that conducted heat like incandescent wire cast in a plaster base to display the sentence "No You Won't." A series of descriptive taglines such as "I will be rich" and "I will succeed" were printed on paper and placed over the wire base, which was then heated until the wire message burned through. The result was a depressing reminder that while you may dream of good things, your dreams will ultimately go up in flames.

Designer / François Xavier Saint Georges

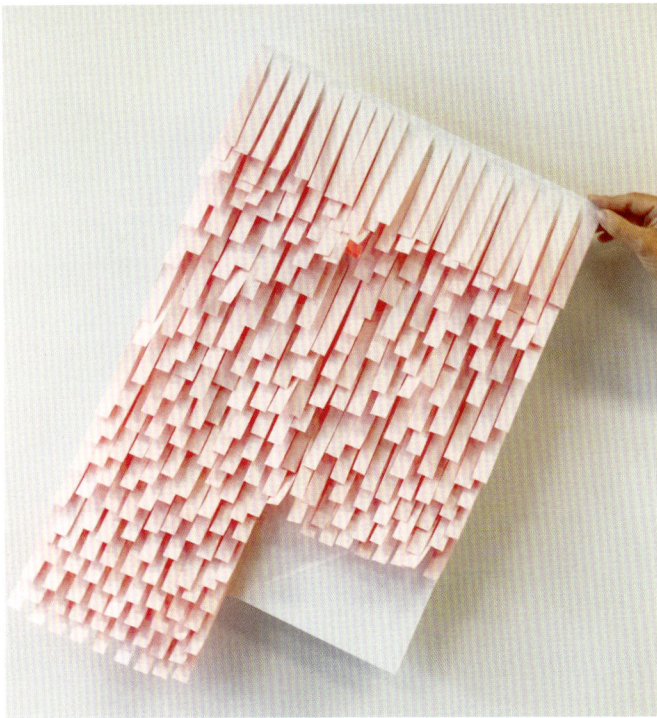

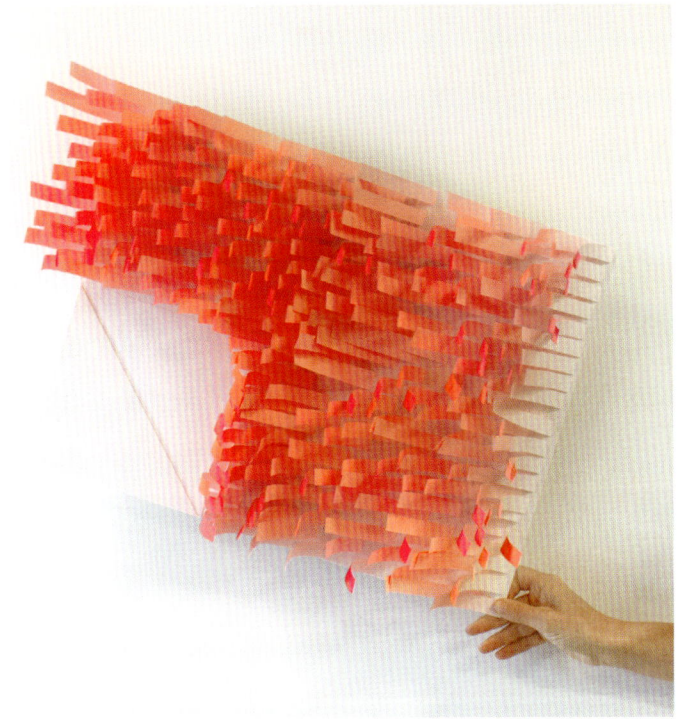

Liliom

This poster aimed to immerse the viewer in a future atmosphere and explore the connection between smell and visual image. The rotation triggered by user creates a cotton candy scent.

Designer / Alexia Roux

CIDIC

The main idea of the design congress was "future." Therefore designer Xavi Martínez Robles created a concept that is to fold up the posters and reveal what lies behind. This system helps to create a dynamic design for congress and establish a strong and recognizable identity.

Designer / Xavi Martínez Robles

Valors i percepció
19 de febrer 2014

08:30	Classes
10:00	Conferència: "Subjectivitat nòmada: Compromís des de la translació" *Dra. Mireia Feliu*
10:45	Pausa
11:00	Comunicació: "Gratis" *Andrés Requena*
11:30	Conferència: "El llenguatge gràfic com a acció política" *Aitor Méndez*
12:00	Taula rodona: *Antoni Mañach (moderador), Dra. Mireia Feliu, Aitor Méndez, Oriol Ocaña, Andrés Requena*
12:45	Pausa
13:00	Classes
15:30	Comunicació ESDi: "Naming" *Dra. Gemma Gómez*
15:45	Comunicació ESDi: "Els blogs de moda espanyols: de l'espontaneïtat de l'usuari a la professió de blogger" *Encarna Ruiz*
16:00/ 18:30	Taller: "KNIT & RUN!" *Marina Castán, Miguel González i Cristina Real*

Tendències de Futur
Future trends

ÖÏ
3r Congrés Internacional
de Disseny i Innovació
de Catalunya

ESDi

De la compra a la venda
20 de febrer 2014

08:30	Classes
10:00	Conferència: "Situació i repte l'actualitat dins del món labo Joaquim Català
10:45	Pausa
11:00	Taller: "Gestió efectiva del professional" Judith Català amb el sup Joaquim Català

Escola
Superior
de Disseny
ESDi

ÖÏ

ESDi

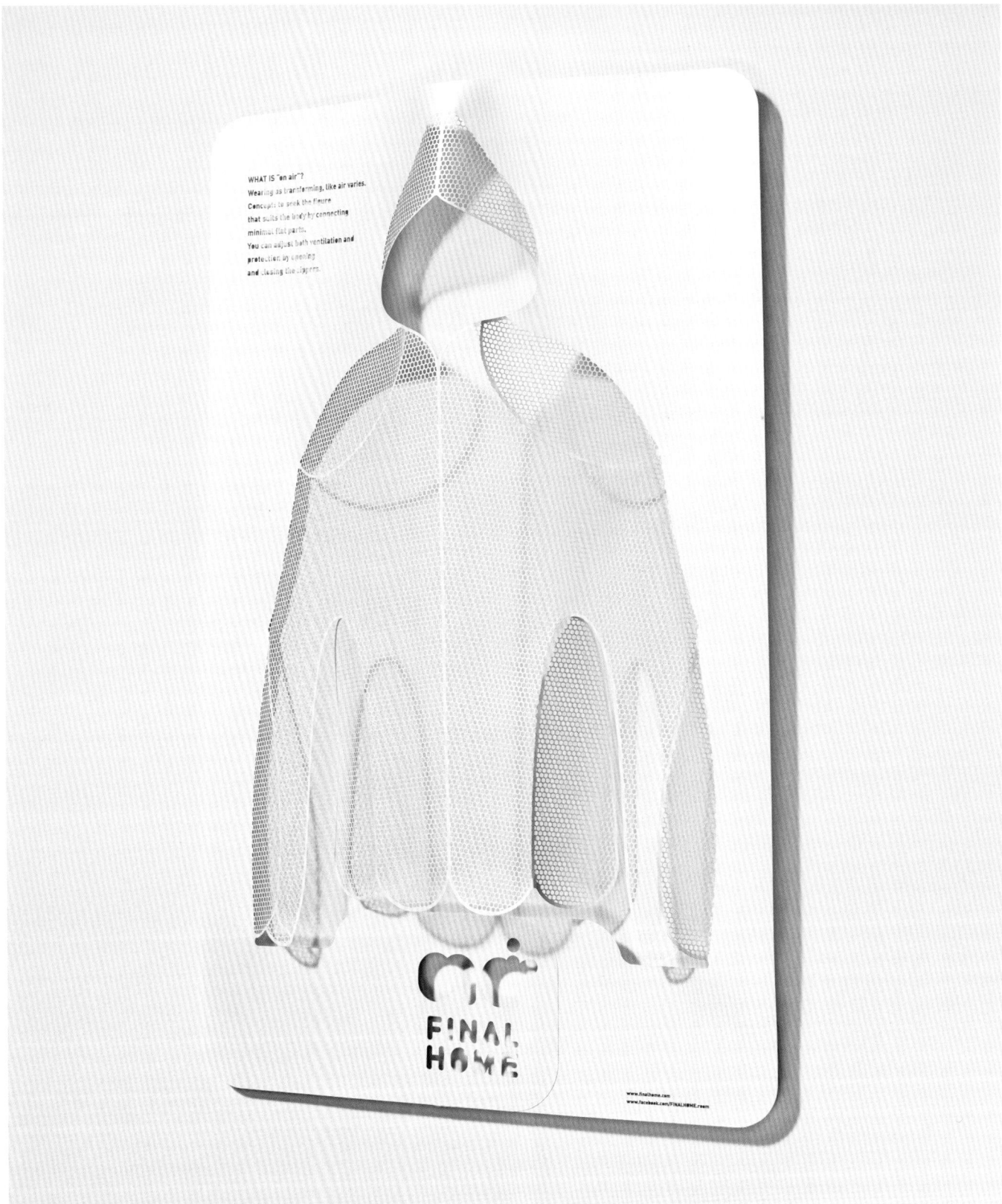

on air FINAL HOME

on air is a jacket that is as light as air and snugly fits the body. Naonori Yago created a "wearable poster" which has the same form, texture, and lightness of a real jacket. It worked not only as a poster but also as a paper mock-up, so the viewer can try the jacket on artificially by fitting the poster over your body. It was a poster to convey something real-life rather than just an image. Many people visited the locations where the poster was placed to touch it and try it on.

Designer / Naonori Yago

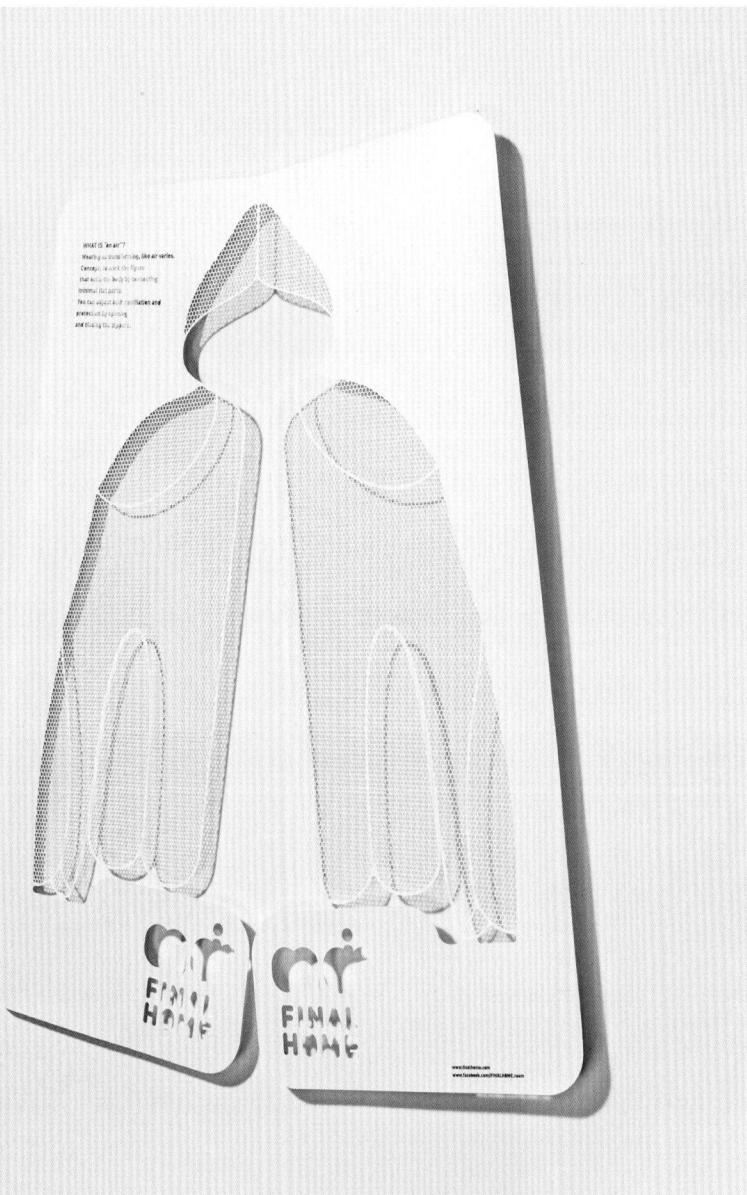

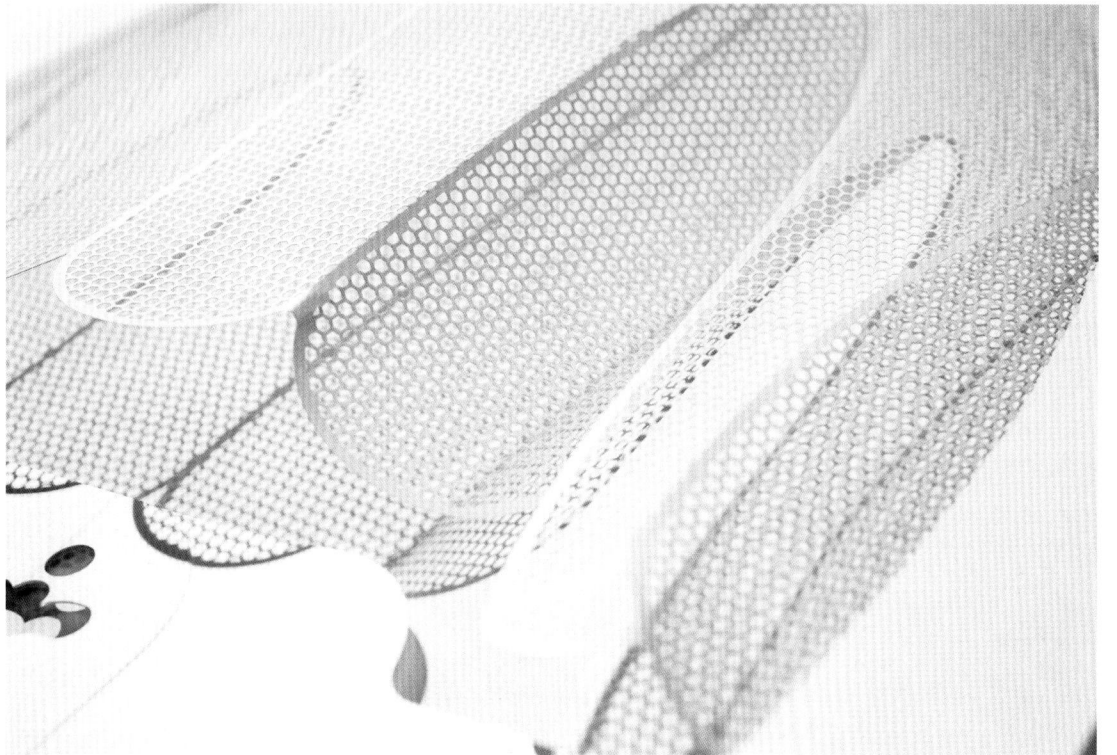

Harriet the Spy Moving Movie Posters

Harriet the Spy Moving Movie Posters is a series of three posters for the film "Harriet the Spy," featuring original illustrations and quotes from Louise Fitzhugh's novel of the same name. Viewers can pull tabs on the posters, which used a custom designed paper mechanic technique, and make transition between two corresponding images to reveal an added layer of information.

Designer / Tree Abraham

Le Reflet

This poster is composed of a cardboard and a mirror on which marks simple lines. Virtual words appear when the abstract lines combine together.

Designer / Alexia Roux

Interactive Poster

The poster was made as a part of author's
exploration of the phenomenon of interaction
in print media. This work is focused on direct
physical manipulation and invites the viewer
to participate in the process by manipulating
the poster's elements in order to get the full
message. The application of such technique
allows the viewer to produce a great variety
of alternative visual combinations that
demonstrates the communicative possibilities
of interaction in print. The handmade poster is
produced with a stencil and acrylic paint.

Designer / Anastasia Itkina

INTER ACTIVITY IS WHAT MAKES A POSTER UNIQUE

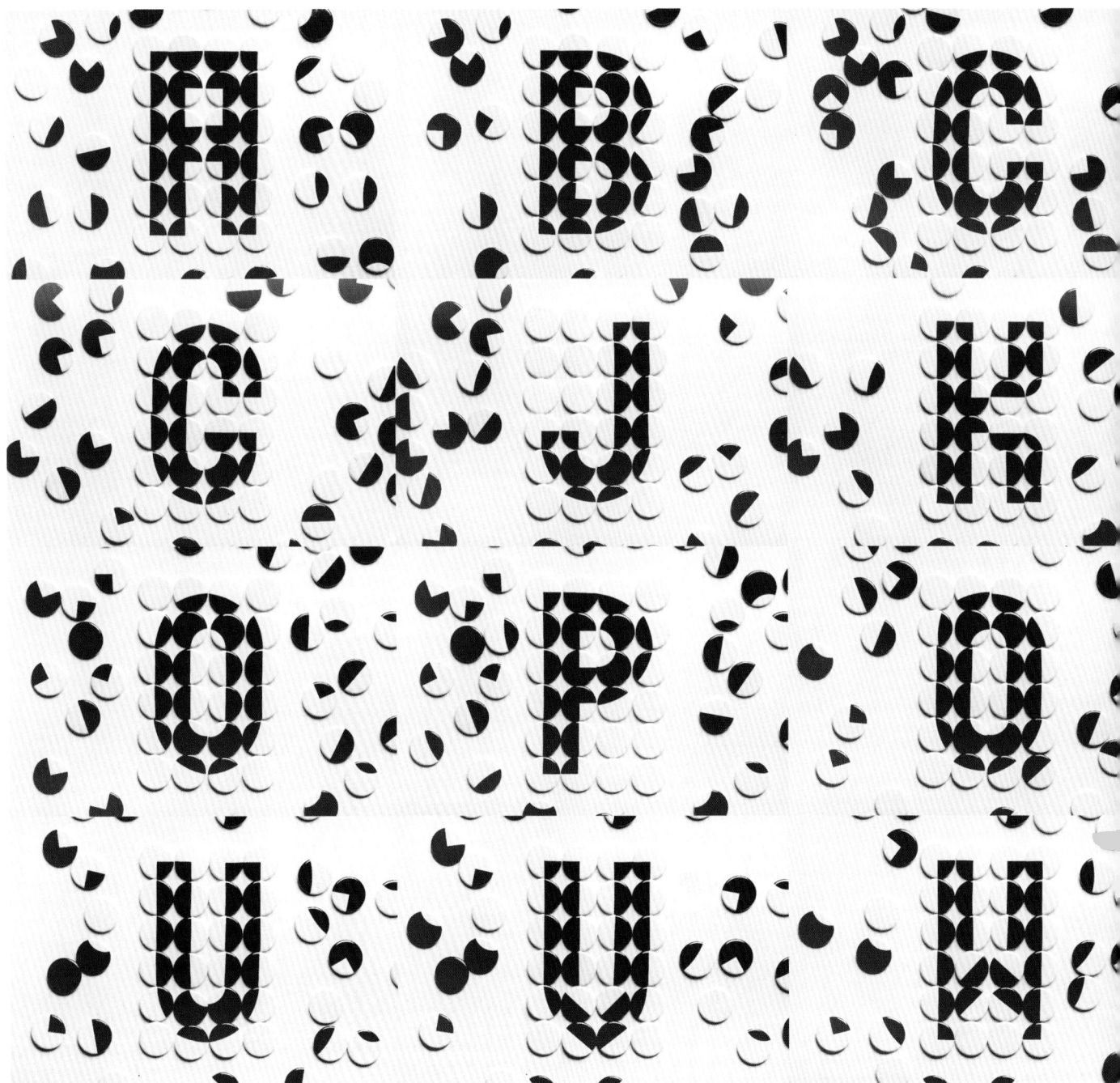

Magnet Typography

This typography was created as a prototype for a fridge magnet spelling game. It was based on six basic black and white shapes that were designed to be swapped, totated and combined together to create all 26 letters of the alphabet as well as other patterns.

Designer / François Xavier Saint Georges

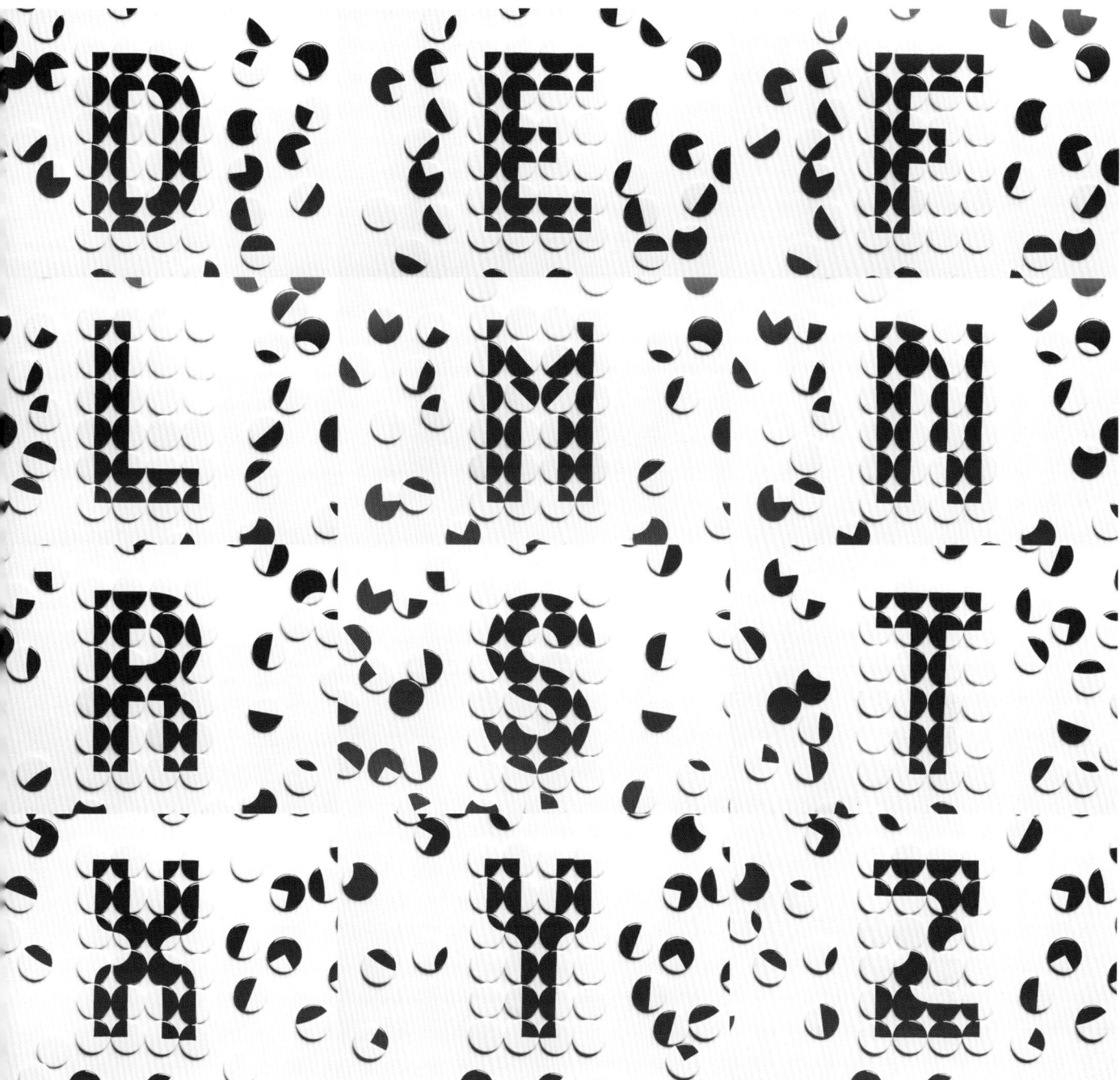

Grid Brick

Based on a font set that fits on a square grid,
Cheolhong Kim came out with the idea to
modularize the font and apply it on playable bricks.

Designer / Cheolhong Kim

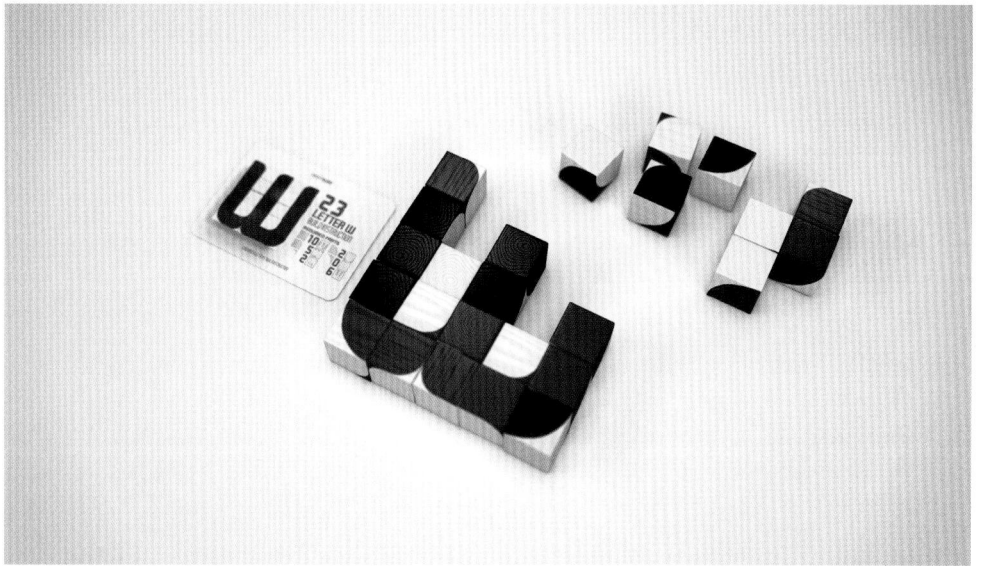

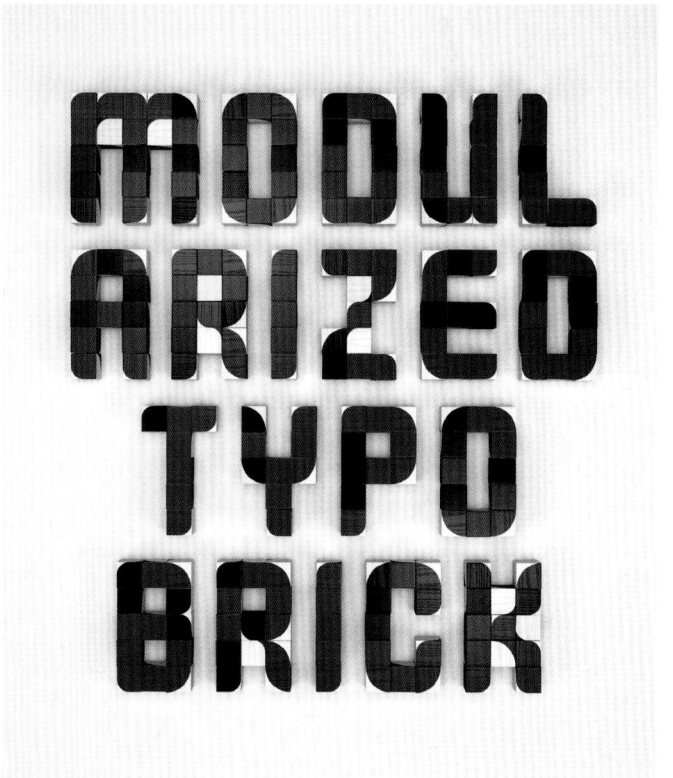

MODUL
ARIZED
TYPO
BRICK

Told Bag

This project is designed for the consumers who want to have a bag with their own signatures.

One can follow the sample provided on the sketch paper, or self-design some unique patterns.

Designer / Tun Ho

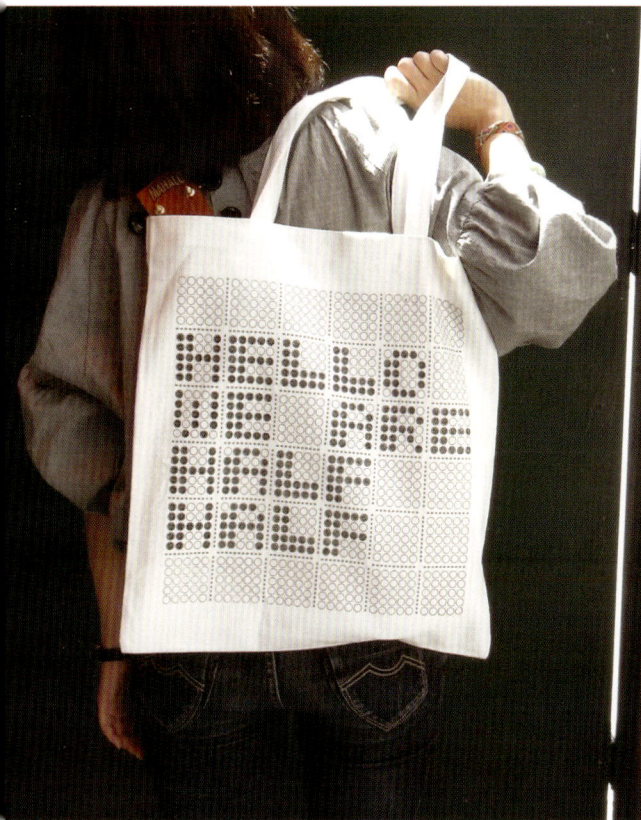

Real Not Ideal

Real Not Ideal is an ongoing pharmaceutical project that focuses on counterfeits in the black market and the effect they are having on the industry today. The idea of the advertising campaign is based on loop holes which are always being found in the black market. It calls for bringing focus to the real product, not just the ideal products.

Designer / George Farrell

The black market is one of fakery.
Between 8 and 15 % of all medicines sold worldwide are fakes.
Concentrate on the real product, not just the ideal product.
There are other alternatives.
www.mhra.gov.uk

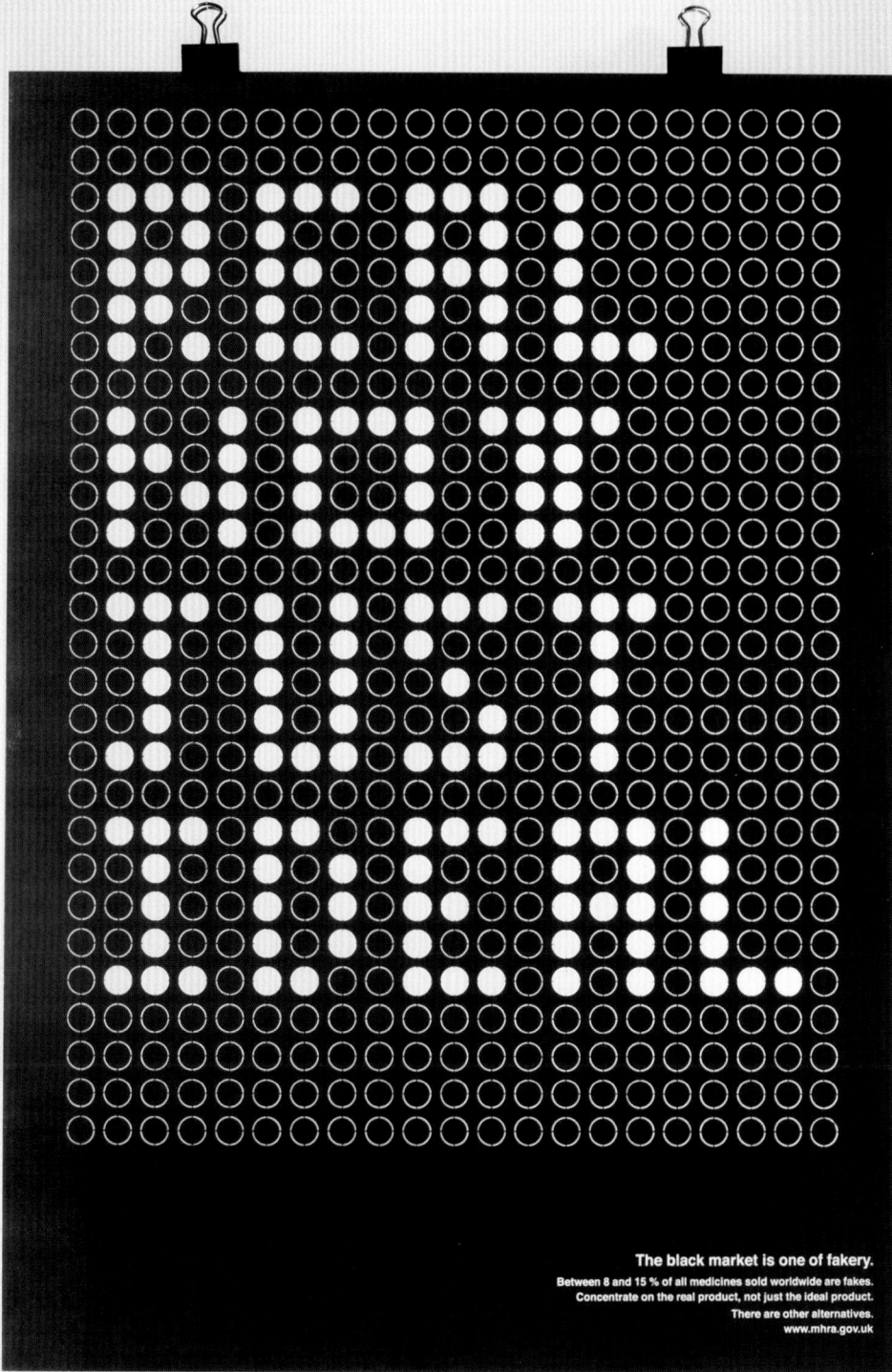

The black market is one of fakery.

Between 8 and 15 % of all medicines sold worldwide are fakes.
Concentrate on the real product, not just the ideal product.
There are other alternatives.
www.mhra.gov.uk

T.K Home Furniture Brochure 2014

A beautifully laser-cut cover design for "T.K Home Furniture Brochure 2014." With the use of die-cut, the cover invites consumers to interact with by pushing out the types and determine the final look. The fusion of black and gold creates a sense of space and conveys an image of high-end furniture brand.

Design Agency / Tu Design Office
Designer / Tu Ming-Shiang

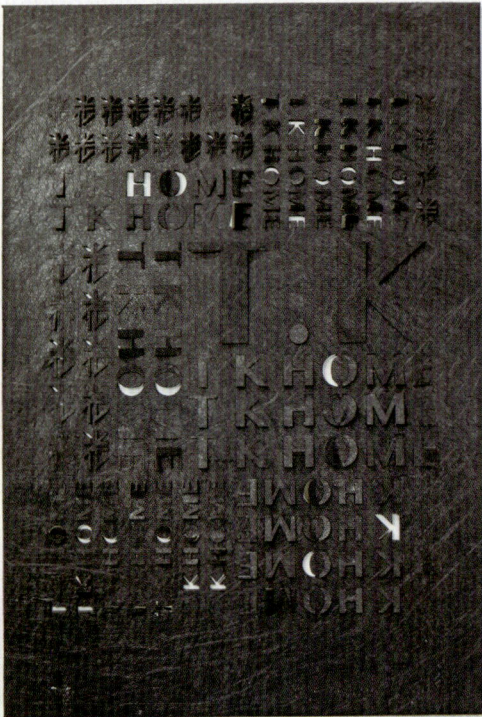

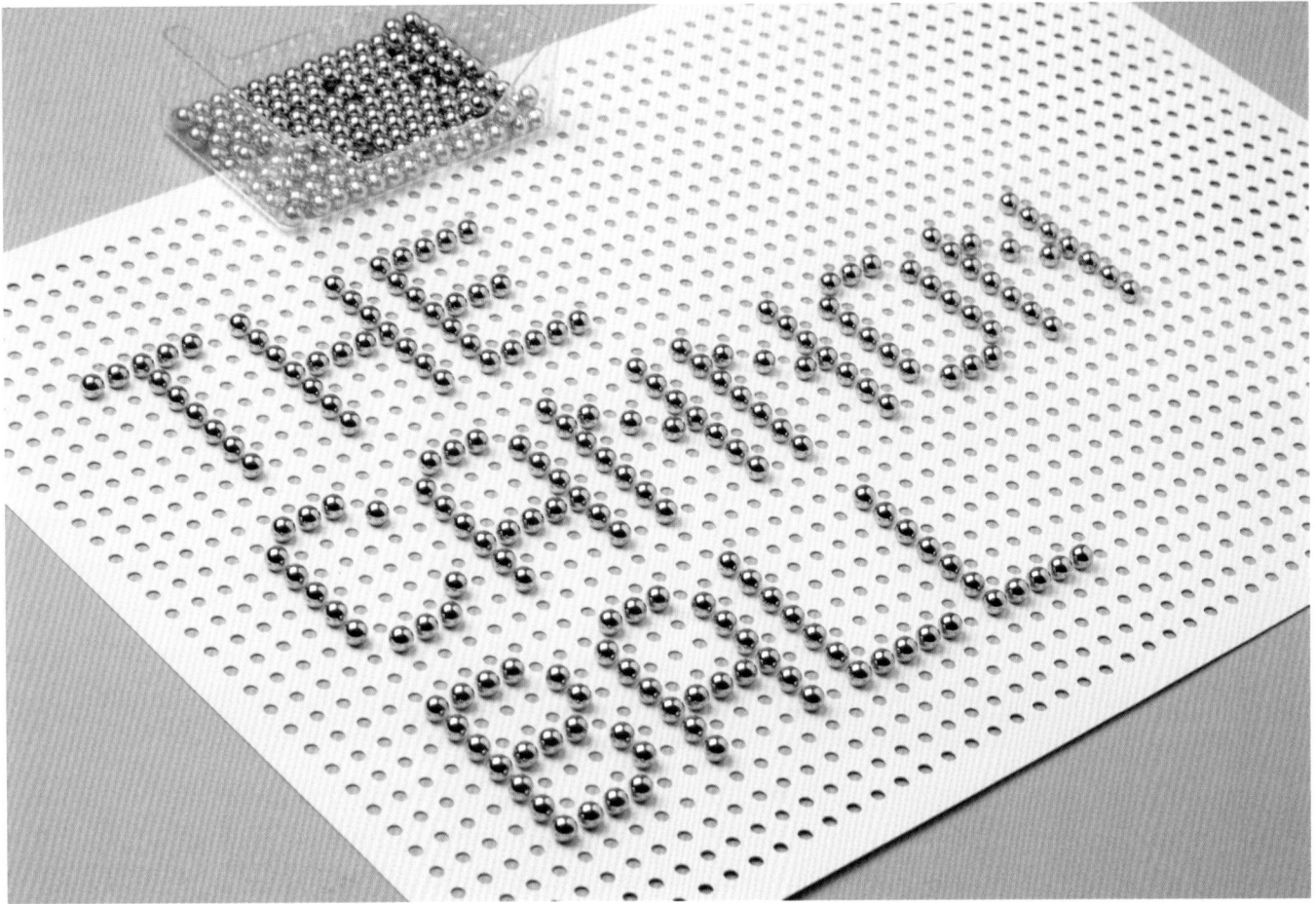

The Cannonball

Lo Siento worked with Dave Sedgwick to create this identity for a production company in Barcelona. They utilized a ball bearing, grid-based concept to give the associated force of the name a precision and a practical sense of creativity.

Design Agency / Lo Siento
Original Idea / Dave Sedgwick

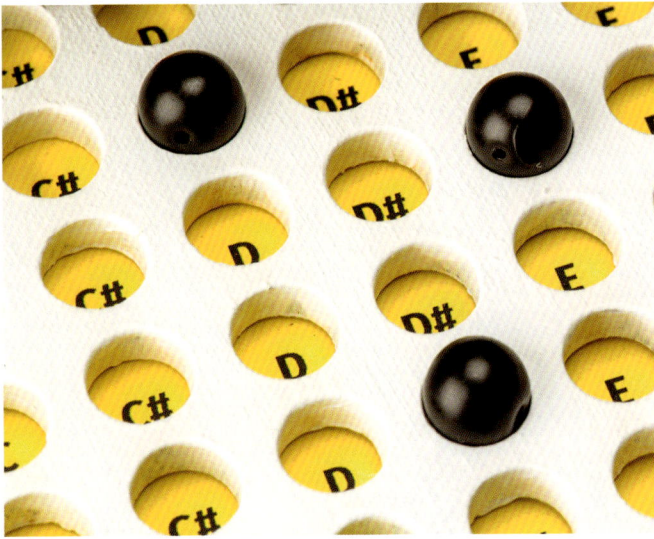

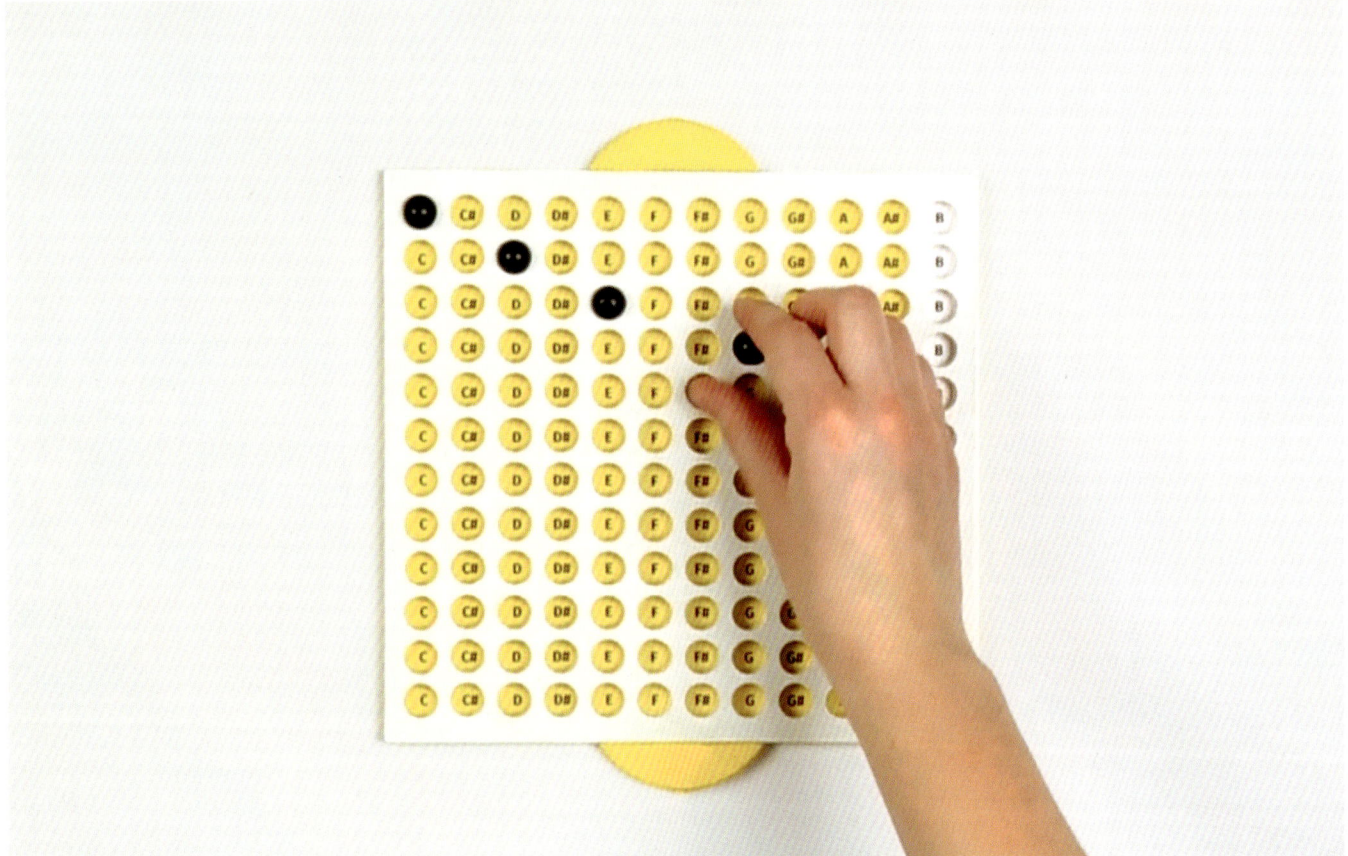

Music Box

The project explores an interactive tool that allows a viewer to produce an unlimited amount of responses. The set consists of a digital music box, a special board with notes and black beads that are used to write any melody. The board covers the 4th and the 5th octaves and there are 23 notes available. Each hole in the board is related to a specific note and placing a bead in this hole means playing the note. The board should be dragged through the box that leads to the beads combination being transformed into the sound.

Designer / Anastasia Itkina

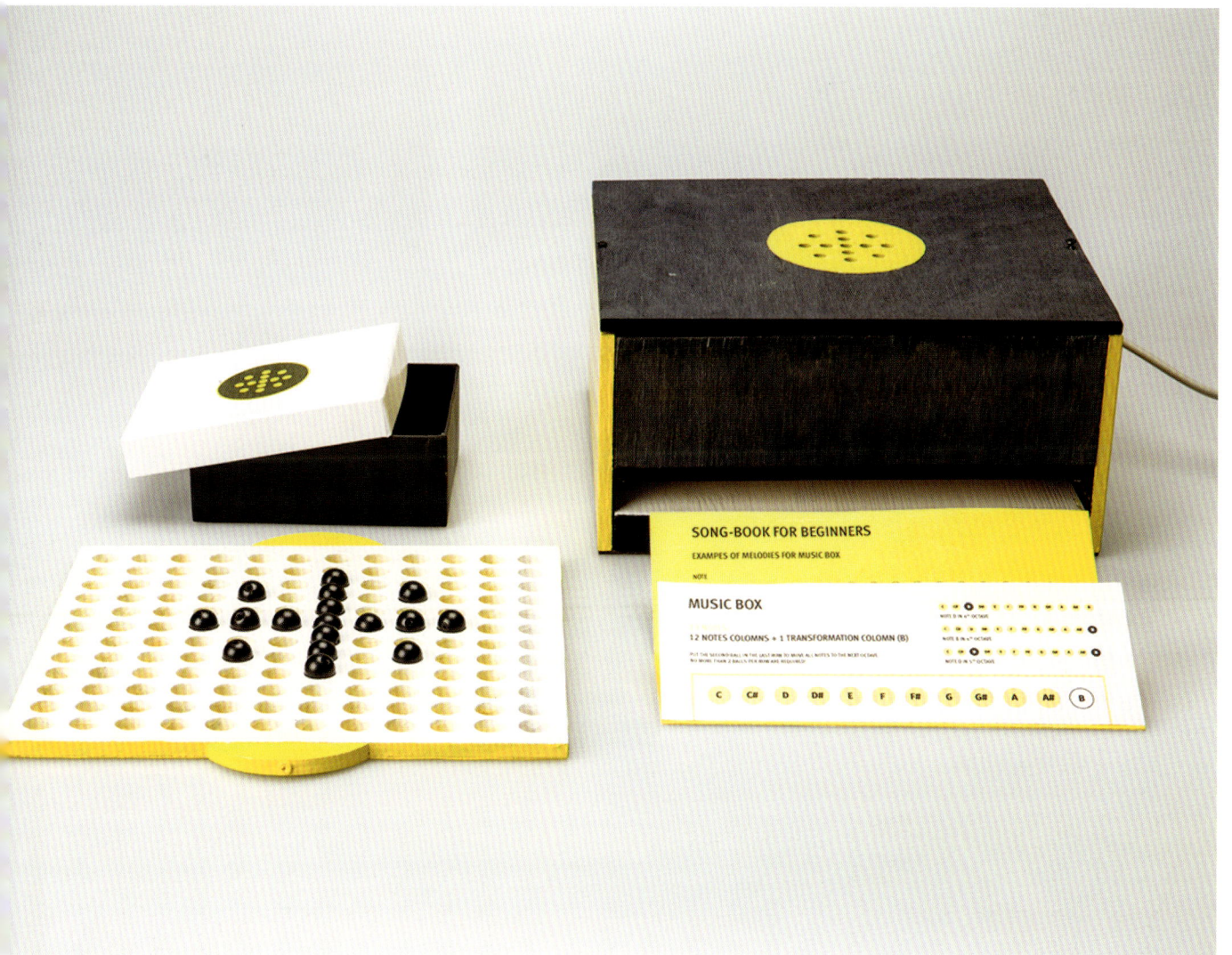

SONG-BOOK FOR BEGINNERS

EXAMPES OF MELODIES FOR MUSIC BOX

NOTE

MUSIC BOX

12 NOTES COLOMNS + 1 TRANSFORMATION COLOMN (B)

PUT THE SECOND BALL IN THE LAST ROW TO MOVE ALL NOTES TO THE NEXT OCTAVE
NO MORE THAN 2 BALLS PER ROW ARE REQUIRED

| C | C# | D | D# | E | F | F# | G | G# | A | A# | B |

Minibar 814

Black die-cut flyers in a one-sided relief paint serve as carriers for the admission chips to the Minibar 814. The chips have been cut from gramophone records by CNC laser machines. All guests should feel like "Glückskinder" (lucky fellows) because of receiving such a personal invitation to this special bar in Heilbronn.

Design Agency / ADDA
Creative Director / Christian Vögtlin
Designer / Christian Vögtlin

10.12.2011
WHO THE FUCK
MUSICLOVERS
FÜR GLÜCKSKINDER
maritim
STEREO
GEMA
DIE 20 BESTEN TANZ- UND PARTY-HITS

FÜR GLÜCKSKINDER

FÜR GLÜCKSKINDER
OWNER OF THE RECORDED WORK RES

Aim For The Day

Aim For The Day is a calendar that creates an experience everyday. It is composed of a dartboard and chest containing 365 dated darts. The dartboard's segments present an aim — "Do something scary," "Take a new route to work," "Learn something," and so forth. Each day the user throws a dart and depending on where it lands, a new aim is given. This calendar encourages the user to break free from routine and explore new experiences. After one year the complete dartboard becomes a showcase of 365 achievements giving the user a great sense of satisfaction and accomplishment.

Design Agency / Trapped in Suburbia
Designer / Cuby Gerards, Karin Langeveld, Richard Fussey & Giacomo Boffo

GAZE

TOUCH

SMELL

Take a Green Break - Poster

Take a Green Break is a project that hopes to encourage and inspire urbanites to incorporate more nature into their breaks. Nature can enhance the effects of taking breaks, and thus in this fast-paced society where our lives are increasingly dominated by work and screen time, urbanites can tap on the restorative power of nature to compliment their stressful living. This project encourages viewers to interact with these posters. Through a haptic and experimental approach, it increases their awareness of the everyday nature.

Designer / How Sok Hwee

· TAKE A GREEN BREAK ·

TOUCH

· TAKE A GREEN BREAK ·

SMELL

an accepted healthcare concept in Japan, is a fore...
...isiting a forest for relaxation and recreation...
...phytoncides (wood essential oils) give...

· TAKE A GREEN BREAK ·

GAZE

...y gazing on forest scenery for minutes ca...
...tration of salivary cortisol, a stress...
...compare to that of people in...

Tree Rain Wear

Tree Rain Wear is a raincoat that was sold at the Echigo-Tsumari Art Triennale held in Niigata, Japan, whose concept was "Humans are part of nature." The aim of this design is to change the impression of melancholy rain into a positive one. It can be folded and packed into a leaf-shaped bag.

Design Agency / Motomoto Inc.
Photographer / Kotaro Tanaka
Client / NPO Echigo-Tsumari Satoyama Collaborative Organization

Smiling Scarf

If you're not happy and you know it, but you really have to show smiles, you can wear this scarf to disguise yourself with a happy face.

Designer / Judith Kroisleitner

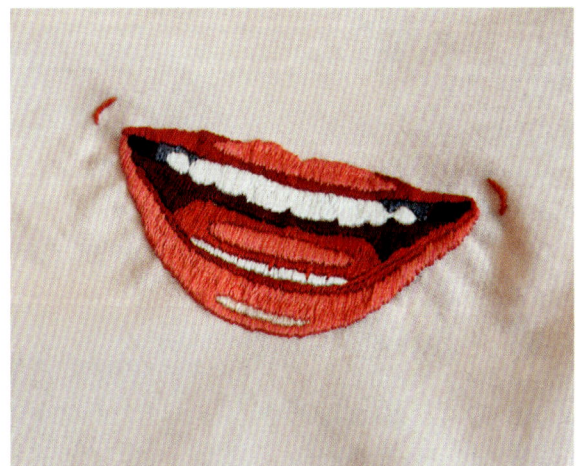

Body & Language

This project explores the conversion of rest and motion. By granting a static object with energy empowered by the play of typography, Yeongmin Won presents the change of a three-dimensional protruded original from a two-dimensional scene. In this way, she expresses that our lives are filled with energy and physicality, instead of being enveloped in "false copies."

Designer / Yeongmin Won

FUN

[rub /runs, run
[ru   g; ran, run

move at a o,   than a walk,
never hav   all the feet
on the gro   e same time.

DANCE

[dans, dah   verb /da   d, danc·ing.

move rh   hmical   to music,
typic ll fo wing
a set se   n   of steps.

I Never Read. I Just Look At Pictures

Taken from the Andy Warhol's quote "I Never Read. I Just Look At Pictures.", the typographic treatment reinforces the message through a optically vibrating graphic. The installation is a vinyl wall application created for the Re/View exhibition at Chicago Design Museum.

Design Agency / Plural
Designer / Renata Graw & Plural
Other / Jeremiah Chiu & Alexa Viscius

READ LOOK TURES

— ANDY WARHOL

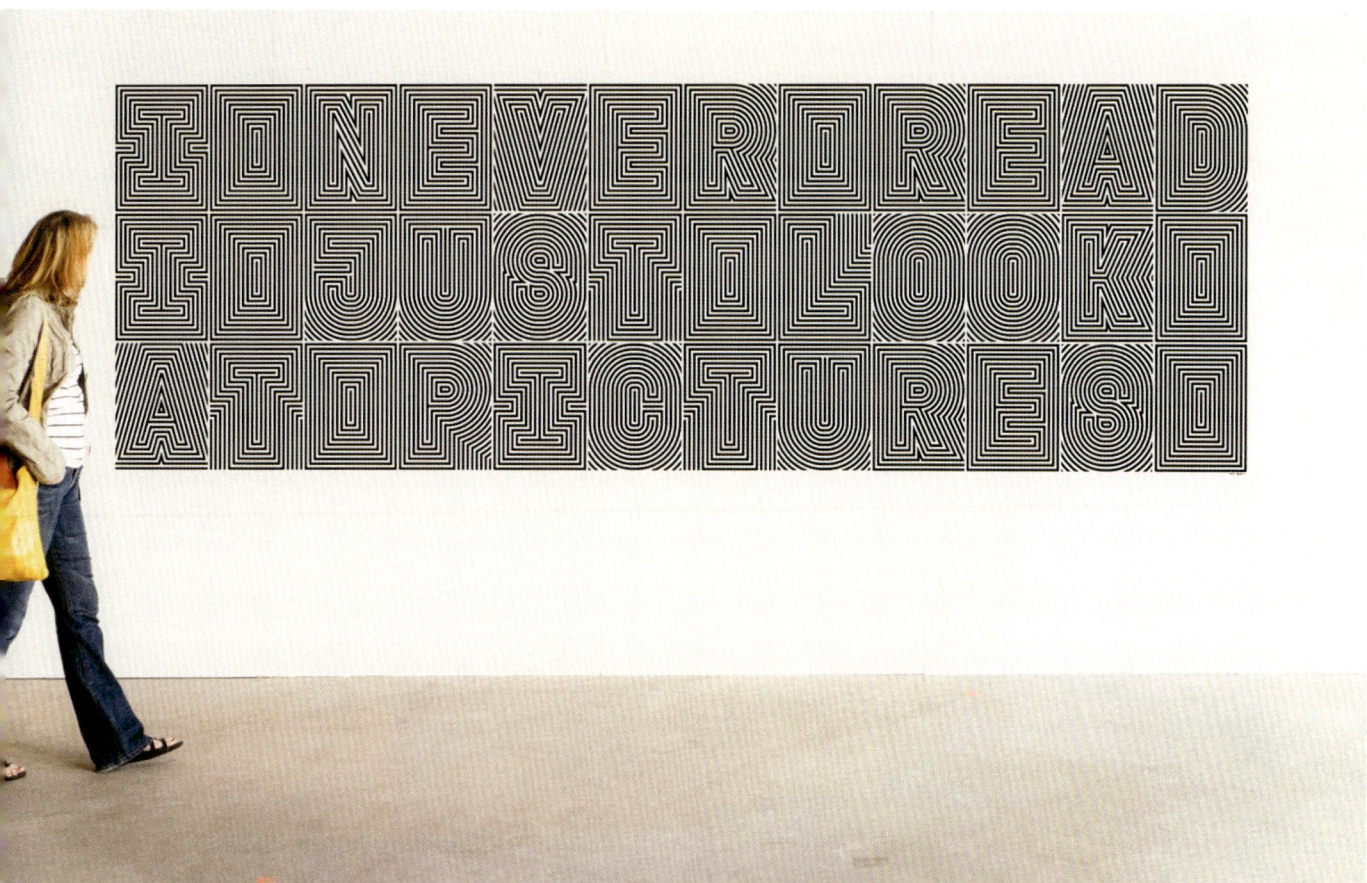

I NEVER READ I JUST LOOK AT PICTURES

The Less Ordinary

The social poster is a set of interactive posters that can be posted. The background is set on Redchurch Street in Shoreditch Central London, where the less ordinary become the ordinary.

By using the postal service to bring back a personal feeling to the social invitation, it enables the locals to visit Redchurch Street and the people who live in the area to organize events or get together in a less ordinary way.

Designer / George Farrell

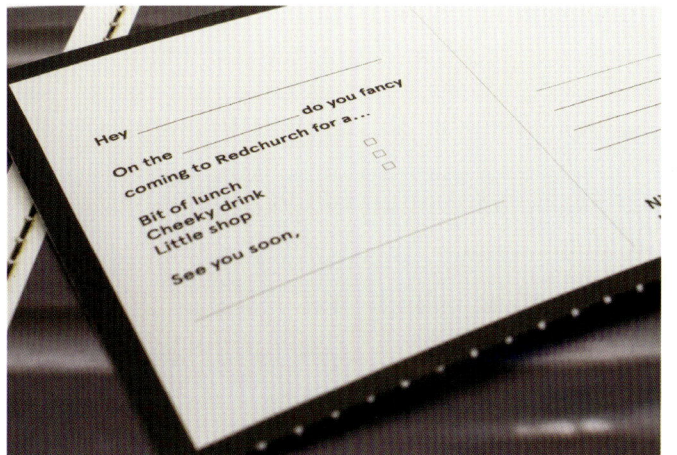

Hey _____ do you fancy
On the
coming to Redchurch for a...

Bit of lunch
Cheeky drink
Little shop

See you soon,

Typography in Spatial Applications

This project started as part of Robert Urban's Bachelor thesis in 2013. Its key concept is that of a spatial visual system with a deconstructed character. The project looks to represent the essence of the possibilities of spatial view — the overall perception of space and the objects contained therein. It is also a tribute to the 25th Anniversary of Deconstructivism at MoMA (1988-2013). The project consists of eight installations using eight different techniques.

Designer / Robert Urban
Photographer / Květoslav Bartoš

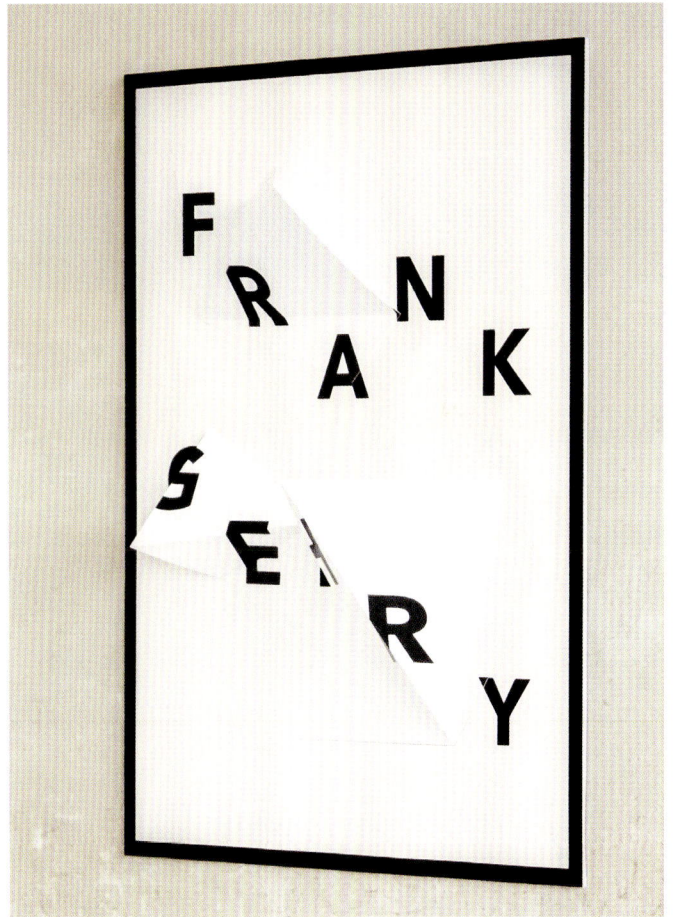

Keep See Seek-ING

To engage audience with graphic design and become a part of it, Keep, See, Seek-ing was created in the poster frame in which audiences become elements of the design. The anamorphic picture was painted on the wall and floor. The audience had to stand at a specific point in order to see the image in the correct shape. The experience of the visual perception contradicts with the observed actual physical characteristics. In graphic design features can be utilized to create visual stimulation and excitement through visual illusion, and also increase the viewer's interest and affinity for design itself.

Designer / Liyuan Tong

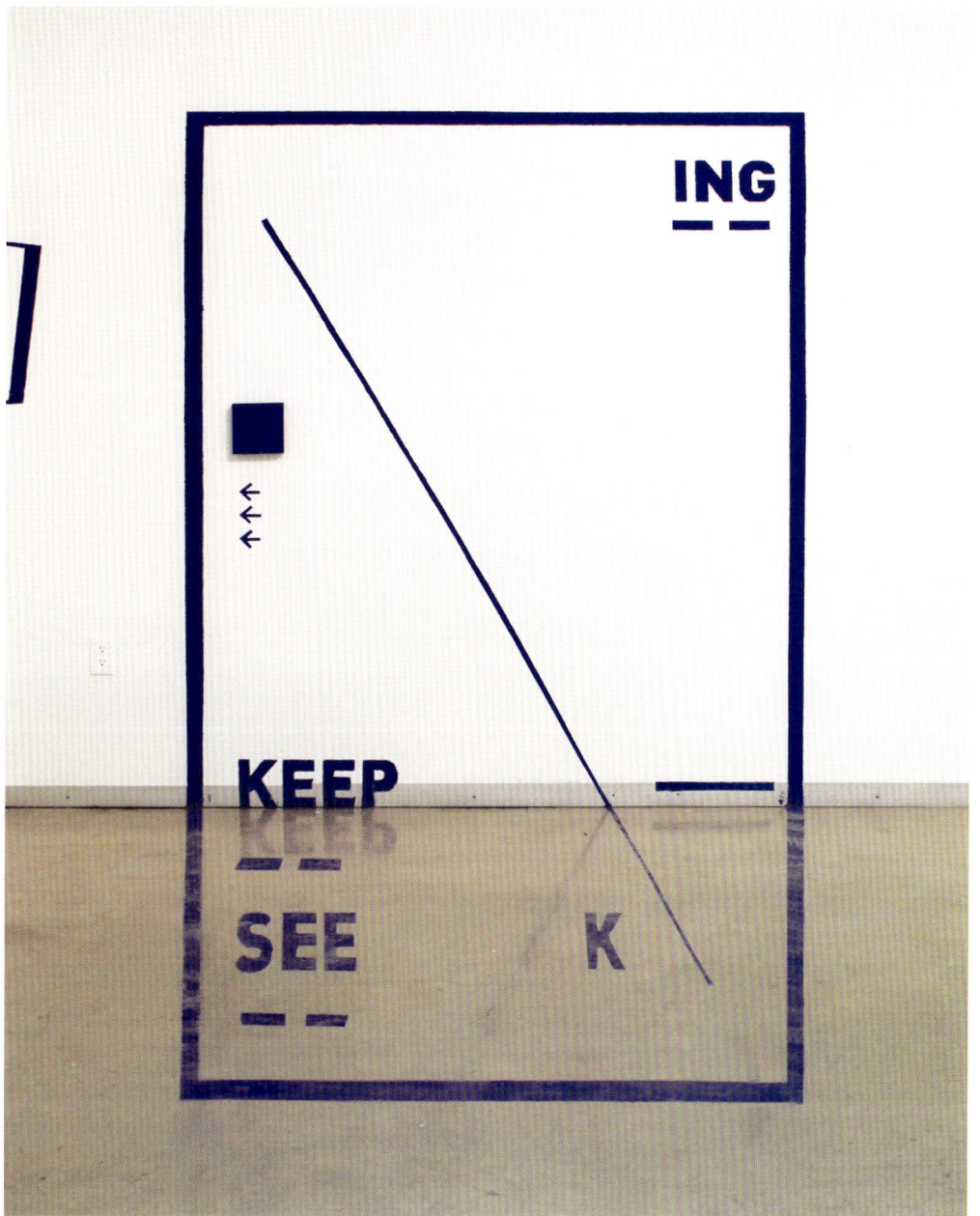

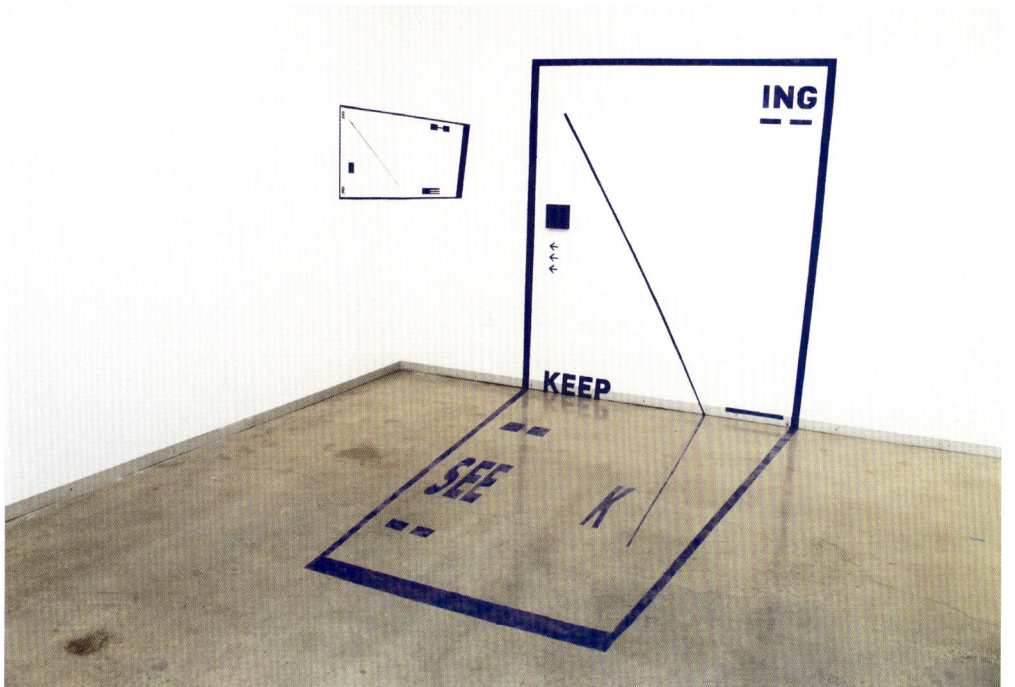

(fos)

(fos) is a visual game between perspective and coloured volumes. The team used yellow duct tape, and yellow painted decor items to create a visual deception as if it had been illuminating for 4 days on the facade of a vegan restaurant Rayen in Madrid.

Design Agency / (fos)
Designer / Eleni Karpatsi, Susana Piquer & Julio Calvo

Linguistic Landscapes of Graz

Linguistic Landscapes of Graz is an exhibition about the variety of languages curated from both a local and a global point of view. The visual identity of the exhibition emphasizes the wide range of languages in terms of sound, visual representation and geographic distribution. Language is represented as an organic and ever-changing system of human communication.

Designer / Georg Liebergesell

Eine Stadt spricht 150 Sprachen.

27.09. – 06.11.2011

Linguistic Landscape Graz – A City Speaks 150 Languages.

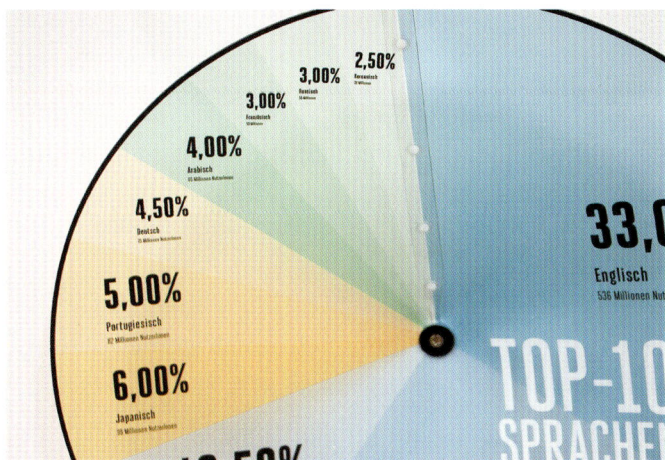

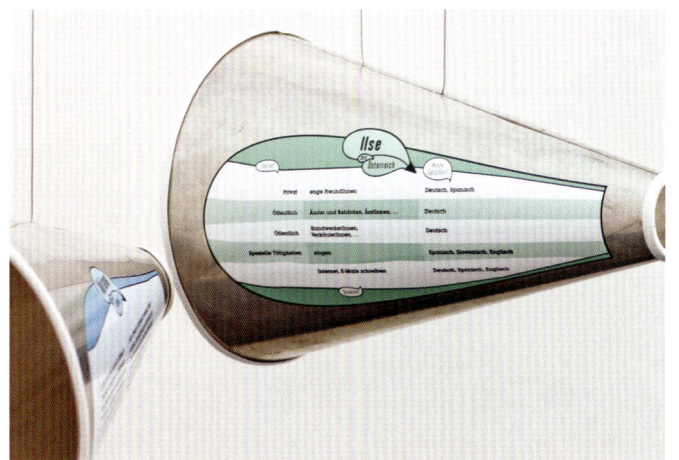

What Made Me

By finding the link between data visualization and spatial design, a three-dimensional and interactive experience was designed, allowing people to become creators of a multi-layered data map. The aim of the project was to explore what shapes the people by asking visitors five simple questions, which could be answered by connecting relevant words together with a coloured thread. Through this visual language, participants were able to share the feelings, influences, thoughts, and inspirations that make them who they are today.

Designer / Dorota Grabkowska
Photographer / Kuba Kolec

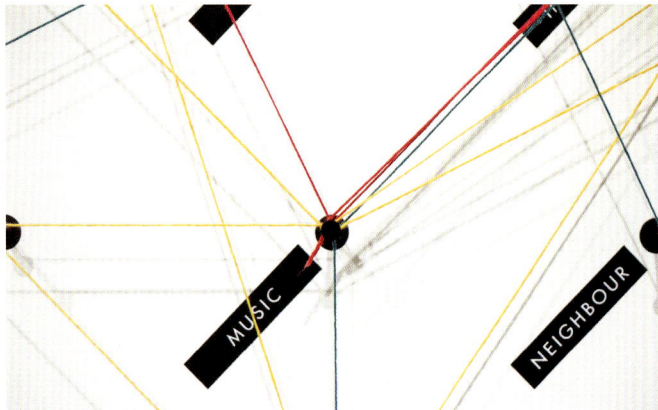

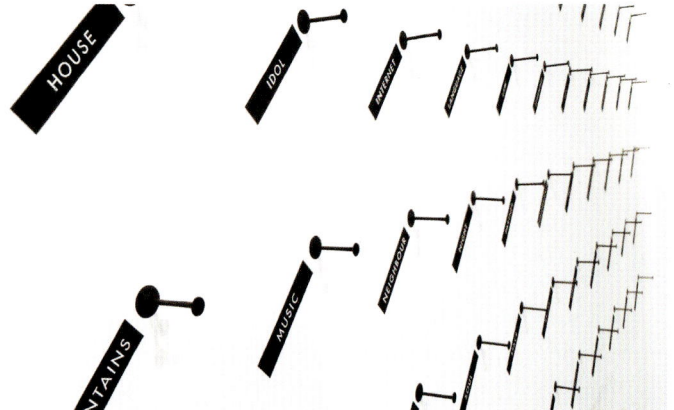

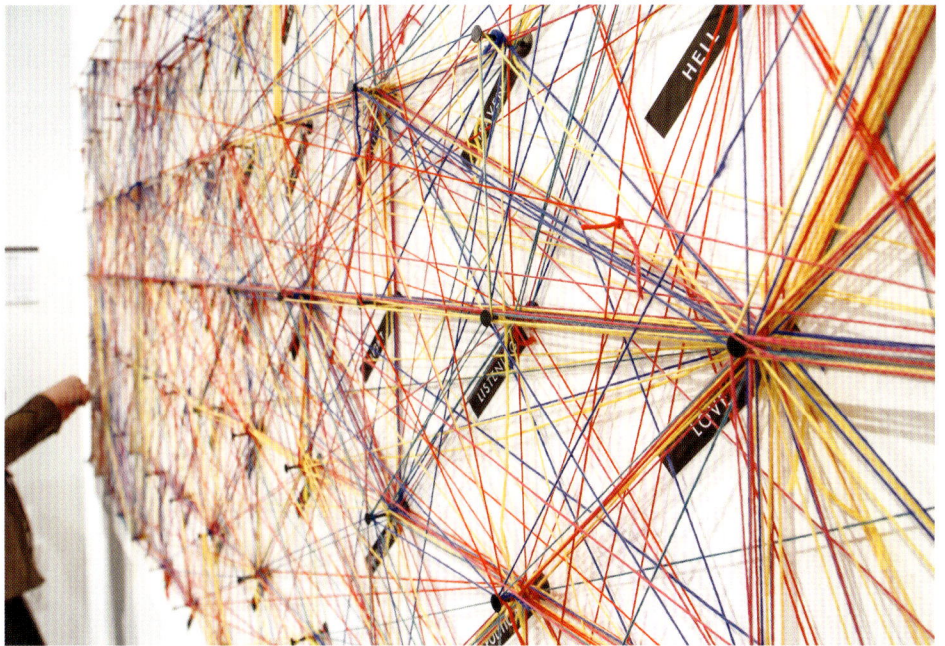

WHAT MADE YOU
CHANGE?

WHAT MADE YOU
HA

INDEX

(fos)

(fos) is a multidisciplinary team based in Madrid and Barcelona, founded by Susana Piquer, Julio Calvo, and Eleni Karpatsi. They are working as independent architects, interior designers, art directors, and visual merchandisers to create design experiences.

cargocollective.com/somosfos

45gradi

45gradi, which means 45degrees, is a graphic design studio based in Milan specialized in "brand care." 45gradi is the acute angle that is not obtuse and far sharper than the right and flat one. They believe that communication is all about choosing the right angle, coming up with striking ideas to be surprising instead of boring.

45gradi.com

A Patent Design

A Patent Design is a studio established by Afroditi Constantinou. She intends to create each project to be "a patent for client": unique, fresh, and conceptually right solution.

Afroditi Constantinou is a graphic designer with a BA with distinction in Multimedia and Graphic Arts. She focuses on branding, advertising and motion design. She is fascinated with typography which is incorporated in most of her work. Exploration and playfulness play a key role in finding a concept and visualization in her projects.

apatentdesign.wix.com/explore

ADDA Studio

ADDA Studio is a Stuttgart-based design agency, specialized in conceptual design, creation and communication. Since 2009, Christian Vögtlin has led it with his holistic principle of creation, and focused on the customers' wishes, ideas and views. ADDA aims to create an emotional and informative benefit to their clients that is homogeneously aligned with corporate values.

www.adda-studio.de

Agnes Herr

Agnes Herr is a Budapest-based graphic designer influenced by Carsten Nicolai, Victor Vaasrely, and Enzo Ragazzini. She is not only interested in graphic design, identity, typography, branding, and web design, but also fond of the trends of optical art, pop art, science based art and other experimental attempts.

www.behance.net/herragi

Alexia Roux

Alexia Roux is a graphic designer based in Montpellier, France.

alexiaroux.fr/

Ali Emre Doğramacı

Born and raised in Istanbul, Ali Emre Dogramacı is a graphic designer predominantly focuses on print medium. He is most interested in the tactile experiences that can be applied to physical design pieces and he experiments with unconventional materials and techniques.

He received his bachelor's degree in Visual Communication Design from Istanbul Bilgi University, and recently graduated with a MFA in Design from The School of Visual Arts.

www.aliemredo.com

Alice Scalfi

Alice Scalfi is a graphic designer based in Brescia, Italy. She specializes in both print and digital design with particular interest in editorial design and illustration. Her aim is always to create works that combine concepts with strong functional and feasible executions.

www.behance.net/AliceScalfi

Amélie Valverde

Currently in the final year of Master in Global Design, Amélie Valverde is a graphic designer specialized in editing and publishing as well as branding.

www.behance.net/amelievalverde

Ana Curbelo

Ana Curbelo is a multidisciplinary designer and art director currently living in London.

www.anacurbelophoto.com

Anastasia Itkina

Anastasia Itkina is a graphic design student from British Higher School of Art and Design in Moscow, Russia. She focuses on the application of interactivity in print and installations throughout her studies, while she is also very interested in branding, typography, and editorial design. She is fond of handmade production and tries to develop and apply these skills in most of her projects.

www.behance.net/anastasiaitkina

Anna Dormer Volgsten

Anna Dormer Volgsten is currently studying a Bachelor of Fine Arts in Visual Communication at Beckmans College of Design in Stockholm.

www.annadormervolgsten.se

artless Inc.

artless Inc. is a multidisciplinary design consultancy, established in 2001 by Shun Kawakami, based in Tokyo and other 7 cities. They perceive "design as a visual communication." They don't differentiate between art, design, architecture, digital and other forms of communication. A diverse challenge extends across different disciplines providing them with an experience that broadens their point of view.

www.artless.co.jp

Bailey Lauerman

Bailey Lauerman is an independent advertising agency headquartered in Omaha, Nebraska. The place has given them an independent streak as wide as the plains. They aren't held hostage to any one perspective, medium, category or holding company. Their only agenda is their clients' success. And their only goal is the relentless pursuit of positively impacting the destiny of the brands they serve.

www.baileylauerman.com

Blink

Blink is a team composed of four multidisciplinary designers from Barcelona. The team works by mixing different areas and disciplines in design in order to explore and communicate new ways of interaction and experimentation within the design field. They concentrate on understanding how people interact with both design and their surroundings.

blink-ignoranceisbliss.tumblr.com/

Bruketa&Žinić OM

Consisting of a group of marketing communications agencies, Bruketa&Žinić OM is one of the 17 world's leading independent agencies according to Campaign magazine. The group numbers some 80 creatives and experts in brand strategy, packaging design, graphic, spacial and product design, strategic planning and every kind of on line and off line marketing communication.

www.bruketa-zinic.com
P168

Bruno Albuquerque

Bruno Albuquerque lives and works in Porto, Portugal. He has established his creative borders through a complex and diversified language marked by the loaded lines and shadows of his works. His aptitude to progressively absorb skills from the wealth of professional experiences and used techniques enhances the construction of his pluridimensional creative sphere. Among these, his music related works must be highlighted, such as posters, album covers, animations, among others, in which he utilizes varied graphical solutions.

www.behance.net/brunoalbuquerque
P100-101

Bureau Rabensteiner

Bureau Rabensteiner is an Austrian design studio that specializes in creative direction and graphic design. The small company structure allows them to work in an inspiring atmosphere, which assures the best results on their clients' projects. The team combines strategic thinking with branding and photography and therefore is able to transport more than just design, but a whole company spirit through different channels. They provide insight into their company life and surroundings. They share the things that inspire them, which emerged as a good way to stay in permanent contact with other designers and interested people all around the world. At the very least, it gives them the opportunity to connect with the right kind of clients, who match their style and thinking and bring interesting new projects and challenges.

bureaurabensteiner.at/
P166-167

Cecília Pletser

Cecília Pletser is a freelance graphic designer from Hungary, Budapest. She graduated in Graphic Design from the Hungarian University of Fine Arts in 2014. Cecília prefers mixing manual and digital techniques in her work so as to touch and smell the results. Although her art is thought over from different perspectives, some of the details are born subconsciously. Her works are characterized by traditional techniques, experimental, and multidisciplinary.

www.behance.net/pletsercecilia
P128

Chantelle Barnard-Rance

Chantelle Barnard-Rance is a graphic designer based in Crawley, UK. She describes her work as clean and minimal, yet still quite quirky with elements of surrealism. She likes to use soft, muted colours and to play with texture and imagery in her work. Meanwhile, she often draws inspiration from other designers, photographers, music, and fashion trends.

www.chantellebarnard-rance.com
P063

Chén Fan & Maxim Cormier

Chén Fan and Maxim Cormier are designers based out of Toronto. They are constant collaborators, working side by side on most projects. They focus on both identity design as well as editorial design.

xuechenfan.com
maximcormier.ca
P116-117; P169

Cheolhong Kim

Cheolhong Kim is a freelancing designer located in Seoul, Korea. He loves typography and intends to astonish and inspire people with it.

www.behance.net/07-73023066
P194-195

Commune

Commune is a creative collective based in Sapporo, Tokyo, and Stockholm. Commune manages the encounter-themed creative salon MEET and organizes a variety of events and exhibitions. They are currently in the process of expanding their activities and building themselves up through the sharing of ideas and technologies.

www.commune-inc.jp
P066; P068; P121

Cosa Nostra

Cosa Nostra is a creative multidisciplinary agency based in Poland with a young team full of fresh ideas that are always open to innovation and collaboration. Driven by a passion for design and commitment to their work, they aim to develop, design and realize creative concepts which are impressive, simple, and elaborate.

www.cosanostracreative.com/
P067

Derek Dubler

Derek Dubler is a professional graphic designer based out of Greater Los Angeles, California. He is currently working towards his Bachelor of Fine Arts degree in Graphic Design. Being well versed in multiple areas of design and fine arts, his approach is often considered minimalistic supported by big ideas. Derek takes a great deal of inspiration from traditional Swiss design, as well as bold colours and plenty of negative space. When he is not designing, Derek surrounds himself with design publications. He is an avid learner who is always looking to discover something new.

derekdubler.com
P056

Designers Anonymous

In a busy world full of messages and chatter, they help consumer brands to stand out so they are seen, understood, loved and talked about.

Their work focuses on capturing and expressing a brand's charisma — the unique qualities and perhaps the touch of magic that set it apart and draw people in.

To achieve that, they explore deep within the brand to discover what makes it special. Then they create inspiring ways to bring its personality and promise to life, seamlessly, across everything from identity and packaging design to film, print, advertising, web, mobile, campaigns, events and environments.

www.designers-anonymous.com
P164-165

Dina Lozovskaya

Dina Lozovskava is a Russian designer specialized in interactive design.

cargocollective.com/DinaLozovskaya
P036

Dorota Grabkowska

Born and raised in Wrocław, Poland, Dorota moved to the UK in 2006 to study Design and Applied Arts with plans in mind to set up her own design studio. After graduation, she started exploring different design disciplines, when she developed a strong interest in graphic design. Additionally, Dorota collaborated on a number of spatial design projects and small architectural commissions, while simultaneously developing her own products. In 2014, she co-founded a multi-disciplinary design consultancy Fanatic House and exhibited a range of furnishing products at the 2014 London Design Festival.

www.fanatic-house.com
P230-232

eskju | Bretz & Jung

eskju is a design factory with its own inhouse printshop, based in Bingen, Germany. eskju was founded in 2013 by Daniel Bretz and Oliver Jung. It is the perfect match between a creative illustrator and a very experienced printer.

www.eskju.com
P041

Evan Pokrandt

Evan Pokrandt is a designer working in Brooklyn New York. His approach is experimental with emphasis on the concept. He inclines to use juxtaposition to deconstruct conflicting cultural conventions, and reconstruct them into cohesive messages.

www.evanpokrandt.com
P104-105

Ewelina Orlowska

Ewelina Orlowska is a graphic designer and artist from Poland. Graduated from the Academy of Fine Arts in Gdansk (Poland) with BA in Interior Design and Graphics. She is currently pursuing her Master's degree in Graphic Design with focus on editorial design and linocut. Multidisciplinary background in architecture, art and graphic design infuse her projects with unique and surprising solutions. She experiments with various tools and media with attention to detail to find a balance between playful and refined design which engages the audience.

www.behance.net/EwelinaOrlowska
P026-027

Filter Studio

Filter is a multi-award winning communication and brand design studio in Brisbane, Australia founded by Claire Hamilton. They specialize in brand identity and creative problem-solving using both print and digital media to help their clients evolve in a crowded marketplace. They work collaboratively with clients as well as other creative businesses, combining experience and skill to develop effective creative strategies that empathize with the end user. They believe in questioning, understanding, researching and developing ideas, as well as ensuring everything they do is crafted and designed meticulously.

www.filterstudio.com.au
P069; P070

François Xavier Saint Georges

Brought up on the land, inveterate experimenter, machine maker, and conceptual artist Francois Xavier Saint Georges (aka FXSTG) uses the natural landscape and the elements as a laboratory for his art and visual research. In recent years he has concentrated on creating systems for exploring the process of art production and the effect of time on objects through two parallel, yet distinct and constant projects. Many of his projects can be seen on major art and design sites.

www.fxstg.com
P180-181; P192-193

Georg Liebergesell

Georg Liebergesell is a designer and art director based in Vienna, Austria. He now works in different fields of visual arts including graphic design, branding, exhibition design, motion graphics and illustration. His client list includes national and international cultural institutions, digital agencies and other businesses.

www.georgliebergesell.com
P228-229

George Farrell

Having trained as a graphic designer at Chelsea College of Arts London, George Farrell has affection to advertising, events and branding which become a focus in his work. His obsession with organization and symmetry, as well as line spacing and simplicity are all contributed to the aesthetic of his work. He aims to evoke a positive reaction from a communication design solutions.

cargocollective.com/georgefarrell
P198-199; P220-221

Gong Xinyu

Gong Xinyu graduated from Visual Communication in Sichuan Art University, specialized in book and editorial design. In recent years, he focuses on transforming the content to a abstract concept with bookbinding.

www.behance.net/leonismyeeg
P062; P152-155

Grabowski Böll

Grabowski Böll develops corporate designs, websites, signage systems, product packaging and more. Their work is characterized by aesthetic independence, radical simplicity and formal clarity.

www.grabowski-boell.de
P102-103

Hachetresele Studio

Hachetresele was established in 2004 by Horacio Lardiés and redefined with the incorporation of Luciana Cartolano (Studio Manager) and Patricio Kolar (Design Director). It aims to develop integrated graphic design projects under the philosophy that strong concepts meets creative thinking. The interdisciplinary team develops commercial and art projects of global significance.

www.h3lweb.com
P040

Helena Morais Soares

Helena Soares is a Portuguese designer currently studying her Master of Communication Design at ESAD - Escola Superior de Artes e Design.

www.behance.net/helenacmorais-s
P012-013

How Sok Hwee

Sok Hwee is a graphic designer based in Singapore. She does a range of design works, which include print and screen graphics, branding and identity projects, publications, packaging and illustrations. In addition, being passionate about anything handicraft since young age, she is always eager to learn new craft techniques in which she believe can aid in her design too.

www.behance.net/sokhwee
P210-211

Interbrand Seoul

Interbrand is the world's leading brand consultancy, with a network of 31 offices in 27 countries. Since it opened for business in 1974, it has changed the way the world sees branding: from just another word for "logo" to a business's most valuable asset to business strategy brought to life. Publisher of the highly influential annual Best Global Brands ranking and Webby Award-winning brandchannel, Interbrand believes that brands have the power to change the world and helps its clients achieve this goal every day. Interbrand's combination of strategy, creativity, and technology delivers fresh ideas and insights, deep brand intelligence, clear business opportunities, and compelling brand experiences.

www.interbrand.com
P044-045

IS Creative Studio

Founded by Richars Meza, IS Creative Studio is an international branding firm with offices in Lima, Madrid and Tokyo. IS Creative has gained a global vision through their 20 years experience working in New York, Tokyo, Madrid and Lima with clients from various industries.

www.iscreativestudio.com
P048; P076; P112-113

Jacy Nordmeyer

Jacy Nordmeyer is a multidisciplinary artist who lives and works in Chicago. She attended The School of the Art Institute of Chicago, and earned a BFA in 2014. She is interested in empathy, functionality, and narrative; investigating these themes through editions of emotionally relatable designed objects. Jacy's studio practice combines illustration, sculpture, and design.

www.behance.net/jacy
P018; P034-035

Ji Yun Kim

Ji Yun Kim is a graphic designer based in New York. She graduated from School of Visual Arts with BFA in Design in 2014. She has explored different areas of graphic design, specifically in digital design and corporate identity. Research is the stage she highly values because it adds accuracy and in-depth meaning to design and communication. In a world of sensory overload, she seeks to discover the unnoticed.

jiyunkim.com

Jonathan Kleinpeter, Chloé Heinis, Lina Kahal

Recently graduated from the Haute Ecole des Arts du Rhin and the University of Strasbourg in France, Jonathan, Chloé and Lina are three young and creative graphic designers.

Jonathan comes from Strasbourg. His internship at Grrr studio in Amsterdam brought him to work on dynamic visual identities and organic systems in graphic design.

Chloé is a Strasbourg-born graphic designer dedicated to incorporating interaction and gamification with print design.

Lina has dual nationality of French and Syrian which motivates her to work on hybrid languages and cultures.

jonathankleinpeter.fr
www.behance.net/chloe-heinis
www.behance.net/linakahal

Joseph Veazey

After growing up in the Atlanta, GA area, Joseph Veazey attended Savannah College of Art and Design. After school he spent two years at Adult Swim designing DVDs, billboards, posters, and a giant inflatable bathing cat. In 2012 he relocated to NYC where he has been assisting Azede Jean-Pierre with the launch of her fashion label and serving as an art director, as well as freelancing for various clients. His work has been selected for Print Regional Design Annual, American Illustration, Creative Quarterly, CMYK Magazine, and more, as well as appearing in multiple national and international design books and magazines.

josephveazey.com

Judith Kroisleitner

Judith Kroisleitner is an Austrian graphic designer living and working in Vienna. Her work stands for a strong concept, precision in detail, the passion for creating unique stuff and an individual approach to clients and briefs.

glueckskinddesign.com

Julie Soudanne

Julie Soudanne is a graphic designer and typographer based in Paris, France.

She studied at École de Communication Visuelle (ECV) in Paris, a visual communication school, and she graduated with a master's degree in Graphic Design and Typography in 2015.

www.juliesoudanne.fr

Juyeon Lee & Hyunseo Yoo

Juyeon Lee and Hyunseo Yoo are currently in their last year of studying Communications Design at Pratt Institute in Brooklyn. They both are multi-disciplinary designers based in New York City, and always explore different concepts and design solutions with creative thinking and reasoning.

juyeonleedesign.com
www.hyunseoyoo.com

Katerina Kerouli

Originally from Greece, Katerina moved to England to continue her studies in 2011. Passionate about craft, illustration and editorial design, she is now a student majoring Graphic Design in Nottingham. She enjoys problem-solving, creative visual communication, and challenges of using new techniques, technologies or materials.

www.katerinakerouli.com

Kevin Harald Campean

Kevin Harald Campean is a graphic designer based in Budapest, Hungary. He focuses on graphic design, packaging, branding and print design.

www.behance.net/HaraldKevin

Kir Rostovsky

Kir Rostovsky is a graphic designer based in Russia.

www.behance.net/kir_u

Kolle Rebbe

Kolle Rebbe conducts business with entrepreneurial intelligence – capitalizing on their cooperative, interdisciplinary approach and transcending boundaries of culture and media.

www.kolle-rebbe.de

Kristóf Kőmíves & Kinga Nyoszoli

Kristóf graduated from the Hungarian University of Fine Arts last year. He works as a freelance designer.

Kinga is a master student of MOME's product design department, while she is working on her own brand, called DEZKA.

www.behance.net/komiveskristof
www.behance.net/kinganyoszoli

Latona Marketing Inc.

Founded in 2008 by designer Kazuaki Kawahara, Latona Marketing Inc. is a Japanese design office adept in marketing. Concentrating on graphic design, website, branding, and marketing, Latona conducts precise marketing in advance, enabling them to correctly pose problems, derive the correct solutions, and reflect these in their designs. Their ultimate objective is to increase the sales and enhance the management of their client.

www.latona-m.com/

Liyuan Tong

Grew up in Shenzhen, China, Liyuan Tong is currently working and living in New York City. She is a young and imaginative graphic designer and printmaker, with experience in production, design, illustration, craftmaking, and printmaking. She received her BA from Guangzhou Academy of Fine Art and her MFA from Minneapolis College of Art and Design in 2014, with a major in Graphic Design.

www.liyuan-tong.com

Lily Kao

Born and raised in Taiwan, Lily Kao is currently a freelance graphic designer and illustrator based in Toronto, Canada. Growing up watching her grandfather does Chinese brush painting and calligraphy, Lily's cultural and visual art background have a impressive influence on her design works in both conceptual and aesthetic way. She mainly focuses on packaging, branding and other print based design.

www.lilykaodesign.com

Lo Siento

In 2005, Borja Martinez on his own founds LoSiento. Nowadays, Lo Siento gathers a team of 5 professionals and continues to work in design projects from the fields of corporative, packaging, editorial and personal projects as well.

The studio is specially interested in taking over identity projects as a whole. Its main feature is a combination of physical and material approach to the graphic solutions, resulting in a mixture of graphic and industrial, and a constant collaboration with the artisans.

www.losiento.net

Lucia Freire Coloma

Lucia Freire is a graphic designer specialized in identity and branding from Spain. Among others, she has worked for clients such as: Coca-Cola, Fanta, Levi's and Telcel.

www.behance.net/dry
P057

Lundgren+Lindqvist

Lundgren+Lindqvist is a design and development studio based in Gothenburg, Sweden. Operating out of a harbour-side rooftop studio in an old sugar factory, their process is based on research and led by ideas.

Through an intuitive approach, they move seamlessly between digital and physical, approaching every project with the same inherent passion and curiosity. Working across a range of disciplines – including identity design, design for print and digital, web development and art direction – they treat problems as opportunities, always inspiring an engaging and well-crafted outcome.

lundgrenlindqvist.se
P049; P075

Mark Wilson

Mark Wilson crafts relevant solutions for clients realised through a practice of analysis, invention and a touch of creative tangents. He typically focuses on the creation of advertising campaigns, branding strategy and experience design.

www.markwilson.graphics
P090

Maryam Khosrovani

As a graphic designer, Maryam Khosrovani uses a concept-oriented approach and illustrates her ideas in non-linear narratives. She earned a master's degree from ESAG Penninghen in Paris in 2011. She has gained her experiences working with artists such as Reza Abedini, SARL LM Communiquer and Michel Bouvet. In 2011 she founded her own studio MiM Studio. Her work has been exhibited in Iran in several galleries.

maryam-khosrovani-owlx.squarespace.com
P050-051

Melodie Eve Pisciotti

Graduated with a Bachelor in Graphic Design from California State University of Long Beach, Melodie Eve Pisciotti is currently a designer and letterer working for WeAreGiants in Los Angeles.

melodiepisciotti.com
P146-147

Mille Windfeldt

Mille is currently living in New York working on her MFA in Design at School of Visual Arts.

www.behance.net/millewindfeldt
P126-127

Mona Leu-Leu

Mona Leu-Leu is a French freelance graphic designer who works mainly on communication and visual identity. Interested in objects that invite users to participate through a visual interaction, she writes and illustrates stories that display different levels of reading and enable the user to discover what lies behind the surface.

monaleuleu.wordpress.com
P162-163

Morphoria Design Collective

The Morphoria Design Collective is a collaboration of seven designers with different specializations located in Germany. They primarily work in the creative fields of editorial, exhibition design as well as animation, interactive design and branding.

They are passionate about every detail of their work regardless of the medium. Convinced that good design comes from good storytelling, Morphoria Collective offers the right expertise in diverse disciplines, including photography, illustration as well as art direction and conceptual design.

www.behance.net/morphoria
P140-141

MOTOMOTO Inc.

Kenichi Matsumoto was born in Tokyo in 1980. In 2004 he received his degree in Graphic Design from Tama Art University and entered E.Co., Ltd in the same year. He established MOTOMOTO inc. in 2013.

www.behance.net/kenichi_matsumoto
P212-213

Mucho

Mucho is a global boutique design studio based in Barcelona, Newark, Paris, San Francisco and New York. Their principals represent multiple cultures yet are dedicated to a singular mission: to define how companies are perceived in the world, so they can stand out and succeed. They offer creative strategy and design for all kinds of clients — from boutique businesses and start-ups to multinational corporations.

By arranging senior positions at the most renowned design studios and work directly with every client from start to finish. Mucho's tight-knit global office network allows their designers to collaborate across oceans and cultures. This continually infuses their work with fresh perspectives and creates an esteemed pool of resources for every project.

www.wearemucho.com/
P052-053

Murmure

Murmure is a creative communication agency, with 2 Art Director: Paul Ressencourt and Julien Alirol. Overturning the limits between art, graphic design and communication, the agency brings together an array of skills paving the way for the production of projects in a creative way. Murmure regards senses, poetry, and elegance of texture as the fundamental principles which are used to create an original and efficient communication.

www.murmure.me
P170-171

Naonori Yago

Naonori Yago was born in Shizuoka, Japan in 1986. He studied at Department of Visual Communication Design, Musashino Art University and graduated in 2009. He is currently working as a graphic designer.

www.naonoriyago.com/
P046-047; P077; P118-119; P186-187

Nendo Inc.

Driven by the desire to create little surprise moments in daily life, Nendo was founded in 2002 by Oki Sato. Overflowing with imagination, Nendo has been responsible for a prolific amount of projects in architecture, interior, product, and graphic design.

www.nendo.jp
P080-081; P136

NOSIGNER

NOSIGNER is a design firm based on the principle of creating "designs that bring positive changes to the society and the future." With a desire of being a team that identifies large challenges and designs ideal relationships requisite for the society, they have been working under the name of 'NOSIGNER', meaning 'professionals who design intangible things'. NOSIGNER provides comprehensive work beyond typical design disciplines, including areas of graphics, products, spatial design, and business models and branding. In addition to design as a business activity, NOSIGNER also creates social innovations in various fields, including local industry, technology, education, sustainability, cultural exchange and open source design.

nosigner.com/
P022-023

Ogilvy & Mather New Zealand

Ogilvy & Mather New Zealand is a full service agency with offices in Auckland and Wellington and is part of the Ogilvy & Mather network with 450 offices around the world.

ogilvy.co.nz
P058-059

Paperlux GmbH

The full circle of natural creativity is completed when the intuitive minds of the 11 pioneering spirits from Hamburg's Schanzenviertel district perform their craft. Here is where inspiration, abstraction, passion, palpability and aesthetics are transformed into concept, branding, corporate and editorial design, event communication, typography, illustration and art. A surge of growth, an indelible imprint, a lasting impression.

www.paperlux.com
P024-025

Pedro Veneziano

Pedro Veneziano is a 22-year old Brazilian graphic designer. He works with 3D language and graphic design constantly to shape materiality, either digital or real. His interest lies in things that create a narrative: things that fold, bend, open, distort, reveal, change, adapt and twist.

pedroveneziano.com
P148-149

Philip Stroomberg

Philip Stroomberg is an Amsterdam-based graphic designer who works primarily in the cultural sector. His clients include universities, publishers and art institutions. Stroomberg regularly creates designs that are used to promote Dutch culture. An important feature of his work is interaction: his designs encourage the user to develop a bond with the object and often challenge the user's imagination.

www.stroomberg.net
P086-087

Plural

The studio was founded in 2008 by Jeremiah Chiu and Renata Graw. Plural is a collaborative art and design practice. Focused on a process of research and experimentation, Plural collaborates on meaningful projects in art, design, interaction, installation, music, new media, and technology. Their works have been widely recognized and exhibited in the worldwide.

weareplural.com
P218-219

Publicis Machine

In a world of digital transformation, Publicis Machine is a rare type of agency: born digital and now fully integrated. Strong digital and design capabilities are now married to the experience and scale of Publicis worldwide. Publicis Machine is a powerhouse on the forefront of communication in Africa and a leader of change within the industry.

www.publicismachine.com
P028-029

Qiang Fu

Qiang Fu is a Chinese designer who studied product design and graphic design in China and UK for five years. He currently focuses on exploring various techniques to transform letters to images through the play of light and shadow.

www.behance.net/FDQ
P096; P097; P098-099

Red Peak

Red Peak is a firm where creativity, design and strategy meet to transform brands. Devoting to solve 21st century problems, they assemble cross-platform teams of award-winning creatives and strategists to develop bold solutions to today's marketing challenges.

www.redpeakgroup.com
P020

René Miní Lázara

René Miní Lázara is a Spanish designer currently working in a parking startup company called Parkapp as a junior graphic designer.

www.renemini.com
P088-089

Robert Urban

Robert Urban is a young Slovak designer with primary focus on the product design, as well as a passion for typography and book design. His work is focused on artistic aspects and a more experimental approach. Robert pays the same rigorous attention to context, process and detail to every project.

roberturban.sk
P222-223

Roberta Donatini

Grew up and studied in Italy, Roberta Donatini is now living in Paris where she works on graphic design and photography.

www.behance.net/ROBSDONATINI
P042

Rong Yan

Rong Yan is a Finnish multi-disciplinary designer living in New York. Her work has been published in several international books and she has won a number of awards and scholarships. She completed a master's degree in Package Design at Pratt Institute, New York and BA in Sichuan Fine Art Institute, China.

www.yanrongdesign.com/
P021

Rubio & Del Amo

Based in Murcia, Spain, Rubio & Del Amo is a design studio specialized in editorial design, brand identity and packaging. Regarding aesthetics and concept are equally important, they are dedicated to providing solutions with highest quality to communication problems.

www.rubioydelamo.com
P150

Saatchi & Saatchi Ukraine

Saatchi & Saatchi Ukraine is a full service, integrated communication agency. Through their creative ideas across all media and all disciplines, they set out to turn brands into Lovemarks, which generate loyalty beyond reason. They believe passionately in the power of ideas to differentiate and motivate, through which they can change the world better.

saatchi.com.ua
P110-111

SAFARI inc.

SAFARI is a Japanese multidisciplinary design studio, whose name represents that they are adventurous to explore the world of design with curiosity.

www.safari-design.com
P030-031; P071

Spread

Spread is a creative unit founded by Hirokazu Kobayashi and Haruna Yamada in 2004. By mixing the concept of landscape design and graphic design, and by dismantling and rebuilding memory, they spread multidisciplinary creations to the future.

www.spread-web.jp
P108-109

Stephan Lerou

Stephan Lerou is a Dutch independent creative studio. Regarding simplification as the key, their design philosophy is clean, minimalistic design with a balance of playfulness and seriousness.

www.stephanlerou.nl
P120; P172-173

Stuart Lamont

With a focus on delivering creative and innovative design solutions through the whole process, Stuart Lamont is a graphic designer especially enthusiastic about exploring the interaction between design and audience to enhance their experience with design.

www.stuartlamontdesign.co.uk
P095

Szani Mészáros

Szani Mészáros is a Hungarian freelance designer specialized in packaging and branding.

www.behance.net/szani_meszaros
P124-125

Tetusin Design Office

Tetusin Design Office is a design studio established by Senzaki Takayuki who works as a graphic designer and art director based in Kyushu. His focus is using plant-theme graphics on design.

www.tetusin.com
P137

The Bold Studio

The Bold Studio is a Russian graphic design studio, which overshadows the minds of the illusory consciousness and creates a critical triangular paradigm.

thebold.ru
P074

Tina Touli

Tina Touli is a London-based graphic designer from Athens, Greece. Graduated with a MA in Communication Design at Central Saint Martins, she is passionate about applying her visual skills with essence in details to make things functional and beautiful.

www.behance.net/tinatouli
P072-073

Trapped in Suburbia

"Tell me and I'll forget; show me and I may remember; involve me and I'll understand." Trapped in Suburbia focuses on human interaction and engaging their audience. They don't expect them to sit back and relax; instead they take them on a graphic journey and surprise them.

trappedinsuburbia.com
P019; P208-209

Tree Abraham

Tree Abraham is a book and cover designer specializing in the areas of illustrative mixed media design, hand drawn type, and paper mechanics. Her projects seek to illuminate universal themes within the human experience in engaging and apt formats. Her previous travels and professional work with different cultures around the world on issues of sustainable development continue to inform her design sensibility. Tree has been shortlisted twice for the Penguin Design Award and her book Earth to Everyone received a Merit Award by the International Society of Typographic Designers.

cargocollective.com/treexthree
P078-079; P188

TU DESIGN OFFICE

Being the founder and lead designer of TU DESIGN OFFICE, Tu,Ming-Shiang graduated from National Yunlin University of Science and Technology with a Master degree in Visual Communication Design. He is also a lecturer at Department of Industrial and Communication Design in National Taiwan University of Science and Technology.

www.tudesignoffice.com
P038-039; P200-201

Tun Ho

Tun Ho is an art director and illustrator based in Macau. He is specialized in branding, graphic design, t-shirt illustration and typography.

www.behance.net/tunho
P196-197

UMA/design farm

UMA/design farm was founded by Yuma Harada in 2007. Currently Yuma Harada is leading a team with 7 members working into various domains including book design, graphic design, exhibition design, space design, and also total art direction.

umamu.jp
P014; P084-085

Vladimir Shlygin

Vladimir Shlygin is a graphic and interaction designer from Moscow. Since 2008 he has worked on different kinds of creative projects in various media, using different production and execution techniques. In recent years his professional focus is brand identity.

www.behance.net/vladimirshlygin
P106

Wooksang Kwon

Wooksang Kwon is an independent graphic designer based in New York. Working primarily in the creative and cultural sectors, his works have received recognition from many international awards such as ADAA and the Type Directors Club.

www.wooxang.com
P094

Xavi Martinez Robles

Xavi Martinez Robles is a graphic designer based in Barcelona. He is specialized in branding and editorial design but he also works on a broad range of projects like packaging, website, motion graphics, and video.

www.xavimartinez.eu
P184-185

Xisco Barceló

Xisco Barceló has more than 12 years of experience working with clients of all around the world: Mexico, Dubai, Brussels and Spain.

www.xiscobarcelo.com
P132

Yeongmin Won

Yeongmin Won is an enthusiastic graphic designer obsessed with finding visual clues to communicate with viewers by experimenting with different media.

She wants to combine craftsmanship with technology to create meaningful art pieces for people.

www.yeongminwon.com
216-217

Yoonshin Kim

Born in Seoul, Korea, Kim is currently a multidisciplinary graphic designer based in Chicago who has a background in Sculpture and Visual Communication Design. Kim has recently completed his master degree in Visual Communication Design from School of Art Institute of Chicago. His work spans many genres — environmental design, branding, poster, book, brochure, packaging, video, UI/UX design, and sculpture.

www.yoonshinkim.com
P082-083; P151

Yurko Gutsulyak

Yurko Gutsulyak is a professional designer with more than 15 years working experience. In 2005 he founded a graphic design studio with his sister Zoryana.

Widely-recognized with about 100 international awards, he has been actively involved in the development of local design and advertising market. He was President of the Art Director Club Ukraine from 2010 to 2012 as well as a representative jury of Ukraine of different international design and advertising festivals.

gstudio.com.ua
P122-123

ACKNOWLEDGEMENTS

We would like to express our gratitude to all of the designers and companies for their generous contribution of images, ideas, and concepts. We are also very grateful to many other people whose names do not appear in the credits but who made specific contributions and provided support. Without them, the successful completion of this book would not be possible. Special thanks to all of the contributors for sharing their innovation and creativity with all of our readers around the world. Our editorial team includes editor Javier Zheng and book designer Yunshu Liu , to whom we are truly grateful.